RAIN FOREST ADVENTURES

A Collection of Stories
by
HORACE BANNER

© Copyright 2001 Christian Focus Publications
Reprint 2001 and 2002
ISBN:185792-6277

Published by
Christian Focus Publications Ltd,
Geanies House, Fearn, Tain, Ross-shire
IV20 1TW, Scotland, Great Britain

www.christianfocus.com
email:info@christianfocus.com

Cover illustration by Graham Kennedy.
Cover design by Catherine Mackenzie
Black and white illustrations by Stuart Mingham.

Printed and bound in Great Britain
by Mackays of Chatham

CONTENTS

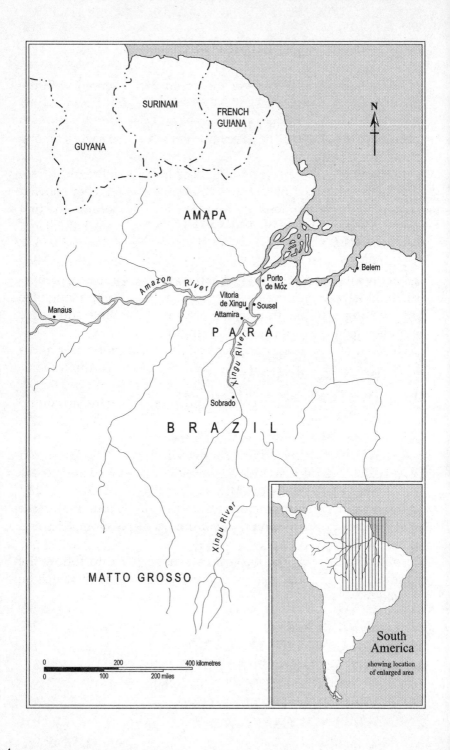

GUYANA

SURINAM

FRENCH
GUIANA

AMAPA

Belem

Amazon River

Porto
de Móz

Vitoria
de Xingu

Sousel

Manaus

Attamira

P A R Á

Xingu River

Sobrado

B R A Z I L

Xingu River

MATTO GROSSO

N

0   200   400 kilometres
0   100   200 miles

South
America

showing location
of enlarged area

About the author...

Horace Banner was a pioneer missionary who served with the Unevangelised Field Mission (UFM Worldwide). He loved the people of the Amazonian Rain forest and for over 40 years, in obedience to God's call, he gave himself to the Lord's work among the Kayapo people.

Called by God to serve among these Indians of Brazil, Horace and his wife Eva joyfully accepted that commission. They showed remarkable courage, tenacity and love as they became the first missionaries to live among the fierce Kayapos in a tribal village.

Horace and Eva, and later their children Jessie Mae and James, identified with these people and entered into their culture. They related well to this tribal people and were loved and accepted by them. Horace began the task of reducing the Kayapo language into writing. Later he translated portions of the Bible and wrote hymns which the Indians are still singing.

Instead of violence, peace became the norm in the area and a number came to know and love the Lord Jesus. To the Indians, Horace was a preacher, teacher, healer, brother, friend and helper in many ways. He became a recognised authority on Indian culture and was made an honorary citizen of Brazil, receiving a citation and a medal for his outstanding service to that land.

Above everything, Horace Banner was a man who knew and loved God. Unassuming and utterly selfless, he looked upon every problem as a golden opportunity to get closer to his Saviour. His delight was to endeavour to bring others to the Saviour. He longed that others would see something of the Lord's wisdom, love and power in his life.

May the Lord of the harvest call many more to follow the example of this godly man and join the Mission with which he served for so long!

George P Rabey
UFM Worldwide
April 2000

VOICES IN THE RAIN FOREST

In the wilds of the River Xingu, life can still be very much what it was almost five centuries ago when white men first discovered what they called the New World. In forests, which from an airplane look like a vast green billiard table or an ocean of interwoven tree tops, there are tribes of primitive Indians who live in a jungle world of bows and arrows, paint and feathers, wooden sword-clubs and stone axes, who still make fire by rubbing one stick into another. What we call civilization has made little more than a finger mark on them.

Planes may fly overhead. From time to time the pounding of the diesel engine of a trader's launch navigating a rapids-strewn river or shots from a hunter's rifle may invade the domain of the forest's wild life, but the voice of the rain forest is that of the thunderstorms which may darken the skies on over a hundred days each year, crashing timbers, bird cries, animal calls and the wheeling, whirring, whistling and chirping of insects.

These are the sounds I hear in the jungle which for many years have been home to me and to my family. To the Indians, I am *Orat*, the nearest they can get to my name. Donna Eva is my wife. Our two children, Jess and Jim, spent their early years in our forest home, though for schooling they had to go to the Mission boarding school in Belem, and then to England.

They are always happy to come "home" to us for their holidays. We ourselves are equally happy to get away from the noisy outside world the moment whatever business takes us to the city can be completed.

During inevitable periods of waiting in Belem, as we make yearly or half-yearly purchases of stores and equipment or visit doctor or dentist, there is nothing we like better than to slip away for an hour to a small "island" or virgin forest within easy reach of the Mission House and city centre. They are carefully preserved memorials of the time when what is now a marvellous capital city was just as much rain forest as our home on the River Xingu still is. Behind a fringe of giant trees and an undergrowth of ferns and palms, and still within range of the noise of passing traffic, are the Para Botanical and Zoological Gardens. The zoo is not a big one but it is unique in that everything there - animals, birds, reptiles and fish - are native to the forests of the Amazon region.

Crocodiles and boa-constrictors laze in near-natural surroundings. Emus (the South American brand of ostrich) strut around with heads high up in the air and, thanks to the periscope of a neck with which nature has provided them, are able to look down on mere visitors like ourselves. Jaguars growl. Red macaw parrots squawk. Armadillos burrow and anteaters sleep under their blanket-like tails. Giant tortoises share a pen with red deer and grey tapirs. There are playful monkeys which chatter and glum ones which howl - according to their species. Sloths and wild boar, leopard cats and porcupines, herons and peacocks, cranes and flamingoes, they are all there. Through the glass panels of the aquarium we can see the killer fish we call piranha being fed or watch the electric eels.

Life in the wilds of the River Xingu has given us close-up contacts with many of these jungle creatures in their natural setting, away from all the pens and cages. Not all of them are in the "All things bright and beautiful" class. Some may not even be either "wise or wonderful" at first sight, but we have lived long enough to see that everything has its purpose.

"Ask the beasts and they shall teach thee," wrote the observant Job. Following his wise and ancient advice, we have kept eyes and ears open and seek to pass on some of what we have learned.

****

"And God said, "Let the water teem with living creatures, and let the birds fly above the earth ... let the land produce living creatures according to their kinds: livestock, creatures that move along the ground, and wild animals, each according to its kind. And God saw that it was good."

Genesis 1: 20-25

SERPENT IN THE RIVER

Here we have cloudless skies for five months each year and, if we feel like it, swimming every day. Except when the river is in flood because of the heavy rains, we have a lovely beach within easy reach of our home.

Early each morning the women go down to the river to fill their clay water-pots and calabashes before the water is disturbed by all the coming and going the day will bring. The men have their little dug-outs moored to pegs driven deep into the sand. Out in the shallows are several table-like contraptions - heavy boards perched on forked sticks - where the women sit in the water while rubbing soap over dirty clothes and then banging out the dirt as they bring the soaking garments swishing down on the table tops. Fish scales on a big, flat stone mark the place where the fishermen's wives and daughters clean the day's catch and prepare it for the cooking pot. The entrails they throw into deep water where lurk the ever-hungry piranha fish.

Towards sunset the men who have been tapping rubber or working in their forest gardens walk down to the beach with clean clothes over their arms. They do not delay in the water because the mosquitoes are becoming too numerous for bathing to be enjoyable unless one's whole body is kept under water.

There are no mosquitoes when the sun is shining, and by day the beach is a favourite haunt of the boys and girls - expert swimmers without exception, though they usually keep to the clear, shallow water where there is no danger of being bitten by the piranha. In the shallows the only dangers are the tawny sting-rays upon which the unwary may tread and get a vicious jab from a poisonous spur.

Chief among the boys is Manuel who loves to come racing down the path from the village and hit the water like an arrow, making barely a splash. Then, for a change, he will take a running leap, somersault and plunge into the water.

Where the beach ends, a pile of huge boulders overshadows the water, robbing it of that transparent freshness that bathers find so enticing on a hot day. By the stones the river runs deeper. There is no DANGEROUS FOR BATHING notice but none of the grown-ups ever bathe there and, from time to time, the youngsters are warned to keep to the beach and shallow water. Pedro the fisherman, who is headman of the village, has heard strange gurgles and splashes at night. Ducks disappear without trace. Nobody has solved the mystery of a missing dog.

Now Manuel is not the kind to be easily scared or put off. He found high diving from the boulders far more exciting than any running leap from the sand. He dived and somersaulted so often that warnings became futile. The killer piranha fish only attack where there is bleeding, he reasoned. And opening his eyes under water he could see no trace of them. So he began to regard as chicken the other boys who would not join him.

Then one day, when Manuel dived, he came up against something long, smooth and supple - something alive! And, before he could come up to the surface, something

11

covered his face and things like knives cut into his cheeks. There can be no describing his feeling as it flashed upon him that an anaconda was getting him - no, had got him! At any moment he expected to feel the serpent's coils fasten round his body. There, in the depths of the river there could be no escape.

In his terror he prayed, "God help me!" and tore at the clammy mask on his face. To his unspeakable relief, it came away and, with his face stinging and streaming with blood, he shot to the surface and scrambled ashore.

It was the headman, Pedro, who offered an explanation to the awed villagers. "These serpents, after getting their teeth into anything, have to get their tails anchored to something solid before they can begin to crush. The one which got our Manuel must have missed the submerged boulder at which it aimed its tail. That gave the boy his chance and he got away, thanks be to God."

Manuel's cheeks will always bear the marks of the river serpent's teeth but he has learned his lesson. He is taking no more risks. And as he tells his story and shows his scars, he is helping others not to make the same kind of mistake.

****

Have you ever thought that every sin leaves a scar?
We can't get rid of the scars of sin ourselves. What we need to do is ask for God's forgiveness.
Hopefully our story will help others not to make the same mistakes as we did and to find the healing and forgiveness that only Jesus can bring.

"Come now, let us reason together," says the Lord. "Though your sins are like scarlet, they shall be as white as snow; though they are red as crimson, they shall be like wool."
                                                    Isaiah 1:18

TREE-FROG'S NEST

I was in the forest with some of the Indians. Reaching a creek, we decided to rest for a while. The Indians took out their gourd bowls and had a hasty meal of farina and water, while I looked round for the place where the water ran clearest. On a sandy beach, where the water was both shallow and clear, someone had walled-off a small, round pool using sand from the river bed.

"This must be the work of the Indians!" I said to myself. "How clever to think of filtering their drinking water through that wall of sand!" And taking out my collapsible aluminium cup I had a good drink of water from the inside of that pool.

When I rejoined my guides I told them of my discovery and my guess that another group of Indians had passed that way.

"Indians don't make pools like that," they laughed. "That is the work of Koo-pok-koo-pok."

I knew that word. It was their name for a tree-frog. Was that pool a frog's nest? Yes, sure enough, nestling in a quiet corner was a cluster of frog-spawn!

The Koo-pok-koo-pok lives in the trees, the Indians explained, and only comes down to make her nest in the water. After laying her eggs she climbs back into the trees and forgets them. I did not really mind the laugh being on me for I am always learning and some of the most important lessons in life don't come from text-books.

A few days later things began to happen in that pool my aluminium cup had disturbed for a moment. What should appear but a tadpole, and scores like him, wriggling up and down as tadpoles have always done. None of them were a bit concerned about all the splashing, gurgling and snapping going on just over the low wall of sand.

But as he grew arms and legs the tadpole found that wall a bit of a nuisance. Whichever way he wanted to go, there it was right in front of him and confining his aquabatics to a space not much bigger than a pancake.

Then one day he found himself amphibious, able to leave the water, climb the wall and see the world outside. There was no glimmer of appreciation in his eyes as he saw the forest beyond, the birds and butterflies, and the little fish with their silvery scales lazing about in the water below. There was no flash of understanding as big fish

came dashing by and the little ones streaked for shelter among the stones or in the shallows where their enemy could not get at them.

It did not dawn on him that there were jaws there which could have swallowed frog-spawn by the barrel had it not been for that little wall which had protected him until he could fend for himself. Frog minds could not be expected to reason that walls don't just happen, that somebody has to build and that, somewhere, somebody has to plan.

As for our former tadpole, he just sat there sunning himself and seeing nothing but the tiny insects he somehow knew were there to be jumped for and devoured. Not a glimmer of wonder in his bulging eyes, not a spark of gratitude in his cold, unfeeling heart as he hopped away towards the bushes and trees destined to be his home for the rest of his life. But one day he will be down by the creek again, helping his mate build the very same kind of wall his unknown parents once built for him. He never saw other frogs at work but when his turn comes he will not hesitate. He will make no mistakes. The wall he makes will be just right in size and shape, in just the right place and at just the right time.

How does he do so well at a job he never learned? Instinct, we say, or nature!

The tadpole's protection came from a wee wall of sand. When God wants to illustrate His care for us He takes us to something more solid.

****

"As the mountains surround Jerusalem, so the Lord surrounds His people both now and forevermore."

Psalm 125:2

WASTED YEARS OF THE TORTOISE

I've been reading about the Royal Tongan Tortoise which, in 1773, was presented by Captain Cook to the King of Tonga and was still living on May 19, 1966!

It set me thinking about the Brazilian tortoise our hunter brought in for dinner. A tortoise gets tough before he is out of his teens and by the time he has made his first half-century his meat is really hard. You need a sharp hatchet, a strong arm and a hard heart to prepare him for the pot. Then with salt, pepper and onions plus the milk from, say, half a kilogram of grated Brazil nuts you have a delicious meal. When the liver is fried separately its taste resembles that of grilled mushrooms. And when the tortoise is female and there are eggs to fry along with the liver the meal is better still.

In the Old Testament the tortoise and his kind are rated as unclean and forbidden. He was never meant to be eaten. With his flat, armour plate below and the rounded, streamlined dome above he has little to fear. Rain cannot wet him or hornets sting him. He is safe from both hawks and dogs. He cannot be crushed by either the peccary's hammer hooves or the anaconda's coils. The fierce piranha fish may snap off a leg as he swims across a river but such a wound is never fatal. And after being once bitten he is more than twice shy.

It isn't just the defensive armour which helps him. Disposition helps his mind as the shell protects his body. He is quiet and easy going. He makes no enemies, never hurries or worries. He makes himself at home anywhere, on land or in the water, in forest, field or back garden, provided it is not too cold. He never works for he makes neither burrow nor nest. He is never bothered with a family. Not that he doesn't mate. The female lays one egg here and another egg there and leaves the rest to nature. From the very first day after hatching out the youngsters have to fend for themselves. The tortoise could not care less about anything or anybody - except when a hunter has him tied up and he feels that his own precious life is in danger. Then he will really work to free himself.

But in spite of armourplate, slow motion and living as a palace pet for nearly 200 years, the Royal Tongan Tortoise died on May 19, 1966. And what did he have to show for having lived so long ? Just nothing!

What a picture of so many humans ! We cannot hope to stay in the world as long as the Royal Tongan Tortoise but God does give to most of us a full seventy years of opportunity, not just to love and die, but to do something really worthwhile in a world full of human need. He means us to enjoy life to the full by living it for Him and with Him.

Jesus said: "He that loveth his life shall lose it but whosoever shall lose his life for My sake, the same shall find it."

I once took an Indian to town to spend some money he had earned. Wanting to help him with the buying, I was shocked when he told me that he had already lost all his money. Then, seeing the effect of what he had said, he went on, "But look what I have found." And he proudly displayed the new clothes, the knife, mirror and other things he had bought.

There are no commercial terms in his language, no words for earning and spending, buying and selling so he was adapting. He had not lost his money. He had spent it. And in spending it he had found something of far more practical value than his coins and banknotes.

And so to lose a life for Jesus is to spend it with Him and for Him. How can young people do that ? First of all by making up your minds that whatever others may or may not be, you are going to be a committed Christian and live your life not just for yourself but for the Lord Jesus who died to make you His own.

****

"I have chosen the way of truth; I have set my heart on your laws."

Psalm 119:30

SQUIRREL AND THE SNAKE

If "every picture tells a story", so does every snake skin we see being stretched in its frame of split bamboo for drying in the sun. The one I found my hunter friend at work on was over 3.5 metres long. He was only too ready to tell me the story.

He had made no noise as he trod the forest's carpet of dead leaves, sodden and smelly after weeks of rain. Game was elusive but he figured that in the nut grove there might be something to kill and take home to his hungry family. Scattered around like so many rusty cannon balls were Brazil nuts, still intact in their heavy outer casing. The hunter walked cautiously for nuts were still falling with a dull thud and he knew that a direct hit could crack a man's skull.

A hundred yards ahead an agouti* was quietly and steadily working on one of the nuts. Brazil nuts are hard and his teeth had been at work since the first light of day. An agouti is a Brazilian ground squirrel the size of a rabbit and ginger-red in colour. Without any tail he has little of the glamour of his bushy-tailed relative, frolicking in the branches above his head. However, he is very cute to watch as he squats on his haunches and nibbles the food he holds in his short paws.

After a time of patient and industrious nibbling, the agouti of our story paused in his work and began to look around. Right then, something caught his eye, something which must have given him a jolt for he at once dropped the nut on which he was working and began running around. Deeply agitated, he lost all interest in what he had been doing - his food, his work, his customary caution, indeed, in everything but the silly little dance he was doing on that stage of wet leaves.

He scurried to and fro, seemingly in a dreadful hurry, but getting nowhere. He would go away but he always came back, his strange circuit getting smaller and smaller and nearer and nearer the spot where that mysterious something had first caught his eye.

Hearing the pitter-patter of tiny feet, the approaching hunter crept forward and saw what the agouti was doing. "That animal is surely bewitched," he said to himself and began to look around to see what was holding it in so strange yet so powerful a charm. Yes, there sure enough, motionless as a tree trunk and with green eyes unblinking waited anaconda, the boa constrictor, all ready to catch, to crush and to kill! Her victims rarely get away. They are doomed even before her teeth bite into their neck. It is enough that she catches their eye. But this time, just as her head was poised to strike and end the agouti's career, the hunter fired.

"And what happened to the agouti?" I asked, as I admired the fine skin and heard his story. "Did you kill him too?"

"No," came the reply. "I let him go."

I found myself feeling glad, relieved that the little fellow should have been given another chance. I was thinking about young Christians at home - and older ones too - who go the same way as the agouti. Busily and happily engaged in Christian service - Sunday School, Christian Endeavour, Youth for Christ, Crusaders and Covenanters - with practical interest in overseas missions and Bible School training, they suddenly see something or hear something which sweeps them off their feet. They drop everything and lose all interest.

This is nothing new and not at all peculiar to this day and age. "O foolish Galatians, who hath bewitched you?" cried the apostle Paul.

His lament was that they had taken their eyes from Jesus and left themselves easy victims when the serpent of error raised its head to strike.

It was good for the agouti that at his zero hour there was someone at hand who was more than a match for the serpent and all its wiles. If ever we find ourselves being caught we may be sure that the Lord Jesus will be a very present help in our trouble, if we will but call upon Him.

****

"God is our refuge and strength, an ever-present help in trouble."

Psalm 46:1

---

* Agouti is the Indian name for squirrel, pronounced 'a good tea'

TAMING
THE PECCARY

It is surprising that in these vast forests there should be no really *big* game, no lions, tigers, elephants, hippos or rhinos. As far as individual animals go, the striped jaguar is king of all the South American beasts.

However, the real terrors of these jungles are the peccary or wild hogs. They are very different from domestic pigs. For one thing, they have no tails! They are black and hairy and have bristles running down their spines. They rove the forest in herds and they are vicious, clicking their teeth and grinding their long, sharp tusks. In the ordinary way, nothing can stand up to them. Small animals get trampled underfoot. Snakes don't often get a chance to bite - and when they do it seems that their poison has no effect. Even the jaguar has to be careful how he sets about getting a dinner of wild pig. He dare not risk a frontal attack but must pounce on a straggler, and, after making a quick kill, be ready to move out of the way until the angry, tusk-grinding pack has moved on.

When hunters are armed with repeating rifles and work together, they can usually kill a big number and send the herd away in confusion. But not always. It depends on how the hairy old boar leading the pack reacts to the shooting and whether he snorts a retreat or a charge! Most of my hunter friends can tell of occasions when, after emptying the magazine, they have had to shin up the nearest tree for safety.

One Indian hunter I know, over-confident in the possession of a shot-gun, delayed just a little too long and was knocked to the ground and badly gored. He barely managed to reach a tree in time to save himself from being trampled to death. His legs will always bear the marks of those teeth and tusks.

One day a big herd had been ravaging the forest gardens of maize and manioc and the Indians went all-out for revenge. Some of them boasted old shot-guns but had few bullets. Those who had arrows carried short clubs too, not wanting to leave themselves defenceless when the last arrow had been shot.

The herd was bigger and tougher than usual and, instead of being routed by the shooting, they charged! One savage creature snapped his teeth right through the leading Indian's hand, although he did manage to stun it with his club. As the hunters trooped into the village with their numerous victims, the women did a burst of wailing in sympathy for the wounded man and also for the gored dogs limping home with drooping tails.

Late that night Donna Eva was called in to ease the Indian's pain. The medicine-man had been along to kipper the wound with tobacco smoke but this was a case for cleaning out, not covering up, and for a shot of penicillin and careful treatment over many days.

Meanwhile, village life was enlivened by the squeaking and grunting of two tiny baby peccaries the hunters had brought home. The women fed them. The children played with them as if they were puppies or kittens.

One morning, when I had been to see the injured man, a little piglet followed me home. Out of the lodge, across the village square, right into our house as if he had known me all his life! I had quite a job to avoid treading on him for he kept right under my feet. He would eat out of my hand and wherever I went he was never more than a few inches from my heels.

After a while, a wee Red Indian boy came along to claim his pet. He looked so cute with his copper-coloured skin, jet-black hair and eyes brimful of sparkle. It was hard to believe that such lovable boys could ever have grown up to be the fearsome, pitiless killers who had terrorized the River Xingu for so long!

I did not say so but I was thinking the boy would not have an easy task in getting his pet away from me and our nice clean house. It was, however, the quickest, easiest thing in the world! All the boy did was to get his feet in between the piglet's snout and my heels! In one moment, it left off following me and followed him out of the house and into the village. And, believe me, if a forest peccary had suddenly cut in between the little boy's feet and the little pig's trotters it would have been back in the jungle in no time and just one more in a big, wild herd.

How do Indians tame peccary? It's easy. They just make the most of that instinct to follow the feet which are nearest. The feet which guide the trotters will decide the future of the tusks.

And who will say that young humans don't have a "follow-instinct" too?

That is why we missionaries are here. We want our feet to be worth following, as we, for our part, seek to follow the One who said, "I am the Way".

****

When Jesus spoke again to the people, he said, "I am the light of the world. Whoever follows me will never walk in darkness, but will have the light of life."

John 8:12

THE ANTEATER

One of the Indians has a wonderful pet. Only a toddler as yet, it is no bigger than a dog although its head is already a foot long, all snout, narrow and tapering like a parsnip. Donna Eva and the children got a fright when it put out its tongue at them. They thought a snake was coming out of its mouth! It's ears and eyes are tiny. The front legs are longer and stronger than the back ones and all four are armed with great claws. The body is covered with long, coarse hair, black and grey. But strangest of all is the flat, bushy tail, big enough to use as an umbrella when it rains and as a blanket at night. When he grows up he will be a great anteater or ant bear.

True to his name, he really eats ants and, as far as I can see, he will eat nothing else. In the zoo he gives his keeper a hard time to keep him fed. For the Indian, feeding his pet is no problem at all for there are ant hills all over the place in these parts. The anteater's preference is for white ants or termites.

Termites are horrible little creatures which work underground and keep us on the alert lest they should gnaw into our boxes, books and furniture or even the wooden framework of the house we live in. Were it not for the problems in looking after such a pet and taking him around with us on our travels, I would be tempted to make an offer for that anteater. How convenient to have him around the house, relieving me of all concern for our wooden possessions.

The anteater's one aim in life seems to be to rid the earth of termites. His strong, hooked arms were built for breaking into ant hills. The tapered snout and snake-like tongue are his equipment for rooting out the ants from their clay strongholds. Angry insects swarm on to the invading tongue as it licks around, thinking no doubt of stinging it into retreat. Retreat it does but only into its mouth, and with it, all the clinging ants as well.

Around it goes from ant hill to ant hill, breaking them open, mopping up their occupants and generally doing a good job. It is a hopeless task though, for ant hills are so many and anteaters so few. And instead of appreciating the good work he is doing, the Indians are all too ready to kill and eat him. How easy it would be for the anteater to get discouraged, to give up his mission and go in for eating bananas or even wild fruits. But he never runs away, either from his work or from his enemies.

Whenever he is attacked he always stands firm, rearing himself on his hind legs and, raising that flag of a tail, he opens his arms wide and makes his claws stick out like the knives in Boadicea's chariot wheels. Even the jaguar will not risk a frontal attack. If he cannot take him by surprise and get him from behind, he will leave him alone for he knows that once that anteater's hooked arms get a hold they will never let go, not even in death.

The Indians have learned a lot from the animals who share their jungle empire, mostly along the lines of camouflage and being wily, tough and relentless. It is from the anteater that they have learned the value of standing firm. Indian boys never run away in a fight, even though they cannot hope to win. They just stand their ground, giving and taking until beaten.

The anteater's tenacity is a lesson to Donna Eva and me as we seek to win these Indians for Jesus. Ant hills of superstition we have demolished by the score but still they appear. The tribe, instead of joining us for a Christian Christmas, staged a week's commemoration of the time when some painted women turned themselves into fish! And how many ant hills of cruelty have we not attacked yet! Most Indians still delight to kill and are amused at the sufferings of others. In their recent feast, scores of big turtles were roasted alive after a hole had been hammered in each shell. Other ant hills still persisting are those of indifference and callousness.

We carry on, trying to be kind among the cruel and loving the unloved, the unloving and the ungrateful. Doing everything in love, just as Jesus did.

****

"Be on your guard; stand firm in the faith; be men of courage; be strong. Do everything in love."

1 Corinthians 16:13,14

THE BOA TURNS TO SOAP

We are in town for a few weeks. We came down the River Xingu in a trader's launch. The days were long, our seats were hard and whenever the owner called a halt for trading the sand flies swarmed on board and piled on the agony until we got going again and the wind could blow them away.

There was more foam on the water than usual and James mistook it for soap suds. I had to explain the difference between soap suds and the kind of foam we see on our River Xingu. Foam might be just air bubbles caused when water runs up against rocks, trees or the prow of a boat. Where there are rapids or falls the whole river may become a seething mass of foam. Eddies and whirlpools make foam too - not very white for they have a way of churning all kinds of impurities out of the water. I suggested that the foam might be coming from Indian fish poison. I told him how all the men in a village will carry a heavy sheaf of poison vines to the water and hammer them to pulp with their clubs. In a few minutes the water is covered by a mass of foam which poisons the water and soon has the poor fish gasping for breath, their tummies turned upwards and providing the Indians with easy targets for their arrows.

Then I remember another story of foam on the water.

There was once a pig - just an ordinary pig wallowing in the mud by the riverside. But his grunts of contentment suddenly became squeals of fright as he felt himself being

hugged by a boa constrictor. Up in the village a man heard the squealing and, guessing what was happening, picked up his gun and raced down the path to the river. Though too late to save the pig he killed the boa and soon had it unwound from the pig and rewound on a long pole for carrying to the village.

Everyone crowded round to watch as he first removed the valuable skin and then sliced the flesh into steaks. That man knew that the boa was as fat as it was long. For every centimetre of her two metres of life she had been piling up the fat as she preyed - first of all on frogs, rats and lizards and then, as she grew longer and stronger, on larger animals. And now the man was going to fry her steaks for the fat they would yield.

What would he do with so much boa fat? People in the interior of Brazil may live right off the beaten track and so have to be as independent as they possibly can in the matter of supplies. They may have to make their own lamp oil from oil-yielding wild fruits. They need to know how to make their own soap too. And it was with the help of a tin of caustic soda that our friend was going to turn the boa fat into soap.

That was the end of the mighty boa constrictor. Nothing but soap suds to show for a whole lifetime! And as the river carried those suds away nobody gave them so little as a look.

****

Have you ever thought about how much people invest in their lives, often without a thought for the future and what will happen when they die? Remember that the Bible tells us that everything we make and buy will perish, even our health and strength will fail. Only the love of God will endure forever!

"As for man, his days are like grass, he flourishes like a flower in the field; the wind blows over it and it is gone, and it's place is remembered no more. But from everlasting to everlasting the Lord's love is with those that fear him."

Psalm 103:15-17

PLAYING POSSUM

We are still away from the Indians and living in our chalet home on the River Xingu. The house has been empty for more than a year and, in our absence, the rats have taken possession. Indeed, the whole town is plagued with them. Our neighbour, who bakes to sell from door to door, has a sack of flour from which she just could not keep the rats away until she and her husband decided to take the flour to bed with them and give it the protection of their mosquito net!

Another neighbour did not take proper care of his artificial teeth and when he awoke one morning he found them gone from beside his bedside table. He spent the whole day on the roof of his home, looking between the tiles and rafters where rats have their hideout during daylight hours. He only got them back after several weeks when the people next door but one had had their roof repaired and the denture was found.

In the chalet young Jim has taken to baiting our rat-traps instead of his fish hooks. One night, when he went to our outside bathroom, he saw a rat as big as a cat. It was not an ordinary rat because, as well as being very big, its hair was longer and its movement slower. It was an opossum.

Like the kangaroo, the female has a pouch in which to carry her babies and when these get too big for the pouch and yet are still too small to fend for themselves they cling to their mother's fur coat wherever they can get a hold.

The opossum did not run away when discovered, so out of pity we took no action against him. However, when next night we saw him there again we suspected that he was making our bathroom his headquarters for raids on our neighbours' chickens. Jim aimed a blow at him with an Indian club but, being rather long, the descending club hit the low roof and broke a tile instead of the opossum's head. The next time we saw him was on top of a fence. Clearly loitering with intent to commit a felony, as the police would say, we decided that the opossum had to die. A single shot from a gun sent him toppling to earth like a stone.

Jim was for climbing the fence right away and hauling out the prize from the clump of foliage into which he had fallen but, opossums being smelly things, I told him to leave it until morning.

But when morning came, there wasn't a trace of the "dead" opossum. He can cleverly pretend to be dead where there is a chance of saving his life and with us his ruse worked all too well and he made a clean getaway.

"Playing possum" is something we humans can do too. If it means an easy way out of a difficulty we can feign dead or sick or pretend not to know something when all the time we do. There are a number of Bible stories of people who could play possum when it suited their interests, pretending to be sick or ignorant of what they knew to be true. There was Peter, for instance, who lay very low when a girl challenged him about knowing Jesus. At that fireside he looked more like a dead sinner than a live disciple of Jesus Christ.

****

"For God did not give us a spirit of timidity, but a spirit of power, of love and of self-discipline."

2 Timothy 1:7

DON'T BE AN ARMADILLO

This is the rainy season and the River Xingu is in flood. With many of the rapids now under water, we find it more convenient than in the dry season for getting around in our little boat and visiting the settlers who have their homes on the river banks.

Below the very last rapid and for nearly two hundred miles before the River Xingu flows into the Amazon, is a long, clear stretch of water which is navigable to big river steamers. In those waters are creatures which fight shy of rapids and rough waters for they are never encountered in the upper reaches of the river. Such are the dolphins (regarded by the natives as being enchanted), the giant cow-fish and the famous tartarugas. These are turtles which may weigh as much as one hundred pounds and are in great demand for the tables of the rich, as the flesh is considered to be a greater delicacy than that of turkeys.

It is not surprising, therefore, that as we travelled through those waters our conversation should be of dolphins and fresh-water turtles.

In the midst of our talking we had to call at one of the riverside homes. As we moored our boat the women of the household were at work on a big pile of fresh meat. There, sure enough, a few metres away, was a real whopper of a yellow, horny shell.

"Stay for a meal," the good folks invited. We did.

"Well," said Donna Eva as the meal over, we proceeded on our way, "If that was the wonderful tartaruga turtle, I just cannot understand people being so crazy about it."

"Tartaruga?" I exclaimed. "Who said that was tartaruga? Do you think that everything in a big shell is turtle? That wasn't tartaruga at all but an armadillo!"

The expression on Donna Eva's face was a mixture of dismay and disgust because she had never eaten armadillo before.

The Indians tell us that he is the most ancient of all animals. He began life, so they say, up in heaven but, being a great burrower from the beginning, he one day burrowed right through the floor of heaven and fell down to earth!

Digging is the armadillo's favourite means of defence even though nature has given him a coat of armour which

covers him from nose to tail. At the slightest alarm he begins to dig himself in and down into the earth he goes with amazing speed. Scratching away with his front legs, he uses his back ones to hurl the dirt clear. Woe betide the hunting dog who gets caught in the back fire from that furious digging!

Fancy living in this vast, wonderful forest yet only venturing out under cover of darkness. Fancy having such a coat of armour and yet not using it except as protection against falls of earth and sand as he digs on and on to comfort and safety. Why, with such equipment, the armadillo could laugh at cold and rain, thorn and thicket, snake and hawk, hornet and nettle and make life one long party!

There is a streak in his inside make-up as yellow as his armour plate. The armadillo is just plain scared of everything and everybody!

As regards diet, he lives on grubs, earth worms and - like the anteater - termites. Of course, the latter has much the harder time with no armour to protect him.

How I wish I could get the two of them together. If only I could encourage the armadillo to face the light of day, to take a stand like the anteater or, better still, to take a stand with him. How cheered the old termite fighter would be to have an ally at his side. If only they would pool their resources. But our two friends are only animals. They haven't the sense to get together and work together. The sad thing is that we humans sometimes try to imitate them.

If there are tough Christians who sing "Stand up, stand up for Jesus" and do it, there are also the other kind, armadillo Christians, armchair ones, whose concern seems to be to keep as safe and comfortable as possible. To say that they are just cautious or tactful in their witness is much too charitable. I know what kind of Christians we need to be.

****

"Finally, be strong in the Lord and in his mighty power. Put on the full armour of God so that you can take your stand against the devil's schemes."

Ephesians 6:10,11

SLOW AS A SLOTH

Hanging upside down from a rafter! My first impression was of an ageing monkey because its dark brown hair was greying. It was a sloth and he was fast asleep. I was glad to see him for he is a rare sight, even in the Brazilian forest.

Fossils show that the sloth family was once numerous with some members as big as elephants. But Providence seems to have fashioned them all on the basis of a gram of brain to each tonne of brawn, which wasn't enough to ensure survival in a competitive world. Perhaps before very long even this Brazilian variety will become extinct too, with nobody at all to lament its passing.

I had no difficulty in getting a photograph for, as regards movement, the sloth is in the tortoise class. And in a flat race the tortoise would win easily because, to get along at all, the sloth needs to be up in a tree. He was born in a tree, he lives in a tree and in the ordinary way he will die in a tree, although it would be exaggerating to add "and all in the same tree". It is pitiful to see him on the ground or in the water because, instead of having hands and feet, he is fitted with big claws which can only be used for hanging on to branches. He cannot walk, stand or even sit. He lives hanging on and upside down he goes, all the way from his cradle to his grave.

He was quite unmoved by my stroking and efforts to show myself friendly. I fancy he would have been just as indifferent to pokes or threats. Though neither hungry nor tied up, he just surveyed me sadly through dull, watery eyes.

"Poor you!" I muttered, as I turned away. "Whoever would want to be a sloth. And yet you must be here for some purpose."

Then I remembered a verse in my Bible: "Not slothful in business." From now onwards I shall want to read, "Not sloth-like."

Let me complete that verse from the Bible: "Not slothful in business, fervent in spirit, serving the Lord." That is being something more than just a human being and not an animal. It means being a Christian and for that, I'm gladdest of all because the Lord gives faith and hope, joy and peace, light and love.

****

"Never be lacking in zeal, but keep your spiritual fervour, serving the Lord."

Romans 12: 11

GOATSUCKER'S BAD NAME

There is never any knowing what Jim will bring home when he goes off with the Indians. He may come in asking for an empty matchbox in which to house a pet frog. Or he may be wanting a piece of string with which to harness a wee trailer to a midget tortoise or a gondola to some strange flying insect.

The other day his trophy was a baby bird, the most unattractive thing imaginable. It had no feathers at all and the only movement made was with its big mouth which gaped hungrily all the time. Jim's first concern was to give it something to eat. He tried it with rice, cooked and raw. He tried it with farina meal, wet and dry. But all to no avail.

It was then that I tried to help. "First of all," I suggested, "we must find out what kind of a bird it is. If it is a hawk, it will need meat, if a gull or heron we must give it fish. If it belongs to the swallow family, we must try it with insects."

When we asked the Indians we were told that the bird was a porro-pot which of course left us none the wiser. Then I went to our home-made dictionary of the Indian language. Over the years we have never heard a new word without writing it down. Well, that dictionary gave us porro-pot's Brazilian equivalent. The rest was easy. Turning up the big Brazilian-English dictionary I discovered that porro-pot is Indian for bacarau which in turn has three names in English - nightjar, nighthawk and goatsucker.

Nothing much to look at, the grown bird is quite drab in this land of so many gaudy feathers. It delights to sit on a patch of bare ground on a moonlit night. Sometimes it gives the impression of not being able to fly properly or that it has a damaged wing, half-flying half-jumping in a way that tempts you to give chase. Usually it is the female bird that does this, endeavouring to lead unwelcome intruders away from her nest.

We mixed some powdered milk and administered it in a small teaspoon. The experiment was not a success. Indeed, it was fatal. The poor bird just gave one long gurgle and died. Milk was clearly NOT its proper food, goatsucker or not.

Now, had there been time for me to check up the facts, I would have learned that the name goatsucker comes from the now disproved tradition that these birds pester mother goats in order to steal their milk. What they are really doing is mopping up the flies, gnats, mosquitoes and other insect pests which are all too ready to torment defenceless animals. In doing their best to help the goats, the poor birds got themselves a bad name which got first of all into people's minds and then into their books.

I was once visiting a colony of leprosy sufferers near the mouth of the Amazon and among them I met several who had recently arrived there from the River Xingu. They were all feeling the separation from home and loved ones as well as the terrible depression which follows the doctor's diagnosis of leprosy. Some of them were Christian believers and the fact that others were not made no difference to the distribution of gifts of money I was able to make. Before coming away I prayed with them, the most and the best I could do for them in their plight.

When the husband of one of the sufferers who was not a Christian heard of what I had done he wrote to me. Not a Christian himself, he complained that I was trying to make a Christian of his wife by helping her. The letter ended with a demand that I should make no further visits and no further gifts without his permission.

There is no need for a Christian to be a foreign missionary to know how easily we can be misunderstood. Just take a stand for Jesus Christ and watch it happen, whether at school, your place of employment or in your own home. The crowd is not always right. Jesus IS always right and nobody ever yet followed Him all the way and regretted it.

****

"Blessed are you when people insult you, persecute you and falsely say all kinds of evil against you because of me. Rejoice and be glad, because great is your reward in heaven, for in the same way they persecuted the prophets who were before you."

Matthew 5:11,12

KILLER FISH FOR SUPPER

On our river journeys we always get very hungry so, as they paddle our boat, the Indians are on the alert for fish and game. One day, as the overhead sun as well as our hungry tummies suggested a halt for something to eat, we were all glad to spot some beautiful, silver fish which were jumping up to snap at leaves hanging low over the water. Very quietly, one of the Indians picked up his bow and arrows. Up to the surface came a fish and in the split second during which it was air-borne, the bow-string twanged. It was a wonderful shot because the arrow transfixed the fish and turned it over on its side.

Next job was to take it from the water but as the current was fairly strong, arrow and fish were being carried downstream. Before we could overtake the still struggling fish the arrow gave a sudden jump and when, moments later, we took it from the water all that remained of our fish was the head! The killer fish were on the war-path and our dinner was gone!

One of our men strode off into the forest with his gun and returned to camp with a bird little bigger than a starling.

Using pieces of the bird for bait, in a few minutes the good man had caught enough killer fish (piranhas) for dinner, and supper too, because of all Brazilian fish, piranhas are just about the easiest to catch. They dash madly at any kind of bleeding bait. The only problem is getting them unhooked without a finger being snapped off!

Some are as grey as lead, some a bright as goldfish. Some are almost 40 centimetres long, others stop growing at 15 centimetres. But all are killers, blood-hungry killers. Their teeth are like newly sharpened rip saws and when they close they click. They hunt in packs like wolves but keep to deep water except when they surface at the noise of a splash or at the scent of blood.

If one has a cut or open sore it is dangerous to bathe in our beautiful River Xingu.

Animals need the river as much as we do. When hunted they always make for the water in the hope of putting the hunter or his dogs off the scent. But should the piranhas

be there, attracted by the bleeding, flesh can be stripped from bone in a few seconds and a living body reduced to a skeleton.

As we watched the fish being prepared for the pot, Donna Eva remarked that she is not surprised that some writers refer to our rain forests, with their killer-fish and jaguars, anacondas and crocodiles, as "Green Hell."

It was not long before we were enjoying our meal of cooked piranha, stripping fish from bone with that enthusiasm born of a good appetite.

"No problem, these killer fish," I said to Donna Eva, my mouth more full than perhaps it ought to have been. "Their human victims are few because they are easily avoided and readily caught. There is nothing we need do about them but keep out of their way. But human beings are different. They can be forgiven, converted, changed, saved!"

And that is our mission in life. In a modern world, haunted and torn by killer-things, inspired by killer-thinking, fed and fanned by killer books and even toys, we know that Jesus alone can give LIFE.

****

Jesus said... "I have come that they may have life, and have it to the full."

John 10:10

BLUE BUTTERFLY?

I have seen the biggest, most beautiful butterfly of a lifetime! It had a wing span of 15 centimetres and, although brown on the underside, the top of its wings was a dazzling blue which sparkled in the morning sunlight. Knowing what a marvellous curio such a prize would make, I dropped the tools with which I was working and gave chase, hoping it would alight on one of our coffee bushes which were in full blossom. However, it flew on, right over the garden fence and into the forest beyond.

Some days after the blue butterfly escaped me, I noticed a tiny caterpillar on our jasmine tree. There is nothing very attractive about its gnarled, crooked trunk and branches but the leaves are a luscious green all the year round and the flowers are as white as Easter lilies and so fragrant that the scent carries more than thirty metres. Flowers are rare on the River Xingu and our jasmine tree can be like a breath of paradise in a dreary world of mud and mosquitoes. We love it.

As I examined the caterpillar, I saw it was

not alone. There were lots of them, tiny creatures decked in black velvet jerseys with gold stripes and lying motionless on the underside of the branches.

The idea came to me that the big blue butterfly might have laid its eggs there while passing through our garden. What matter that the caterpillars should be black and gold and the parent blue and brown? The caterpillar need bear no resemblance to the butterfly into which, one day, it will be transformed.

So the caterpillars were allowed to stay, even when they began to rear their heads and jab at the leaves like hungry woodpeckers. They simply gorged themselves and grew at the rate of nearly an inch a day. By the end of the week they were six inches long and almost an inch in diameter. If I had never seen so big a butterfly, I was now seeing the biggest caterpillars too.

"Who would have thought it?" I said to myself as our once lovely tree was stripped of its leaves and the ground below it became littered with stalks and droppings. "To think that those cute, gay, innocent-looking little fellows should grow up into such terrors!" One morning the children came in to tell me that all my pet caterpillars, as they called them, were going away. I went into the garden and found the jasmine tree as bare of caterpillars as it was of its leaves. Some were hurrying down the trunk, others were hunching themselves along the ground in the direction of the fence. Some had already climbed the fence and were arching their heads as if looking for other jasmine trees to conquer.

Finding an old iron pot, I lined it with leaves and went round collecting as many caterpillars as I could, picking them up between two sticks, placing them in the nest and covering the pot with a roofing tile. When the children asked me what I was doing, I told them how we were going to have a wonderful object lesson of how God can change bad things and make them good, and how He changes bad people too.

"We'll look at them every day," I said. "One day the nasty things are going to be changed into wonderful butterflies and then they will flit around in the sunlight like the bees and humming-birds."

Next day the caterpillars were dull and listless. Their once gay jerseys were losing their shine. Their appetites had gone too, for not a single leaf had been nibbled, but they still reared their heads angrily when lightly touched with a stick.

A few days later, they had become chrysalides. The caterpillar skins and legs were dry and shrivelled and had been cast aside like old clothes. Jim picked them up and handled the black chrysalides without fear.

Each day we peeped into that iron pot, all eager to be on the spot when the great change should take place.

At last it happened. The hard black shells split from end to end. There was movement inside. Would the first glimpse of wing be blue or brown?

It was neither. Instead of the exquisite blue we expected to see, there emerged the ugliest, most horrid, loathsome moths I have ever seen! The children were disgusted.

"Witch-moth!" cried Jim's Brazilian playmate.

Even when they emerged from their coffin-like shells, the creatures made no effort to fly away. To the witch-moth, the brightness of the sunshine, the fragrance of flowers, the company of honey-bees and humming-bees and hummingbirds mean nothing at all. It was not until after sunset that they showed signs of movement and we watched them unfold their wings and flutter clumsily away into the darkness.

This had been an object lesson very different from what I expected. Butterflies and moths, there is always an opposite.

There is nothing at all a caterpillar can do about its future state. It either becomes a butterfly or a moth, according to its kind. It cannot choose between light and darkness. We can. We can be good or bad. We can obey God or disobey Him. We can be saved or lost. And it is for us to choose.

****

" Now choose life, so that you and your children may live and that you may love the Lord your God, listen to his voice, and hold fast to him."

Deuteronomy 30:19,20

TWO BIRDS IN ONE

Donna Eva stood by an open window, looking up into the sky and shading her eyes from the glare.

"Look at those birds," she said, "Oh, to be able to fly so high where there's a cool wind and the air is so fresh and untainted by the things of earth!"

The birds certainly made a fine sight. There were perhaps a dozen of them, gliding majestically at a great height, with only the occasional flip of a wing to show that they were birds and not machines.

"You've seen them many a time on the fence at the foot of our backyard. They're vultures!"

Donna Eva did not try to hide her surprise. She knew the vulture well enough. There is no mistaking him, with his dull, black feathers, his bald pate and hooked beak. His favourite perch is the branch of a lofty tree from where his eye can cover a wide area. He may often be seen on a fence or roof overlooking a kitchen door. There he will sit for hours on end, waiting for scraps of offal or garbage. He has no appetite for the daintier scraps thrown out to the sparrows and starlings. He is a scavenger, only wanting that which is smelly and in decomposition.

He has a clumsy, lurching way of walking. His take off from the ground is a real effort, with nothing graceful about it. As he moves from scrap to scrap or fights for his share of the victim, he has a way of half-jumping, half-flying.

His sense of smell and sight is truly amazing. He is quick to see any sick or wounded animal likely to die and the smell of death guides him unerringly through any covering of thicket or forest roof-top of foliage, no matter how dense these may be. With his sharp hooked bill and strong talons, his meal does not take him long. His companions are always so many and so hungry. There is rarely enough meat to go round.

After feeding, he makes for the river and spends some

time splashing his great wings in the water and sunning himself on the shore or on a convenient branch of a tree. Then up he soars, to heights unreached by any other bird. If among the rubbish he is loathsome, in the air he is superb!

He returns to earth after a while and then, blue skies,

clean air, washing and sunning seemingly forgotten, he is back to his scavenging among the garbage and offal.

"How strange!" murmured Donna Eva. "What a queer mix-up of two natures in the one bird. How can he be so much at home in two such opposite spheres? How can he fly so high, and then, so quickly afterwards, be ready to stoop so low?"

It is clear to me that there are two natures common to all men. If we are honest with ourselves we can recognize their presence in our own hearts. We can see them at work in our children. In young and old alike is the conflict between good and bad. Few will dare say that they are all good, yet none will denounce themselves as wholly bad. Who never wants to soar? But who never comes down to the level of the mean and unworthy?

God never meant us to live like vultures, up and down, now soaring, now stooping, now glorying, now grovelling. There is a way, not only to get away from sin but also to keep away. Paul gives us the answer: "I thank God, through Jesus Christ our Lord."

****

"Submit yourselves, then, to God. Resist the devil, and he will flee from you. Come near to God and he will come near to you."
James 4:7,8

THE ELECTRIC EEL

There are days in these rain forests when Donna Eva is unable to make the grade in the kitchen. It is not enough to be able to cook a meal. A really good cook must know how to catch something to cook!

That is how a friend of ours came to be wading in the river an hour before supper time. Mosquitoes were few so he was not wearing a shirt. Over his shoulder, a shot-gun hung by a leather strap. Over his arm was folded the fishing net he was all set for casting as he moved stealthily towards the spot where he calculated the fish might be. Suddenly, with a yell like someone mortally wounded, he went down like a shot, arms and legs flailing in the water. His leg had brushed against an electric eel! Thankfully for him, the water was shallow enough to lie there until the first effects of the shock had passed. Then, with all thoughts of kitchen and evening meal forgotten, he made for the house and his hammock to seek relief from the aching leg.

I had often heard stories of electric eels but this was the first case personally known to me and, after seeing a victim, I became keener than ever to examine an aggressor.

The opportunity came one Sunday morning. Our morning service had been disappointing for all the boys were absent. Waking up very hungry, they decided to go fishing. They had not been away for long before they returned home and we all knew they were not coming empty-handed. When there is no kill, or when the catch is small, Indians are ashamed and try to sneak into the village without being seen. When the haul is a big one, they make a lot of noise. That Sunday, the shouting was so loud they might well have been bringing in a jaguar.

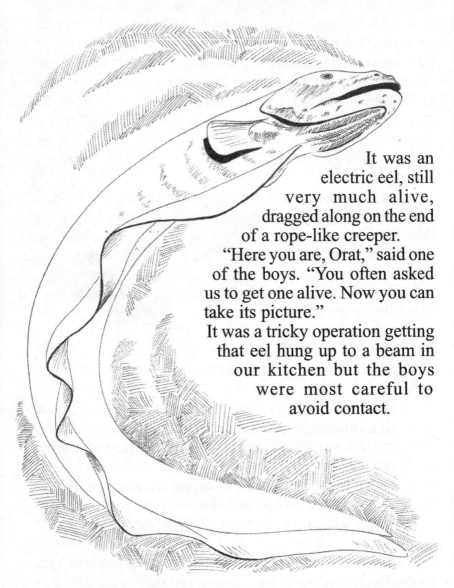

It was an electric eel, still very much alive, dragged along on the end of a rope-like creeper.

"Here you are, Orat," said one of the boys. "You often asked us to get one alive. Now you can take its picture."

It was a tricky operation getting that eel hung up to a beam in our kitchen but the boys were most careful to avoid contact.

I noticed that the drag rope was quite dry. Experience has taught the Indians the ABC of insulation. After all, their ancestors knew all about shocks before ours did!

The eel was not a big one, just over a metre long and as thick as a man's arm. The dark green body had no scales and there was a soft, rippling fin stretching along the underside from head to tail. The head was flat with a gaping mouth and the tiniest of eyes. The drag-rope had somehow been threaded through its gills.

I was looking at the wonderful creature which is dynamo, battery and discharge coil all combined. For the first time ever, there was electricity in our kitchen! Having read somewhere that the current produced is as much as 500 volts, I went for a voltmeter. Maybe I could get some response on the dial.

"Don't touch it! It will knock you down!" yelled the Indians.

In due time the eel died and was cut down and handed back to the boys who, hungrier than ever, prepared for a feast. I watched very carefully as they did the cutting and slicing, but saw no clue as to the source of the creature's power.

Indians believe that they become like the things they eat. They eat the howling monkey to be resistant and tough, the jaguar to be fierce, the electric eel to make their presence felt and feared. The stronger and wilder they can become, the better their chances of one day becoming a chief.

I suppose we have all met people who would make good Red Indians, and chiefs at that! They never saw an electric eel, much less ate one. But they have a way of throwing their weight about in a way that hurts. Things they say, looks they give - words, looks, deeds can hurt just as much as live wires.

For the Indians, the heroes of their legends were all fierce warriors with super-strength, magic weapons and a bent for killing. Now they are hearing of Someone who was different. No-one but Jesus could say "All power is given unto Me, in heaven and in earth." Yet, for all that power, He was so kind and wonderful to know.

For instance, there was that poor woman we read about in the Gospels. Desperately ill for twelve years, all her money gone in doctors' bills, yet without relief. Hearing of Jesus and His power, she crept forward in the crowd, reached out and touched the hem of His garment. She was not hurt, but healed.

The Indians often ask me why God made this and that. If I were to ask them why God made electric eels I think I know what many of them would answer: "To show us how to be!"

Everything must have been made for a purpose although very often we cannot understand what that purpose may be. As for me, I can think of at least one reason why God made electric eels: "To show us how NOT to be!"

****

" Be kind and compassionate to one another, forgiving each other, just as in Christ God forgave you."

Ephesians 4:32

PUTTING UP THE GREEN PARASOL

"Whatever makes you grow your cabbages and lettuces on those big tables?" asked our visitors. No wonder they were surprised. Just as ancient Babylon had its Hanging Gardens - whatever they were - here in interior Brazil we have our gardens on stilts!

This is because of the parasol-ants. The land is honeycombed with their burrows. If we made our kitchen garden at ground level they could strip it in a single night. Parasol ants are so called because they are usually seen carrying pieces of fresh leaves like so many green sun-shades.

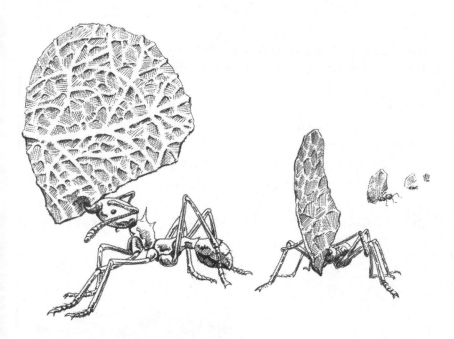

The Bible says, "Ants are creatures of little strength, yet they store up their food in the summer" (Proverbs 30:25). "Go to the ant, you sluggard; consider its ways and be wise!" (Proverbs 6:6).

Here we have stood amazed at their industry, at the way they can work round the clock to lay up leaves in their underground storehouses. They never seem to get discouraged, not even when the wind gets into their parasols and bowls them right over or when a grain of maize, maybe ten times the midget carrier's weight, just won't stay put on its back.

We can hardly blame them for coveting the greens in our garden. Why lay up any old thing when there are luscious cabbage and lettuce, mango and orange leaves about? But with the garden and the work being ours, we could not just stand by and see our precious greens disappearing. The table idea was our last resort after everything else to beat the parasols had failed. We had flushed their burrows with soapy dish water. We salted their trails with D.D.T. We lit the blow lamp and poured fire into their dens. But if we managed to flood or fumigate one store, they would work on another. They just kept to their job, laying up with all the zeal and persistence of Joseph in Egypt.

So I did what I had seen our Brazilian friends do in other parts of the River Xingu and made some rustic tables. The legs were of forked sticks, of a kind of wood the white ants would not devour, let into the ground. The table tops were of rough wood, covered with old mats and fitted with side pieces to prevent the soil from falling off. Thanks to this device, our greens were thriving.

But a few days after our visitors left these ants discovered our secret and swarmed up these table legs in their thousands.

I could not but admire their nerve and courage. Some, I noticed as I stood watching, did nothing but lop leaves. Others did the carrying down the legs and along the trail to the underground store. Talk about team spirit!

What those ants had carried off in the way of lettuce leaves, they more than repaid in the lessons they had taught me. People, like ants, need to "lay up" in a storehouse open to us all through Jesus Christ - a storehouse which cannot be destroyed.

****

"Do not store up for yourselves treasures on earth, where moth and rust destroy, and where thieves break in and steal. But store up for yourselves treasures in heaven, where moth and rust do not destroy, and where thieves do not break in and steal. For where your treasure is, there will your heart be also."

Matthew 6:19-21

THE TRIUMPHANT FROG

The rainy season is just ending and we are glad. The seven wet months are a dreary time for most forest dwellers, ourselves and the Indians included.

Almost alone among jungle creatures, the frog is in his element. The more it rains, the happier he seems to be and he lets everybody know how he feels. There is a swamp just outside our village and we sometimes get the impression that it is the home of a million frogs. All night long, right through the rainy season, that swamp echoes with a mighty chorus of croakers. And, strangely enough, they sound as if they are calling the Indian word for water - *n'go . . . n'go . . . n'go.*

When the rains finish, the swamp begins to dry up and, if its inhabitants are to survive, they must scatter. So away they go in search of water holes which do not dry up during the months when rain is but a dream.

Many a time, on our journeys through the forest, we have been grateful for those water-loving frogs. Travellers can get dreadfully thirsty on the trail and it often happens that it is the croaking of some lone frog which guides them to a spot where there is still water enough to dampen their parched tongues.

The frog has found water, or rain is coming, and he wants to share the good news.

Now, the other day, Donna Eva called me to see a frog she had discovered trying to hide in her kitchen. It was as black as coal and as flat as a pancake. Donna Eva suggested that the poor thing had somehow been crushed. What impressed me was that crushed or no, the frog was keeping his chin up! Quite unconcerned at our presence, he hopped away into the shadows behind our five-gallon jar of drinking water, where it is not only dark but cool.

"Let him stay," pleaded Donna Eva, as I prepared to throw him out. "This is only the kitchen and, after all, even frogs need somewhere to live."

However, later in the day I was recalled by an indignant wife who had found the frog in our bedroom. From time to time the kitchen water-jar had to be taken down for refilling, and this, no doubt, had disturbed him and given him undesired publicity. Hence his desire to explore the bedroom.

This seemed to be imposing on good nature, and picking up a broom, she took action and most unceremoniously brushed him out of the house altogether. As far as we were concerned, he must join the rest of his kind in their search for suitable accommodation by a water-hole. Once installed, he would soon settle down and join his mates in the evening chorus of *n'go . . . n'go . . . n'go. . .* which during the dry months must needs be on a greatly reduced scale.

However, we had not seen the last of that flat, black frog!

At supper time, I lit the pressure lamp and we sat down to a meal of boiled fish and manioc cereal, grateful for a light good enough for us to pick out the bones. Then, would you believe it, in came that frog, his chin higher than ever, as round the room he made his way mopping up mosquitoes!

There he was, rooting them out of their hideouts in the clay walls with his long tongue. If he spotted one out of range, up he would jump and get it while still in the air!

"Good old fellow," I muttered, "there you go, crushed, sat on and kicked out, yet with no ill feeling at all, getting on with the good work while the rest of the world takes it easy!"

If a puny creature like a frog can refuse to be discouraged, if he can keep his chin up in the face of misunderstanding and opposition and not let it interfere with his programme of doing good, if he can be at his best when the weather is at its worst and never tire of sharing his good news, then surely we humans can take courage.

****

"Blessed is the man who perseveres under trial, because when he has stood the test, he will receive the crown of life that God has promised to those who love him."

James 1:12

BATTLE OF THE BATS

Our house has been plagued by a whole squadron of bats. Once the light from our pressure-lamp is extinguished, there is a swishing and a swooping, a flapping and a fluttering and the nightly invasion is on. We have been afraid lest during our sleep our fingers, elbows or toes should touch the flimsy muslin of our mosquito nets and get nipped by bat teeth! We have tried to keep them away be leaving a storm-lantern burning but this has been ineffective.

The Indians did not seem concerned when we told them. One of them had arrowed a bat he had found

sleeping in an orange tree just outside our back door. It had a wing-spread of half a metre, and ugh, the teeth!

"But there is nothing for you to be afraid of," he assured us. "This kind doesn't bite. The blood-drinkers are small."

We were quite aware that most of the world's bats are

harmless and live on insects and that not all our Brazilian ones are vampires. But why should those teeth have to be so big and sharp? And what attraction could the few mosquitoes in our house have for so many bats?

Then we noticed that a big bunch of bananas in our storeroom had been well nibbled overnight. Here, among the Indians, we get plenty of bananas. We eat them singly and we eat them by the dozen. We eat them baked and boiled. We squash them and make them into porridge, cut them in strips and fry them in oil or dry them in the sun until they turn brown and taste like seedless figs.

"Bats like bananas too," said the Indians.

My problem was how to keep those bats away from ours! Next day I decorated the house with tufts of sharp sword grass, just as if it might be with holly and mistletoe at Christmas time. I thought that this might cut their wings

as many a time it has cut my feet, ankles and fingers. But no. Even in the dark, the bats' built-in radar enables them to avoid the traps hanging for them, eat their fill of ripe bananas and take off again without receiving a scratch.

Then came an Indian hunter with another suggestion. "Try prickly bobs. They get under the bats' wings and stick fast. Then they'll go away and not come back."

We tried it but that idea did not work. The bats were there to the last ripe banana!

I could not admit myself beaten. I would make a screened pantry, absolutely bat-proof. And meanwhile I would thank those bats for the lesson they had given me in sheer tenacity of purpose. We must take a hint from our battle with the bats and go on to beat our trials and difficulties. Whether overseas or on the home front, we Christians are called to a big task; that of making Jesus known and winning others for Him. May He keep us all from discouragement and give us something of the toughness of the apostle, Paul.

"Knocked down but never knocked out."

"Ready for anything through the strength of the One who lives in me."

****

"I can do everything through him who gives me strength."

Philippians 4:13

EAR OF THE TAPIR

On a river journey I made with four Indians, we had been living for days on snacks and were longing for a really good meal - one which would last all day and even then leave something over for supper!

As our boat rounded a bend in the river, a big animal was having a quiet bathe. "Tapir!" breathed the Indians in one breath.

The tapir is as tough-looking as his flesh makes tough eating. His head is big, hard and stream-lined, a wonderful provision for life in the jungle because it can crash through the densest thicket.

His skin is so thick and tough that he is indifferent to thorns and stings, and even arrows and buckshot if these are shot at random. His legs are short and powerful, hoofed and very sure-footed. The cutest thing about him is a short trunk, enough to cover his mouth and leave an inch or two over. He raises it when he eats and when he whistles to his mate. When danger is in the air, sensitive as an aerial, the same raised trunk sniffs around and keeps him informed.

Those Indians had not made a sound but that aerial was already alerted for danger. His big hard wedge of a head was raised, his oval ears had stiffened while the short trunk twitched and sniffed the air. And before anyone could reach for a gun, he was away, his legs working like piston rods and his hooves making no mistake for all the slipperiness of a river bank.

"I'm going after him," whispered an Indian. "Give me the new gun and you wait here with the old one in case he takes to the water." I gave a grudging consent, because I had purchased the gun for a special friend, handed it over and watched him scramble ashore and disappear into the jungle.

I had half hoped that we had seen the last of that tapir. Once back in the river he would almost certainly escape

us. He swims like an otter and the Indians tell me that he can actually walk underwater along the river bottom. However, after a few minutes, we heard a shrill tapir call, then another and another. There was a pause and then, from quite a different direction, a responding call. This was repeated, call and counter call getting nearer to each other as the minutes went by. Then suddenly, there was a bang!

When the hunter pushed his way back to the boat, it was to report a kill and to get his companions to sharpen their knives for the skinning and quartering. My own first thought, peevishly enough, was for the new gun I was wanting to return to its wrapping paper. To my dismay, I saw that the wooden ramrod was now minus its metal head! The hunter explained that he had loaded the gun in a hurry and that the ramrod head must have broken off as he had rammed the wadding on top of the charge of powder and shot. With so much meat in prospect, none of the Indians could understand why I should be so concerned about such a trifle as a broken ramrod!

When, later on, I reached the scene of the kill, I found the tapir already skinned and the tough hide serving as a mat on which the cutting up was to be done. I noticed with amazement the size of the beast, the massive head and the thickness of the skin. However could a single shot from a muzzle-loader have been so deadly?

I asked the hunter to show me the bullet hole. Glad to see me thawing out, he said with a smile, "If you want to get a tapir with a single arrow or charge of buckshot, there is only one place. You must get him in the ear. The big job is to get him to turn his ear your way. That is why I gave him a call. He is a lonesome animal. He is not really wild or as tough as he looks. He took my call as being friendly. I kept calling until I got his ear. The rest was easy."

"That's true with people as well as with tapirs," I said to myself. "If I am to catch anyone for God, whether here in Brazil or at home in England, I must somehow get his ear. Behind many a tough look there can be a lonely, friendly heart just waiting to respond to the right approach. The thing for me is to be patient, to go all out to get his ear and then to trust God for the right word."

The hunter was poking his knife into the soft flesh just under the tapir's ear. A couple of deep probes and he felt the point touch metal. Putting in his fingers, he brought out the missing brass head of the ramrod!

"Now you can be happy again," he said with a grin. It took me only a few minutes to dig out the broken wood end and put the brass cap back where it belonged. The gun was as good as new again! And as I washed my hands after operation tapir-ear was over, I said to myself, "No wonder the tapir dropped like a stone! And if I can only remember what I have learned today about the importance of ears, I shall be more than repaid for any damage done to this muzzle-loader!"

****

"Faith comes from hearing the message, and the message is heard through the word of Christ."

Romans 10:17

JUNGLE TURNCOAT

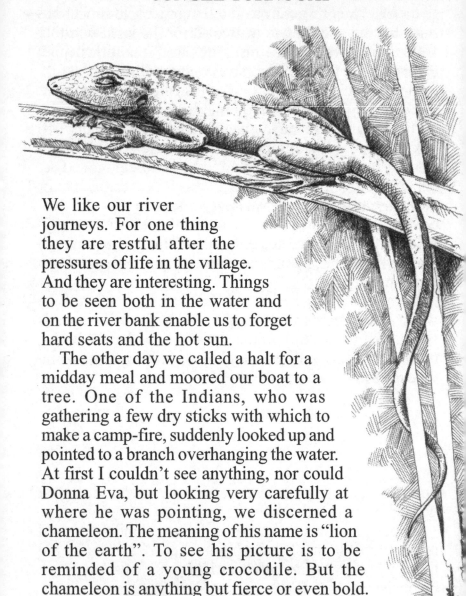

We like our river journeys. For one thing they are restful after the pressures of life in the village. And they are interesting. Things to be seen both in the water and on the river bank enable us to forget hard seats and the hot sun.

The other day we called a halt for a midday meal and moored our boat to a tree. One of the Indians, who was gathering a few dry sticks with which to make a camp-fire, suddenly looked up and pointed to a branch overhanging the water. At first I couldn't see anything, nor could Donna Eva, but looking very carefully at where he was pointing, we discerned a chameleon. The meaning of his name is "lion of the earth". To see his picture is to be reminded of a young crocodile. But the chameleon is anything but fierce or even bold.

He was holding on to that branch as if his very life depended on it. And, as if his four legs and feet were not enough, he was making extra sure by using his long tail as a hook. How different from the playful, daring monkeys we see hanging by the tip of the tail, many metres above the ground!

We had found it hard to see him for as he lay on that branch he was as green as the leaves which almost hid him. But he is not always green. He can look anything from a dirty white to almost black and sometimes quite brown. It is said that he is able to change colour at will, just to match his surroundings. That is because he does not like being seen. He does not want his enemies - particularly hawks - to know he is there. Another opinion is that his colour is determined, not so much as by where he happens to be, but by how he happens to feel. It depends on whether he is warm or cold, wide awake or sleepy, scared, angry or hungry.

But in the ordinary way he looks very green and feels very cold. I once handled a live chameleon and, although the day was very warm, his body was as cold as a dog's muzzle.

Being a reptile, he is cold-blooded. Any warmth he wants must come from outside, which is why he spends so much time basking in the sunshine. And as he basks, he dozes. Poor fellow, should a hawk or a prowling wildcat catch him unawares.

It would seem that it is not the cold blood which is the cause of the chameleon's being so changeable. Warm-blooded human beings can be every bit as changeable! Wherever the chameleon is known, he has become the symbol of those who can make a quick change of opinions, attitude, political party or even religion, just whenever it suits them.

Nobody admires a turncoat and the kind most despised is the religious one. What a hindrance to Christianity are those who profess to be Christians but whose lives are inconsistent.

In the Bible, Peter once gave a solemn promise that he would never forsake Jesus, even though it might mean dying for Him. But that same night, Jesus was arrested and Peter, who was there, began to feel cold. There was a fire in the high priest's courtyard and he went to warm himself. But his coldness was such that no fire on earth could deal with it. He was afraid. All the warmth and fervour he felt when with Jesus had disappeared. His whole appearance changed with his circumstances and, when taunted, the testimony of a Christian disciple became the lying and swearing of an ungodly man.

But it only needed one look from the Lord Jesus to bring tears to Peter's eyes and a deep sense of shame and sorrow to his heart. He still believed. He still loved but he was weak and prone to change with changing circumstance.

Only on the day of Pentecost did Peter find the fire he needed to deal with his problem. It was spiritual fire. With the other believers, he was filled with the Holy Spirit, "baptized with the Holy Ghost and fire" as Jesus had promised. Peter the fearful became a good soldier of Jesus Christ, never again to deny his Lord.

****

"Watch yourselves closely so that you do not forget the things your eyes have seen or let them slip from your heart as long as you live."

Deuteronomy 4:9

SNAKES ALIVE

"Snake!"
is a common cry in
these parts but it
never fails to alert
people and a crowd soon gathers.

The other day the shout went up from our kitchen and I ran in to find Donna Eva pointing excitedly to a loop of snake, clearly visible between two layers of the palm-leaf thatched roof. The Indian boys were quickly on the scene, some with sticks, one with a bush knife and all with plenty of noise and enthusiasm.

What shall we do? A quick slash at the exposed coil or a well directed poke with a stick to bring it down to earth where the actual killing will be easier?

The latter is what we did and the boy made no mistake as he brought down his stick on the scaly body. But the shouts which followed were those of disappointment. What came tumbling down to earth was not a live snake but an empty skin, light and transparent as a plastic bag.

Snakes have the habit of shedding their skins from time to time. Spiders do too. So do caterpillars when they become chrysalides and in turn the ugly chrysalis is shed when the beautiful butterfly emerges. But when a snake sheds its skin, what emerges is just the same old enemy with a new look, a new lustre in its scales, a new gleam in its eye.

If that empty skin meant disappointment for the Indians, it meant far more for Donna Eva and me, living in that primitive house with the straw roof and clay walls which makes the best kind of hideout in the world for this enemy. When other enemies get the worst of an encounter, they will run or slink away and not return. But nobody wants a snake to get away. The only snakes you can be happy about are dead ones. The snake that gets away is soon ready to stage a come back!

So both indoors and outside, with the Indian boys to help, we cleared away everything in which the snake might be lurking. He was still alive and not too far away from the old coat he had discarded. We realized that there could be no once for all freedom from snakes as long as our home was the jungle.

It is just the same with sin and temptation. The Bible refers more than once to "that old serpent" which is Satan. We would like to think either that he does not exist or that he will never bother us, but that would be very wishful and very foolish thinking indeed.

In the story of our Lord's temptation in the wilderness Satan had in the end to retreat, a defeated foe. But Luke is careful to tell us that his departure was only for a season. Time and again he returned, nothing discouraged and always with a new look. On one occasion he used Peter himself as his mouthpiece, just as later on he entered into Judas Iscariot and caused him to betray Jesus to His enemies.

The only One Satan truly fears is the Lord Jesus and safety for us lies in walking and working with Him, following closely all the time, eyes and ears alert and taking no risks.

****

"Be self-controlled and alert. Your enemy the devil prowls around like a roaring lion looking for someone to devour. Resist him, standing firm in the faith ... and the God of all grace ... will himself restore you and make you strong, firm and steadfast."

1 Peter 5:8-10

CALLING THE JAGUAR

When the Indians are away fishing or hunting, the empty village at Smoking Waterfall can be a creepy place, especially at night. Above the ceaseless rumble of water tumbling over the falls comes the croaking of countless frogs, the grunts of foraging pigs, the hooting of owls and the weird cries of twittering bats.

One night, over and above the usual queer sounds, Donna Eva could make out the short, throaty grunts of a jaguar. She did not wake me, for with the stout fence around our house and the closed bedroom door, she felt quite safe. But as she told me next morning, she was pretty confident there would be plenty of jaguar tracks to confirm her story. But for once, Donna Eva was wrong. It turned out that all the 'jaguar calls' had come from a lone hunter named Koory-ko, one of the very few men to remain behind.

In the ordinary way, the Kayapo Indians fish and hunt as a pack. Koory-ko is learning to work alone and very successfully too. Whenever we see an Indian wanting to be different we try to help him, for it shows that he is beginning to think, as well as act, for himself. How pleased we were the other day when we heard Koory-ko telling a visitor that he is a Jesus-hearer! That is surely a decision we can only make for ourselves.

Koory-ko is good at making things as well as decisions. At one time it was model airplanes. On one particular night he was practising on his home-made *rencadeira*, a gadget which can imitate to perfection the call of a jaguar. It is just a wooden drum, 20 centimetres in diameter by 40 centimetres long and left open at one end. Through the dried skin which closes the other end, a nail is driven into a loose wooden rod inside the drum. When this rod is coated with bees-wax and rubbed with the fingers, it causes the skin to vibrate and produce a sound so realistic that any jaguar within range takes it as coming from either

a mate or a rival. It is in fact the hunter's challenge to the jaguar to come out into the open and fight!

It seemed that Koory-ko was looking for trouble as he set out in the hope of bagging a jaguar. While the pack was asleep by the camp fires, he paddled his canoe into the darkness to sound out his challenge. The wait was long, cold and hungry but, in the end, he heard a jaguar call back and begin to come nearer, slowly at first and then at speed. Then came the moment of confrontation. Swapping his *roncadeira* for his gun, he held a flashlight against the barrel, took quick aim and pressed the trigger. The shot did not drop the jaguar right away and he had to wait for daylight before he dare follow the blood-splashed trail to where it was lying dead.

It was a very exultant Indian who returned to the village with his trophy. As we saw the pelt and heard the story we could see that Koory-ko's looking for trouble had been well worth while.

We saw our own need of patience and courage as we proclaim the Name of Jesus to the Indian tribe. We have been missionaries long enough to realize that, except where the Holy Spirit of God is working in the hearts of men and women, they can make themselves feel satisfied with their way of life - sin, darkness and all.

****

"For God, who said,'Let light shine out of darkness,' made his light shine in our hearts to give us the light of the knowledge of the glory of God in the face of Christ."

2 Corinthians 4:6

THE GRASSHOPPER MIND

We were just about ready for bed one night when Donna Eva pointed to a big green insect perched on the mosquito netting. The mosquitoes were buzzing around and we were wanting to get that net between us and their stabbing proboscises. And now there was this suspicious-looking creature, seated on the net and looking as if he were all set for eating a hole in the net so that the hungry mosquitoes could get in and at us.

Flashing the light, I could see that it was only a Brazilian grasshopper. Insects in Brazil are quite in keeping with the size of the country and grasshoppers are no exception. He was much bigger than the kind we have at home but a grasshopper for all that. "Nothing to be afraid of," I called out. "Only rats, beetles and white ants will damage our net. The grasshopper only eats green leaves." Donna Eva was not easily convinced. "That may be true," she said, "but do put him out of our bedroom. There's no grass in here."

So I gave the net a shake as I do when I want to clean the bits of straw the wind blows down from our thatched roof. The grasshopper was quite unmoved by my shaking. I then gave him a flick as if he were a wasp, fly or beetle. He did not budge. Finding an old magazine, I made it into a roll and gave him a swipe. But never an inch did he retreat. Finally, I seized him between my thumb and forefinger and pulled. Even then, the grasshopper was most reluctant to let go. Then I noticed that his legs were fitted with grips like the teeth of a saw - not for cutting but for holding on.

Seeing himself overpowered, the grass-hopper hopped, and a real good hop it was. I went after him to see that he hopped again until he was right out of the house. Imagine my surprise to find him waiting for me, with his head turned my way. Far from waiting to be poked in the back, he was already turned right round and facing whatever might be coming, like a boxer coming in for another round. I poked him again, and again he hopped but made another complete turn in mid-air so that when he landed he was already facing his foe!

"Your game and no mistake," I muttered. "Your motto seems to be 'Only give way when you have to, and even then, keep facing the enemy'."

Did you ever come across the word "backslide"?

A backslider is a professing Christian who doesn't stand firm when tempted and tested but gives up and goes back. Now whatever unkind things may be said of the grasshopper, he cannot backslide. His legs were built for standing, not sliding. His direction is forward, not backward. If we see him hopping around, he is looking for something. He will hop around until he finds it. Then he stays put. He plants his feet and those non-skid legs of his and there is no moving him until he is through. Hit him, beat him, knock him down or chase him out, he is tough. When he moves, it is forward. He is game. When he comes up again he is facing the enemy. That is what I have seen in these Brazilian grasshoppers.

There was a time when great multitudes followed the Lord Jesus because He had fed them with loaves and fishes. When later He applied the lesson and spoke to them of the Living Bread and of eternal life, the crowds disappeared. We read that many went back and walked no more with Him. (John 6:66-69). Turning to His disciples, Jesus asked them point-blank whether they would go too.

Peter replied for them all: "Lord, to whom shall we go? You have the words of eternal life. We believe and know that you are the Holy One of God."

They were not casual Christians.

They were not Christians for the sake of loaves and fishes.

They wanted eternal life, and, having found that in the Lord Jesus, they were His for ever.

****

"Lord, to whom shall we go? You have the words of eternal life. We believe and know that you are the Holy One of God."

John 6:68,69

GUIDANCE FROM THE GECKO

On a Saturday morning Donna Eva and Jess were washing up the breakfast things. Jim and his friend Simon were stacking firewood. I was out in the village.

Our kitchen is ten paces from the dining room where the china is kept in a home-made cupboard. Jess brought in a trayful of washed cups, saucers and plates and was arranging them on the shelves when she spotted what she took to be chewing gum - it was white, rounded and apparently sugar-coated as she had so often seen and tasted before.

She popped it into her mouth and promptly gave a squeal that brought Donna Eva dashing along the corridor from the kitchen and Jim and Simon from the wood-pile. They found Jess quite speechless and pointing to a creature like a baby crocodile which lay quivering on the floor. Beside it lay the broken shell of the "chewing gum"!

"It looked for all the world like a sweet," breathed Jess, "but when I put my teeth into it, out came that animal!"

It was an egg, of course. Jim had found it in a wall which was being repaired and had taken it into the house to ask me whether it belonged to bird or snake. The "animal" which had popped out was a baby gecko, a member of the lizard family.

When night fell there was more than the usual interest in the geckos which, as we lit the pressure lamp, came creeping down the walls from their hiding places in the roof. Only three or four inches long, they are miracles for speed, agility and holding on. Their feet are like hands, complete with five fingers, all of which are needed for the very tricky business of running up and down sheer wall at high speed without falling.

Whenever a fly, moth or mosquito touched down for a few moments within range of the pressure-lamp's bright light, two or three geckos would creep in from different directions, advancing so slowly and silently that the victims never suspected their presence. The first gecko to get within range would make a lightning pounce and with a quick snap of its tiny jaws, the catch would be complete.

The strange thing about geckos is that you rarely see them at work away from a good light and a smooth wall. We have lots of insects in this home of ours but very few in comparison with what the Indians have to contend with in their lodges and primitive houses with straw roofs, rough, clay walls and only say a smoky paraffin lamp at night. Where walls are smoothed off and given a coat of whitewash like ours, there are few places where insects can hide away and go to sleep in the daytime, so out they must go. But in the nooks and crannies of those hovels, the walls are simply alive with insects of all kinds, by day as well as by night. Yet in such houses, from my own observation, geckos seem few and far between. What hunting is done at all, is done by the spiders and the driver ants.

No doubt the geckos existed long before men learned to smooth their walls with plaster and illuminate their houses with pressure-lamps and electric light. The gecko pioneers may have been tough but it seems to me that with progress in the way of more modern homes, they lost the spirit of adventure and began to look round for an easier time. Why work in rough, hard places when one can live quite usefully in some well-lit, comfortable spot where the going is easier on hands and feet?

The gecko is small and exceedingly wise but it seems to me a pretty worldly kind of wisdom, the kind which is only thinking about self. He is willing to work - and work hard - but with a preference for the easy, straightforward task and right in the limelight. That is all very well for a mere insect (or is it a reptile?) which cannot be expected to do other than follow its own instincts but it is surely not good enough for Christians wanting to serve their Saviour and Lord to the utmost. There is plenty to do in church and Sunday school but how much more outside?

At family prayers that night, still thinking about Jess's gecko, we read together our Lord's testimony concerning John the Baptist. "What went ye out into the wilderness for to see? A reed shaken in the wind? A man clothed in soft raiment? Behold, they that wear soft clothing are in kings' houses."

What a tough pioneer John the Baptist was! He preferred the wilderness to the king's court and yet, when the need arose, he was quite ready to face Herod and reprove his sinful ways. For John, it was the life of discipline, hardship and sacrifice. He did not hold back from burning himself right out for God.

****

Then Jesus said to his disciples, "If anyone would come after me, he must deny himself and take up his cross and follow me."

Matthew 16:24

TIP FROM THE TERMITES

Returning to the village after weeks of river travel, we had a surprise when we opened our front door and the shuttered windows. Perched on top of the low wall which separates living room and bedroom was an unsightly growth as big as a football. Donna Eva, who was the first to see it, excalimed, "Isn't that a nest of those white ants you write your stories about? Root them out before they bring this house down!"

There was no danger, I assured her. The walls are of puddled clay and the only part that white ants destroy is the wooden reinforcing which had really served its purpose once the clay had hardened.

Seeing that to demolish the ant hill would make a mess in both rooms, we decided to let it stay until a more convenient time. So weeks passed and then, one very wet evening, we saw a multitude of strange insects flying around. Thinking they were coming in from outside, we hurriedly closed doors and windows but it made no difference. They were parachuting down from that nest on top of the wall! The whole house was at their mercy for with there being no ceilings they could fly over the walls from one room to another. They were swarming everywhere.

I had that nest down in a hurry, regardless of the mess it made and found it alive with white ants all sprouting wings in readiness for their mass descent to earth. It did not take long to destroy them and clean up the mess, after which doors and windows were opened again. But now the things began to come in from outside. At that very same hour, every ant-hill in the neighbourhood was unloading its winged commandos! One would have thought those termites were in league with each other and following the carefully made plans of a supreme command. Down they swarmed from nests in the forks of trees. Up they came from ant hills on the ground.

From a window we watched the swallows and nightjars mopping them up in mid air. Our neighbours' chickens were eating their fill. Mud and puddles destroyed untold thousands. But still they came. At lighting-up time they were everywhere. They fluttered round our pressure lamps. They fell in the soup and spoiled our evening meal. They got in Donna Eva's hair and crawled down the open neck of my shirt. We swatted them with rolled newspapers and bombarded them with insect-killing spray. And still they came!

It was the termites' mammoth reproduction act, their annual drive to found new colonies. How any of them survive is a miracle but survive they do. As they contact Mother Earth, they shed their flimsy wings and the parachutists become infantrymen. They dig in, get under cover, link up, advance in single file and, in next to no time, new colonies of white ants are formed all over the place.

Wrapping my head in a towel and sipping my tea with the saucer covering the cup, I surprised Donna Eva by telling her that I had often had the same kind of feeling when at home in England!

"These termites," I explained, "are a kind of parable. I often found my eyes, ears, and mind and even home invaded by hosts of silly little things which used to come parachuting down on me from the hoardings, or bouncing up at me from newspapers and magazines or being shot at me from TV screens. At times the very air seemed alive with them - advertisements for this, that and the other and all making the most fantastic claims."

I must have sounded very enthusiastic.

"Commerce knows all about this termite technique," I went on. "Why cannot we Christians challenge the world in the same way? The apostles not only filled Jerusalem with their doctrine but turned the world upside down! God bless the people who today are attempting really big things for God!"

"Yes, God bless them indeed," said Donna Eva. And then, after a little pause, "But we cannot all do things in a big way, can we?"

I have to admit that she is right. So out here we keep on with our God-given task of making Jesus known to Indians who never saw a poster, could not read a tract, have no radio and would never have had a Christian hymn or verse of Scripture had we not come.

****

Jesus said ... "Therefore go and make disciples of all nations, baptising them in the name of the Father and the Son and the Holy Spirit, and teaching them to obey everything I have commanded you. And surely I will be with you always, to the very end of the age."

Matthew 28:19,20

WHAT TOUCAN DO!

Saying goodbye to Brazil has not been easy. We have many friends here and there has been much to do before we can get away on our furlough. We were glad to be able to arrange a final outing to the Para Zoo to see all the animals there once again: tapirs and turtles, anteaters and armadillos, sloths and jaguars and lots more besides.

Everything but the jaguars and birds of prey seem to be quite happy, with regular meals, good shelter, freedom from fear and the sheer fun of seeing so many human beings. Surely far better than life in the jungle.

Perhaps most at home are the toucans, those marvellously coloured birds with the outsize bills. Most of them have bright blue feet with rings exactly the same hue around their eyes. Some have white bibs, some gaudy yellow, with a red splash here and there. Their black and white fan tails are long, their wings short. But it's always the curved beak you notice most, red or yellow - or both - and huge, out of all proportion to the rest of its cute little body.

The toucan has always appeared to me as being severely handicapped for life in the wilds. However he manages to survive in those jungle tree tops is a miracle. Hawks are so many, so fast and always so hungry and relentless. For the toucan, with his beak so big and his coat so gay, there can never be any hiding, no pretending to be foliage or a knot of wood. His beak is merely for swallowing palm berries as big and as hard as marbles and is too unwieldy to be much use as a weapon, although he certainly can nip unwary fingers when he wants to. As for outflying an enemy, that is out of the question for the toucan is not in the fighter class either for speed or acrobatics. For him, no lovely poise in the air, no imposing wingspread. His design seems to contradict all the laws of aerodynamics.

Yet fly he does, just as he manages to keep so fit and look so smart always. Of course, he cannot soar to great heights like the eagle and vulture. He could never tackle an ocean flight like the swallow, nor could he even attempt the shooting star tactics of a hawk. No, he has to go slow, to look well ahead, to think things out before he takes off and to plan all his flights in easy stages.

And, believe me, he always makes it. Away he goes, alternately flapping his wings and gliding towards the next cluster of palm trees, calling the while, "Tou-can, tou-can, tou-can". That's how he gets his name.

Now, *tou* not only rhymes with *you*, it actually means *you* in the Brazilian language, although we write it *tu*. So if only you have ears to hear, you can hear the toucan calling "You-can, you-can, yes, you-can".

There he goes, overcoming his handicaps and limitations, making the most of what God has given him, going ahead cheerfully and confidently, getting there himself and calling down, "You-can, you-can, yes, you-can too!"

Many a time, during our years in the Amazon rain forests, Donna Eva and I have felt handicapped and quite unequal to the task before us; to facing the constant journeys, sometimes by plane, yes, but more often than not by river and forest trail, to enduring the climate with its heat, damp, mosquitoes and malaria, to maintaining a many-sided missionary witness - preaching and teaching, healing the sick and feeding the hungry, to building and repairing, translating, composing and recording, working in three languages all the time.

Sometimes we have thought how much easier it was for the apostle Paul to be a pioneer with no language study necessary, no family to plan for on his missionary journeys, no children to educate. But if the great apostle was able to do so much for God, it was not just because he was single and a lone pioneer by nature - not because of his natural gifts and qualifications. Here in his own words is the great secret of his success. "I can do all things THROUGH CHRIST which strengtheneth me." And isn't that as good as saying "And if I can, then you can too"?

So we look back and see how the Lord has been with us. His goodness and mercy have followed us all the way, giving us victory over all kinds of circumstances, in spite of our weakness and the odds against us.

The God who calls you and me is the God who enables. Jesus said, "Follow Me and I will MAKE YOU . . . . . !" And with Him to help you, you-can . . . . you-can. . . . yes, you-can!

There's no limit to what toucan do!

****

"I can do everything through him who gives me strength."

Philippians 4:13

To find out more about UFM Worldwide, with
whom Horace Banner was a missionary,
please contact:-

UFM Worldwide
47a Fleet Street
Swindon
Wiltshire
SN1 1RE

Tel: 01793 610515
Fax: 01793 432255

email: ufm@ufm.org.uk

website: www.ufm.org.uk

UFM Worldwide

UFM Worldwide began in 1931 as "The Unevangelised Fields Mission". The mission is committed to taking the Gospel to unreached people around the world.

The first UFM missionaries worked in Brazil and Congo. Today the work involves 85 missionaries working in 16 countries in Africa, Asia, Asia Pacific, Europe and South America.

UFM missionaries are evangelical Christians who have a clear sense of call to missionary service which has been confirmed by their local church.

UFM's priority is to take the Gospel to people who have had least opportunity to hear it. They concentrate particularly on evangelism, church planting and leadership training.

UFM works in partnership with churches believing that churches, not mission agencies, send missionaries. They co-operate with national churches in pioneer evangelism. They work on an interdenominational basis with all who affirm the evangelical faith. They are happy to enable missionaries to go to any country in the world.

You can obtain further information about UFM by writing to their Swindon headquarters or by looking at their website at www.ufm.org.uk.

CHRISTIAN FOCUS

Good books with the real message of hope!

Christian Focus Publications publishes biblically-accurate books for adults and children.

If you are looking for quality bible teaching for children then we have a wide and excellent range of bible story books - from board books to teenage fiction, we have it covered.

You can also try our new Bible teaching Syllabus for 3-9 year olds and teaching materials for pre-school children.

These children's books are bright, fun and full of biblical truth, an ideal way to help children discover Jesus Christ for themselves. Our aim is to help children find out about God and get them enthusiastic about reading the Bible, now and later in their lives.

Find us at our web page:
www.christianfocus.com

Portrait of William Butler Yeats, 1933

The Poems of W. B. Yeats

Deeply involved with Irish culture and history, W. B. Yeats (1865–1939) is one of the most influential poets of the last two centuries.

Taking the form of a sourcebook, this guide to Yeats's powerful and haunting poems offers:

- extensive introductory comment on the contexts and many interpretations of his work, from publication to the present
- annotated extracts from key contextual documents, reviews and critical works and full or extracted texts of the key poems
- cross-references between documents and sections of the guide, in order to suggest links between texts, contexts and criticism
- suggestions for further reading.

Part of the *Routledge Guides to Literature* series, this volume is essential reading for all those beginning detailed study of Yeats's work and seeking not only a guide to the poems, but a way through the wealth of contextual and critical material that surrounds them.

Michael O'Neill is Professor of English at the University of Durham. He has published widely on major poets and in 1990 received a Cholmondeley Award for his own poetry.

Routledge Guides to Literature*

Editorial Advisory Board: Richard Bradford (University of Ulster at Coleraine), Jan Jedrzejewski (University of Ulster at Coleraine), Duncan Wu (St. Catherine's College, University of Oxford)

Routledge Guides to Literature offer clear introductions to the most widely studied authors and literary texts.

Each book engages with texts, contexts and criticism, highlighting the range of critical views and contextual factors that need to be taken into consideration in advanced studies of literary works. The series encourages informed but independent readings of texts by ranging as widely as possible across the contextual and critical issues relevant to the works examined and highlighting areas of debate as well as those of critical consensus. Alongside general guides to texts and authors, the series includes "sourcebooks", which allow access to reprinted contextual and critical materials as well as annotated extracts of primary text.

Available in this series:

* Some books in this series were originally published in the Routledge Literary Sourcebooks series, edited by Duncan Wu, or the Complete Critical Guide to English Literature series, edited by Richard Bradford and Jan Jedrzejewski.

The Poems of W. B. Yeats

A Sourcebook

Edited by Michael O'Neill

Routledge
Taylor & Francis Group

LONDON AND NEW YORK

In memory of my mother's father, Revd Charles Ellis,
and my father's mother, Maud Adelaide O'Neill

First published 2004 by Routledge
11 New Fetter Lane, London EC4P 4EE

Simultaneously published in the USA and Canada
by Routledge
29 West 35th Street, New York, NY 10001

Routledge is an imprint of the Taylor & Francis Group

Editorial material and selection © 2004 Michael O'Neill. For copyright details of
poems, see acknowledgements

This volume first published as *A Routledge Literary Sourcebook on the Poems of W. B. Yeats*

Typeset in Sabon and Gill Sans by RefineCatch Limited, Bungay, Suffolk
Printed and bound in Great Britain by TJ International Ltd, Padstow, Cornwall

British Library Cataloguing in Publication Data
A catalogue record for this book is available from the British Library

Library of Congress Cataloging in Publication Data
A Routledge literary sourcebook on the poems of W. B. Yeats / edited by Martin O'Neill
    p. cm.—(Routledge literary sourcebooks)
Includes bibliographical references and index.
1. Yeats, W. B. (William Butler), 1865–1939—Poetic works. I. O'Neill, Michael, 1953–   .
II. Series.
PR5908.P58R68 2003
821'.8—dc21   2003013092

ISBN 0–415–23475–1 (hbk)
ISBN 0–415–23476–X (pbk)

Contents

2: Interpretations

3: Key Poems

4: Further Reading

Annotation and Footnotes

Annotation is a key feature of this series. Both the original notes from reprinted texts and new annotations by the editor appear at the bottom of the relevant page. The reprinted notes are prefaced by the author's name in square brackets, e.g. [Robinson's note].

Acknowledgements

I should like to thank the University of Durham for a period of Research Leave in 2002 during which I was able to work on and complete the first draft of this book. For the opportunity to discuss Yeats's poems in detail, I am particularly indebted to students who took my Special Topic course on Yeats in 1999–2000 and 2001–2. For their helpful comments and suggestions, I would like to thank the publisher's readers. Duncan Wu, who also commented valuably on my typescript, has been a most supportive and encouraging general editor.

The author would like to thank the publishers and copyright holders for permission to reprint extracts from the following works:

A. P. Watt for permission to reprint the work of W. B. Yeats throughout the world except the United States of America. Copyright Michael B. Yeats.

Extract from *Yeats* by Denis Donoghue reprinted by permission of HarperCollins Publishers Ltd © Denis Donoghue 1971.

Extract from 'The Last Poems' by J. R. Mulryne from *An Honoured Guest: New Essays on W. B. Yeats* ed. Denis Donoghue & J. R. Mulryne (Edward Arnold, 1965) reprinted by permission of the author.

Extract from *Running to Paradise: Yeats's Poetic Art* by M. L. Rosenthal, © 1994 by M. L. Rosenthal. Used by permission of Oxford University Press, Inc.

Extracts from *Between the Lines: Yeats's Poetry in the Making* by Jon Stallworthy (1963) reprinted by permission of Oxford University Press. © Oxford University Press. 1963.

Richard Ellman, *The Identity of Yeats*, 1954, Macmillan. Reproduced with the permission of Palgrave Macmillan.

Poems of W. B. Yeats reprinted in the United States with the permission of Scribner, an imprint of Simon & Schuster Adult Publishing Group, from *The Collected Works of W. B. Yeats*, ([1933], second edition 1950) by William Butler Yeats. (New York: Macmillan, 1933, 1950).

Extracts from *Reveries Over Childhood and Youth* by W. B. Yeats reprinted in the United States with the permission of Scribner, an imprint of Simon & Schuster Adult Publishing Group, from *The Autobiography of William Butler Yeats* by William Butler Yeats (New York: Macmillan, 1938).

Extract from 'Magic' and from 'A General Introduction for My Work' reprinted in the United States with the permission of Scribner, an imprint of Simon & Schuster Adult Publishing Group, from *Essays and Introductions* by William Butler Yeats. © 1961 by Mrs. W. B. Yeats.

Extract from 'Anima Hominis – V/VI' reprinted in the United States with the permission of Scribner, an imprint of Simon & Schuster Adult Publishing Group, from *Mythologies* by William Butler Yeats. Copyright © 1959 by Mrs. W. B. Yeats.

Extract from *The New Poetic: Yeats to Eliot* by C. K. Stead 1964 reprinted by permission of the author.

Extract from *Gender and History in Yeats' Love Poetry* by Elizabeth Cullingford, reprinted by permission of Syracuse University Press and the author.

Extract from *The Waste Land*, *Collected Poems, 1909–1962* by T. S. Eliot, 1992. Reproduced throughout the world except the United States of America by permission of Faber and Faber Ltd.

Every effort has been made to trace and contact copyright holders. The publishers would be pleased to hear from any copyright holders not acknowledged here so that this acknowledgements page may be amended at the earliest opportunity.

Introduction

W. B. Yeats, whose poems are the subject of this volume, was born in 1865 and died in 1939. His life and career spanned momentous literary, cultural, political and historical events. When he was born, Ireland was under English rule. By the time of his death the greater part of the island of Ireland had achieved independence, in a series of events catalysed by the Easter Rising of 1916 and including a guerrilla war with England, which in turn led to the Civil War between those who accepted a treaty leaving six counties of Northern Ireland as part of the United Kingdom and those who did not. Yeats himself was involved in and commented on the huge political changes in his country of origin. In the 1880s he appears to have joined the nationalist organization, the Irish Republican Brotherhood; in 1922, he was elected a senator in the Irish Free State. Yet he is never simply a propagandist or political poet. Behind his response to contemporary events lies a wish to understand the workings of all events, a wish shown in his attraction to magic and his creation of a quasi-astrological system in *A Vision* (first edition 1926; second edition 1937) that seeks to explain human behaviour and history.

This wish to explain is hardly rationalist, however, since Yeats challenges his own and others' scepticism. The supernatural fascinates him, in flight from the nineteenth century's growing scepticism in religious matters, but cut off by temperament and upbringing from any established church. As a young man he joined esoteric societies, including the Order of the Golden Dawn, an elaborately secretive and disciplined society devoted to hermetic matters and involved in the 'practice of ritual magic'.[1] At the same time, however occult the regions he explores, he never strays far from a powerful, often shrewd awareness of the human heart, its passions, desires and fears. In a time of fragmentation, he strives to unify his feeling and thinking, to be a 'finished man among his enemies' ('A Dialogue of Self and Soul', II. 9), to reconcile 'reality' and 'justice' – his words for the opposites that he sought to unite in *A Vision*.[2] And yet he is simultaneously a poet of endless

---

1 Terence Brown, *The Life of W. B. Yeats: A Critical Biography* (1999), Oxford: Blackwell, 2001, p. 69.
2 W. B. Yeats, *A Vision* (1937), London: Macmillan, 1962, p. 25.

conflict, one keenly alive to his 'blind struggle in the network of the stars'.[3] Above all, he is a great artist, who toiled arduously to attain a degree of verbal and structural finish that is at once bewitching and formidable.

Yeats's poetry is profoundly concerned with the making of poetry, with the friction between inner consciousness and external event, the struggle between aesthetic achievement and raw, pre-processed emotion ('masterful images' and 'the foul rag and bone shop of the heart', as he puts the opposition in 'The Circus Animals' Desertion', III. 1, 8). His career begins with an attempt before and after the fall of Charles Stewart Parnell (1846–91), the leader of the Irish Parliamentary Party and a figure for many of heroic status, to shape an Irish cultural consciousness out of legends and myths. It passes through phases of disenchantment with contemporary Ireland during his attempt to develop a specifically Irish dramatic tradition; and it concludes with a return, in his later years and after the setting up of the largely Catholic Irish Free State, to an affirmation of his Protestant and Anglo-Irish background. A poet immersed in the past, he is also very much of his own time, associating in the 1890s with poets of the 'Tragic Generation' and, later, with the arch-advocate of modernism in poetry, Ezra Pound, who helped Yeats to achieve the marked change in style typical of his mid-career. Yeats's sense of difference from Pound and T. S. Eliot is strong, however. His Irishness, for all its complexities, contrasts with their cosmopolitanism; his love of traditional form, driven by a compulsion to find order, contrasts with their formal experimentalism. Yet the poets have much in common, too. Pound's use of personae and Eliot's notion of impersonality share with Yeats's theory of masks and self-remaking a recognition that the presentation of self in lyric poetry is a matter for endless reflection and poetic labour.

Yeats is central to the development of not only Irish but also European literature. His early poetry represents an Irish version of the Symbolist movement to be found in European writing of the latter part of the nineteenth century. Reacting against the 'scientific movement', as he calls it, which brought with it 'a literature always tending to lose itself in externalities of all kinds', Yeats recommends and practises a poetry that relies on symbols, 'the element of evocation, of suggestion'.[4] The rhythms of this early work are wavering, opposed to the declamatory; they attempt, as he expresses it in the same essay, 'to prolong the moment of contemplation'.[5] Later, he altered his style, making it less incantatory, more dramatic, closer to speech. Mature Yeats is typified by what he calls (in an extract from 'A General Introduction for My Work') 'a powerful and passionate syntax, and a complete coincidence between period and stanza'.[6] The later work reveals a desire for 'passionate' control. Whatever the conflict of feeling it expresses, the

---

3   W. B. Yeats, *Per Amica Silentia Lunae* (1918), in W. B. Yeats, *Mythologies*, London: Macmillan, 1959, p. 328. *Per Amica Silentia Lunae* is a phrase from Virgil, *Aeneid*, II. 1, 255: 'Tacitae per amica silentia lunae' ('through the friendly silences of the soundless moonlight').

4   W. B. Yeats, 'The Symbolism of Poetry' (1900), in W. B. Yeats, *Essays and Introductions*, London: Macmillan, 1961, p. 155.

5   Ibid., p. 159.

6   W. B. Yeats, 'A General Introduction for My Work', in W. B. Yeats, *Essays and Introductions*, pp. 521–2. 'Period' means a complete sentence.

poem is artistically shaped, much as the poet, in his work, is 'never the bundle of accident and incoherence that sits down to breakfast; he has been reborn as an idea, something intended, complete'.[7] Yeats expresses here a view one associates with his doctrine of the mask, the idea that the self is 'reborn' in poetry, both to escape the fragmentation of ordinary experience and to open up the possibility of 'new experiences'.[8] In particular, the mask is at once an expression of and a partial solution for 'disappointment': 'The poet finds and makes his mask in disappointment', Yeats writes in *Per Amica Silentia Lunae*.[9] In later poems 'disappointment' turns into 'tragic joy', acceptance of and exultation in suffering and defeat, and such a stance dominates, somewhat controversially, Yeats's poems in the politically fraught 1930s when Europe was in turmoil with the rise of fascism and the Spanish Civil War.

This Sourcebook makes available in the Contemporary Documents section a sample of Yeats's prose covering the range of his career. My aim here is to furnish relevant contexts for an understanding of Yeats's central ideas and to stimulate further investigation of his prose writings. This is followed by a selection, in the Interpretations section, of early reviews and more recent critical analyses. Readers may find it most beneficial to read the poems and the accompanying commentaries (in the Key Poems section) before they turn to these more recent critical analyses. The section devoted to Key Poems consists of poems from Yeats's career, with headnotes and footnotes. This central section of the book contains a considerable amount of detail in its analyses, in the belief that such detail is essential for introductory and more advanced understanding of a verbally subtle and powerful lyric poet. The high cost of reproduction fees has meant that the texts of a number of Yeats's most famous poems have had to be omitted. These texts are widely available elsewhere, however, and commentary on these poems is retained in the present volume. A final section offers suggestions for further reading.

Throughout, the texts of the poems are taken from Yeats's *Collected Poems* (1933, 2nd edn, 1950).

---

7 Ibid., p. 509.
8 Terence Brown, *The Life of W. B. Yeats*, p. 177; see the same work, pp. 176–8, for relevant discussion.
9 *Per Amica Silentia Lunae*, in W. B. Yeats, *Mythologies*, p. 337.

1

Contexts

Contextual Overview

Recognition of their literary, biographical, intellectual, cultural and historical contexts enriches any reading of Yeats's poems. Yeats himself was much concerned with the making and re-making of identity; indeed, as a number of the extracts assembled in this section reveal (**pp. 25, 26–7, 30, 30–2 and 33–4**), identity for Yeats was a question of incessant conflict and re-construction. There is in this process of self-making a marked self-awareness, possibly the key feature of Yeats's poetic personality. As Katharine Tynan (1861–1935), a poet and friend of Yeats, once remarked, 'He had an uncanny way of standing aside and looking on at the game of life as a spectator'.[1]

Self for Yeats is never merely personal; it always links with wider cultural and political formations. From his youth, he displays a longing for connection with tradition and ancient belief, partly in reaction against his father's lack of religious belief. As a young man Yeats joined esoteric societies, underwent initiation rites and participated in seances, one of which in January 1888 went disastrously wrong, troubling Yeats because of the energies it released and leaving him with a question that runs through his life and work, 'what was that violent impulse that had run through my nerves?'[2] Sometimes regarded as a symptom of impossible feyness ('not everyone', wrote an early reviewer of *The Secret Rose*, 'can be brought to take spirit-raising seriously'),[3] this fascination on Yeats's part with occult matters is very much of its time and has recently been linked to what Roy Foster calls 'Protestant Magic', a specifically Anglo-Irish alternative to Catholic forms of spiritual knowledge.[4] The essay on 'Magic' from which an extract is provided shows Yeats's belief, or wish to believe, that 'the borders of our mind are

---

1 Quoted in A. Norman Jeffares (ed.), *W. B. Yeats: The Critical Heritage*, London: Routledge & Kegan Paul, 1977, p. 181.
2 Quoted in R. F. Foster, *W. B. Yeats: A Life: I: The Apprentice Mage 1865–1914*, Oxford: Oxford University Press, 1997, p. 51. Foster gives an account of the seance in question on the same page.
3 *W. B. Yeats: The Critical Heritage*, p. 95.
4 R. F. Foster, 'Protestant Magic: W. B. Yeats and the Spell of Irish History', *Proceedings of the British Academy*, 75, 1989, pp. 243–66. Foster explains Yeats's fascination with the occult thus: 'For a Catholic, religious authority provided the arbitrary [for which Yeats expresses a wish]; an Irish Protestant had to look elsewhere. Yeats found it in magic' (p. 254).

ever shifting, and that many minds can flow into one another, as it were, and create or reveal a single mind, a single energy', that a similar fluidity holds true of memory, and that the depths of this 'single mind' can 'be evoked by symbols' (**pp. 23–4**). Here fascination with the occult criss-crosses with interest in the non-rational powers of evocation accorded to 'symbols'. As one of the extracts below reveals, Yeats attributed to his father a dislike of 'the Victorian poetry of ideas' (**p. 33**), a dislike that he shared. This is not to overlook the fact that Yeats's writings are full of 'ideas', but to point up his trust in metaphors and symbols as allowing escape from the mere statement of convictions. This trust remains throughout his work, for all the changes it underwent – principally in the direction of a harder, more assertive style that leaves behind the dreamily lyrical nature of the earlier work, even as the political dimensions of that work, as critics such as Stephen Regan have shown, should not be overlooked.[5]

There is, arguably, a political dimension to Yeats's concern with esoteric matters, in that it represents a challenge to 'English' logic and rationalism. Certainly this concern derives from and reinforces his Romantic conviction that a poet was a prophet, able to intuit and articulate deep forces at work within his culture. Yeats's hostility to the merely rationalist allies him with Blake, for whom the subjective imagination is the source of value, or Shelley, who urges in *A Defence of Poetry* (written in 1821) a recognition of poetry, the creative principle, as the spring of significance. To these Romantic beliefs Yeats adds a trust in the mind's capacity to tap into collective mythic or historical experiences. Such experiences often reach the poet in the form of powerful images. Later masterpieces such as 'The Second Coming' explicitly evoke the poet as a seer at once summoning up and overwhelmed by the contents of his mind: 'Hardly are those words out', he writes, 'When a vast image out of *Spiritus Mundi* / Troubles my sight' (ll. 11–12). 'Troubles' recalls the Wordsworth of *The Prelude* for whom 'the huge and mighty forms' experienced after his stealing of the boat were 'the trouble of my dreams';[6] but the '*Spiritus Mundi*' to which the poem refers comes straight out of the poet's occult researches into 'the great mind' mentioned in the extract from *Magic* (**p. 24**).

Yeats's interest in the occult links with his early researches into Irish folklore and legend, touched on in the first extract from 'The Celtic Element in Literature' (**p. 22**), researches that display his desire to establish a national literature. Yeats wished to free the word 'Celtic' from overtones of sentimentality or irrationalism. True, he was engaged throughout his career with an attack on blinkered reliance on intellect, disliking the work of his fellow Irishman George Bernard Shaw as glibly logical and mechanical: 'It is as if a watch were to try to understand a bullock'.[7] But in works such as 'The Celtic Element in Literature', he revises the

---

5   Regan argues that the value of Yeats's 1890s poetry 'has less to do with illustrating aestheticism than with challenging and complicating our understanding of what it means to be Irish', 'W. B. Yeats and Irish Cultural Politics in the 1890s', in Sally Ledger and Scott McCracken (ed.), *Cultural Politics at the 'Fin de Siècle'*, Cambridge: Cambridge University Press, 1995, p. 82.

6   *The Prelude* (1805), I. 425, 427; quoted in Stephen Gill (ed.), Oxford Authors edition. Oxford: Oxford University Press, 1984.

7   Quoted in A. Norman Jeffares, *W. B. Yeats: A New Biography*, London: Continuum, 2001, p. 140.

way Celtic (that is, Irish) culture could and should be viewed, rescuing it both from condescension and feelings of inferiority.

In this sense, Yeats is a writer who deals from the beginning with a recognisably colonial dilemma. Ireland was still under British control, struggling towards some greater sense of national identity. Yeats as a young man participated in the cultural aspect of this struggle, stressing the significance of Irish subject matter in literature. Moreover, he associated closely with nationalist figures such as the veteran freedom-fighter John O'Leary (1830–1907) and the political activist, muse-figure and love of his youth and middle-age, Maud Gonne. Through the relationship with O'Leary, Yeats is likely to have become involved in the Irish Republican Brotherhood in the late 1880s, and yet his political attitudes were rarely straightforward. In 'A General Introduction for My Work', he described himself as 'no Nationalist, except in Ireland for passing reasons',[8] which captures both his fundamental hostility to partisan politics and his passionate attachment to Ireland. Gonne, by contrast, was dedicated to the cause of violent political revolt against England.

Yeats's relationship with Maud Gonne involved him in an unresting cycle of intimacy and apartness. One senses throughout his relations with her a division between the suffering lover and the poet for whom experience is converting itself into material for lyric poetry. He first met Gonne in 1889, and fell in love with her, proposing marriage to her for the first of many times in 1891. Gonne repeatedly refused Yeats's offers of marriage, though in 1898 they entered into 'an asexual commitment to each other, heavily reliant on the idea that they had been paired in a previous life as brother and sister'.[9] On Gonne's side, the sexual aspect of their attraction was scarcely existent or was strictly repressed, but they do seem briefly to have had sexual relations in December 1908.[10] She had, in fact, two children (George, born in 1890, and Iseult, born in 1894) by the French anarchist newspaper editor, Lucien Millevoye: a state of affairs of which Yeats was unaware until 1898. In 1903, to Yeats's disbelief and disappointment, Gonne married John MacBride (a member of the Irish Republican Brotherhood and the 'drunken, vainglorious lout' of 'Easter 1916', l. 32); she would separate from MacBride in 1905 because of his domestic cruelty.

Intimacy with Gonne brought Yeats close to questions of politics and fanaticism, and in a number of places (see 'No Second Troy' (**pp. 113–14**) and 'A Prayer for My Daughter') he deplores Gonne's nationalist extremism. Gonne, born in England and the daughter of a British army officer, attached herself to the cause of Irish freedom with a fervour that shows in her letter (included here) rebuking the questioning ironies of Yeats's 'Easter 1916': 'you who have studied philosophy & know something of history know quite well that sacrifice has never yet turned a heart to stone though it has immortalised many & through it alone mankind can rise to God' (**p. 35**). The comment shows the kind of contentions

---

8 W. B. Yeats, *Essays and Introductions*, London: Macmillan, 1961, p. 526.
9 R. F. Forster, *W. B. Yeats: A Life: I: The Apprentice Mage 1865–1914*, Oxford: Oxford University Press, 1997, p. 203.
10 Ibid., pp. 393–5.

with others that Yeats experienced in his attempt to articulate complicated views: here, the mixture of admiration and qualification in his response to what the leaders of the Rising had achieved.

Central to such complications was his conception of 'Ireland', a single word with many resonances. If Yeats's early writings participate, as Edward Said has suggested, in the process of 'decolonization', 'restoring a suppressed history, and rejoining the nation to it', their author's relation to Irish and English culture is rarely straightforward.[11] Born in 1865 to John Butler Yeats and his wife Susan, who came from the Pollexfen family in the west of Ireland, Yeats experienced, from the start, tugs, tensions and dualities in his sense of identity. He grew up in a Protestant, Anglo-Irish family, living as much in England as Ireland. Sligo in the west, where he spent early summers, was a place of dreams, fairies and magic. It was also associated, for his father, with the silence and gloom he attributed to his wife's family. There is no doubt that Yeats inherited from his father a natural tendency to think in contraries and oppositions, a tendency sharpened by his reading of Blake (whom he co-edited, publishing a three-volume edition in 1893). 'Without Contraries is no Progression', Blake's assertion in his work *The Marriage of Heaven and Hell*, could serve as a motto for Yeats's writing. In *A Vision* Yeats writes, 'my mind had been full of Blake from boyhood up and I saw the world as a conflict . . . and could distinguish between a contrary and a negation'.[12] Awareness of 'contraries' – of equal and opposite goods – supplies the dynamic driving his poetic career. It can be related to his hyphenated cultural status as Anglo-Irish, which led to the 'cultural dilemma' that Timothy Webb describes thus: 'He was born a subject of Queen Victoria, he received from 1910 a Civil List pension, and he was even offered a knighthood by the British government during the First World War; yet he was by birth, by choice and by temperament an Irishman'.[13] He pursued a literary career in London, helping, among other things, to establish the Rhymers' Club in 1890, and consequently getting to know many of the principal writers of the day, including Lionel Johnson, Ernest Dowson and Arthur Symons.

Involvement with the London literary scene blended with his desire to create what A. Norman Jeffares calls an 'audience for a reborn Irish literature'.[14] In 1891 he also co-operated with John O'Leary in setting up a Young Ireland League that attempted to bring together different Irish literary societies. The idea bore fruit in a National Literary Society the following year, but involved Yeats in bitter controversy with figures such as the nationalist hero Charles Gavan Duffy (1816–1903), who was out of sympathy with the young poet's attempt to recover a heroic, mythological past. It is a feature of Yeats's literary career that he was frequently embroiled in controversy concerning Irish literary politics.

Such disputes often focus on divergences between Yeats and others about the

---

11 Quoted by Robert Welch in his edition, *W. B. Yeats: Writings on Irish Folklore, Legend and Myth*, Harmondsworth: Penguin, 1993, p. xxxv, n. 11.
12 *A Vision*, p. 72.
13 Timothy Webb (ed. with introduction and notes), *W. B. Yeats: Selected Poems*, Harmondsworth: Penguin, 1991, p. xxxi.
14 *W. B. Yeats: A New Biography*, p. 51.

forms a new Ireland should take. Yeats's involvement in setting up an Irish theatre that used recognizably Irish modes of speech and turned to the language of the peasant as a cultural ideal was influenced by – and led him to recognize the value of – work by J. M. Synge and Lady Gregory. The three figures, he would write in 'The Municipal Gallery Revisited', 'thought / All that we did, all that we said or sang/Must come from contact with the soil' and must be motivated by the 'Dream of the noble and the beggar-man' (ll. 41–3, 47). However, Synge's play *The Playboy of the Western World* (1907) caused uproar when it was first staged in Dublin. Its mixture of comedy and irony was found offensive by many nationalists who felt that it was a slur on the good name of Irish people.

Much later in life, in 'Beautiful Lofty Things', Yeats depicts his father speaking out at a debate about the play: faced by 'a raging crowd' J. B. Yeats first placated it by referring to 'This Land of Saints' before mischievously teasing it with the rider, 'Of plaster Saints'. However reshaped the poem's anecdote, it reminds us that, in the first decade of the twentieth century, Yeats had begun to conceive of the Irish poet's task as involving disdain of the crowd, heroic loneliness and struggle: a struggle explicitly directed against Catholic nationalism, with its wish to impose – as Yeats saw it – a priestly censorship and conformity. One can see in a poem such as 'September 1913' (**pp. 115–17**) a sharp dislike of the new nationalist middle class, caricatured as 'Paudeen' in the poem of that name (**p. 117**) (though Yeats transcends his initial rancour) and held responsible for the death of 'Romantic Ireland'.[15] The year involved bitter dispute about the proposed bequest of Hugh Lane's collection of Impressionist paintings to Dublin provided that the city build a suitable gallery to house them. Lane would have liked a gallery bridge to be built over the River Liffey by Sir Edwin Lutyens; the fact that Lutyens was an Englishman did not help Lane's case in the eyes of many Dubliners. Yeats fervently supported the proposal, but it was opposed by the likes of William Murphy, a leader of Catholic Ireland and an industrialist responsible for the lock-out in 1913 in an effort to destroy the Irish Transport and General Workers' Union.

These feelings help to explain the desire expressed in 'The Fisherman' (**pp. 125–7**) for a wholly new kind of audience. In the poem Yeats turns his back on 'the reality' of an Irish literary and cultural scene in which a principal feature was 'great Art beaten down', and begins to imagine as the addressee of his poetry 'A man who does not exist, /A man who is but a dream' (ll. 12, 24, 35–6). The sense that Yeats's poems give us of searching for an audience adequate to their own high style stems from his almost Utopian wish to 'write for my own race' ('The Fisherman', l. 11), where 'my own race' is by no means a given, but is an idea in the process of being constructed. In his poetic epitaph 'Under Ben Bulben', Yeats addresses his poetic heirs as needing to prove that they belong to 'the indomitable Irishry' (V. 16): by this stage of Yeats's career a far from inclusive category. 'The indomitable Irishry' probably alludes, in the main, to the Protestant, Anglo-Irish 'stock' that Yeats began to exalt after the setting up of the Free State. So, in a Senate

---

15 'Paudeen', a contemptuous nickname for 'Patrick', has more than a hint of anti-Catholic prejudice.

speech of 1925, objecting to legislation that made divorce virtually impossible, Yeats asserted in terms that sharpened the division between his Protestant world and the new, largely Catholic state: 'We against whom you have done this thing are no petty people. We are one of the great stocks of Europe.'[16]

It would be wrong, however, to try to categorize Yeats's political beliefs too quickly. A reason why the Easter Rising of 1916, when various armed Republican groups occupied the centre of Dublin for a few days towards the end of April, made such an impact on Yeats is that it caused him to revise his sense of contemporary Ireland. His initial response on hearing the news (in England) was one of distress; he felt that 'all the work of years has been overturned, all the bringing together of classes, all the freeing of Irish literature and criticism from politics'.[17] But despite Gonne's reservations about his poetic response, 'Easter 1916' reveals an openness to experience and a readiness to undergo inner conflict and emotional change that are the hallmarks of Yeats's finest poems. He may have once thought that extreme nationalist aspirations were the stuff of ironic comedy. After the executions of the leaders, however, he realized that 'A terrible beauty is born' ('Easter 1916', l. 80). Many poems by Yeats involve shift, growth, change and conflict. As a result, the reader of Yeats should be wary of making the poems conform to some pre-conceived system of ideas and prejudices. Some of his finest political poems respond with first-hand uncertainty to the turbulence of the Anglo-Irish War and the subsequent Civil War.

That said, there are evident shifts of emphasis in Yeats's outlook. The friendship with Lady Gregory marks an important re-orientation of his sense of political identity. The widow of a former governor of Ceylon, Lady Gregory owned Coole Park, where Yeats found refuge for many years after his first long stay in the summer of 1897. The poet and landowning patron encouraged one another's interest in folklore and the establishment of an Irish theatre. The cultural and political vision he developed over these years moves away from his earlier nationalism towards a growing appreciation of the virtues of the Anglo-Irish aristocracy. Generally, women were important for Yeats as muse-figures, enabling or incomprehensible others. Gregory, however, acted with maternal, even proprietorial firmness, rescuing him from his despair over Maud Gonne and providing him with a refuge and emotional security.[18]

In his early middle-age Yeats expressed disillusionment with 'Theatre business, management of men' ('The Fascination of What's Difficult', l. 11) (**pp. 114–15**),

---

16 Donald R. Pearce (ed.), *The Senate Speeches of W. B. Yeats*, London: Faber and Faber, 1961, p. 300.

17 Allan Wade (ed.), *The Letters of W. B. Yeats*, London: Hart-Davis, 1954, p. 613.

18 Other women important in Yeats's life (apart from his wife – for whom see below) include Olivia Shakespear, Mabel Dickinson, Margot Ruddock and Dorothy Wellesley. Olivia Shakespear was the mother of Dorothy Shakespear who married Ezra Pound; Yeats had an affair with Shakespear in 1896–7, the probable subject of the lyric 'Pale hair, still hands and dim hair' (**p. 107**), and resumed a friendship with her later in life. Mabel Dickinson was a woman with whom Yeats had what appears to be a strongly physical relationship in 1908 (she contrasts pointedly with Maud Gonne in this respect). Margot Ruddock was a young actress and poet with whom Yeats became infatuated in 1934. Dorothy Wellesley was a young poet with whom Yeats had an important friendship in the last years of his life.

referring to his involvement in the setting up of a new Irish theatre. Indeed, Yeats began to withdraw from management of the Abbey Theatre in 1910. The theatre, however, offers many of his most positive images for the life of the writer. This is observable in his essay *Per Amica Silentia Lunae* (1918), which gives stylish expression to his lifelong preoccupation with poetry as conflict and anticipates the system he sets out in *A Vision*. The current volume contains two extracts from the essay. In one, Yeats recalls the following from 'an old diary', a device that asserts continuity between past and present selves: 'If we cannot imagine ourselves as different from what we are, and try to assume that second self, we cannot impose a discipline upon ourselves though we may accept one from others. Active virtue, as distinguished from the passive acceptance of a code, is therefore theatrical, consciously dramatic, the wearing of a mask' (**pp. 26–7**). The idea that the poet should seek to 'assume [a] second self' evidently owes much to Yeats's experience in the theatre. It also has much in common with the Modernist reaction against any naïvely sub-Romantic notion of poetry as being a 'spontaneous overflow of powerful feelings', as Wordsworth puts it in his Preface to *Lyrical Ballads* (1802),[19] and may, in addition, show the influence of the thought of Friedrich Nietzsche, the German philosopher, whose writings emphasize the importance of will and opposition to 'the passive acceptance of a code'. In the other, Yeats expresses a view that distils much of his poetic practice and thought about poetry: 'We make out of the quarrel with others, rhetoric, but of the quarrel with ourselves, poetry' (**p. 25**).

Two points are significant here. One is the recognition that poetry springs from 'the quarrel with ourselves'. Yeats's poems are often about the quarrel he experiences with himself, but they are never artlessly so; 'consciously dramatic', they often build into themselves an awareness that self-quarrelling is the mainspring of poetic creativity. The second point to observe is that Yeats's view of poetry in this essay is pervaded by his hostility to 'rhetoric', to the 'confident voice' of those 'remembering the crowd they have won or may win' (**p. 25**).

Such hostility suggests Yeats's allegiance in his maturity to certain literary tenets he developed in his youth. Among these is an opposition between the 'world' and poetry, an opposition spelled out in 'Adam's Curse' (**pp. 111–13**), where Yeats asserts that 'to articulate sweet sounds together' is 'to work harder' than those engaged in harsh manual labour, 'and yet/Be thought an idler' (ll. 10, 11, 11–12) by the middle classes. Poets, he frequently intimates, engage in a kind of labour that performs a vitally important role. They make sense of experience; indeed, they create the possibilities of experience because through them, as he will argue in 'A General Introduction for My Work', 'nature has grown intelligible' (**p. 31**).

A Vision, his prose attempt to systematize history, culture and personality, is Yeats's version of what the American poet Wallace Stevens (1879–1955) would call a Supreme Fiction, that is, a structure of belief that knows it is an imaginative construction. The catalyst for this work was his wife's use of automatic writing on

19 Stephen Gill (ed.), Oxford Authors edition, p. 598.

their honeymoon in 1917 to conduct an apparent conversation with spirits. Automatic writing is a practice associated with spiritualism; it involves writing without conscious thought, as though a spirit were holding the pen. It appears that George Yeats's initial intention was to stir her husband from his despondency about the failure of his relations with Maud Gonne and her daughter Iseult, both of whom had rejected proposals of marriage from him. George was an intelligent student of Yeats's work, and the exact degree of manipulativeness she exercised in the automatic writing sessions is hard to gauge. She herself said that, to begin with, she made 'an attempt to fake automatic writing' but that she had found herself 'seized by a superior power'.[20] The result was many question-and-answer sessions with spirit instructors, in which George acted as the medium. From these sessions emerged 'the system of historical and psychological schematization' contained in *A Vision*.[21] The centre of the work is the belief that all human meaning is constructed though engagement by self or historical era with its opposite. The self wishes to be or is haunted by its opposite; a period of history emerges in reactive formation from its predecessor and gives way to its opposite as its power wanes.

A Vision is in many ways an off-putting book, with its tables and diagrams, and esoteric jargon about reincarnation. But the fascination of the work lies in Yeats's quality of intent reflection on history and personality. The reader new to the work is best advised, first, to read Yeats's account of how he came to write the work and what he sees its scope as being (see **pp. 27–8**), and, second, to plunge into Book 2, part 3, one of the more accessible sections. Here Yeats categorizes personality types according to the twenty-eight phases of the moon, tracing a waxing and waning of 'subjective' and 'objective' (or what he sometimes calls 'antithetical' and 'primary') tendencies, the former occupying phases 8 to 22, the latter phases 22 to 8.[22] By 'primary' Yeats means something given or natural; by 'antithetical' he means something deliberately shaped and created. Some of the most enthralling writing of *A Vision* occurs here, as Yeats describes the characteristics shown by exemplars of each phase. The total form of the self is sometimes described by Yeats as the 'Daimon', a composite of Four Faculties: Will, Mask, Creative Mind and Body of Fate. A key struggle in each person is that between Will and Mask (or, as Yeats puts it, 'the will and its object, or the Is and the Ought', the usual ego and its compensating dream of what it might be). To this conflict Yeats adds a further struggle between the Creative Mind and the Body of Fate ('thought and its object, or the Knower and the Known'), allowing in this second struggle for the contest in any person between the sum of 'ideas' (a word Yeats uses to mean 'universals', something that holds true permanently) that the mind can have access to and external reality, 'events forced upon him from without'.[23] The clue to Yeats's sense of self is the belief that the self pursues its opposite in order to

---

20 Terence Brown, *The Life of W. B. Yeats* (1999), Oxford: Blackwell, 2001, p. 232. For more discussion of George Yeats, see Brenda Maddox, *George's Ghosts: A New Life of W. B. Yeats*, London: Picador, 1999, and Ann Saddlemyer, *Becoming George: The Life of Mrs W. B. Yeats*, Oxford: Oxford University Press, 2002.
21 Ibid., p. 256.
22 *A Vision*, p. 88.
23 Ibid., pp. 73, 83.

attain a wholeness that eludes it. So, the typical figure from phase 17 (where Yeats places Dante, Shelley and himself) experiences at the level of Will 'a falling asunder', and takes as a Mask one of 'simplicity that is also intensity'.[24]

In Book 5 Yeats turns his attention to historical periods and maps a series of historical gyres. The gyre, meaning a whirling cylinder with a broad base and narrow head, is Yeats's image for the way each era develops. History is made up of interlocking gyres, the head of one resting against the base of the other, and as each gyre completes its whirling journey it passes into its opposite. In Book 5 Yeats offers a brilliantly impressionist account of world history. He himself addresses in an extract included on **pp. 27–8** the question of whether he believed in his quasi-astrological scheme and compares the system to the search for order found in Modernist sculpture and painting (see **pp. 27–8**). He mentions, too, the message conveyed through the automatic writings that he was being brought 'metaphors for poetry' (**p. 27**). What matters about *A Vision* is less its historical or biographical accuracy than its capacity to impose shape on the multiform nature of experience.

The craving to impose experience on chaos can be connected, in the political sphere, to the rise of strongly authoritarian movements in the 1920s and 1930s, and Yeats's own dealings with fascist movements in the 1930s (including General O'Duffy's 'Blueshirts', sometimes seen as an Irish version of Mussolini's Fascism) have been the matter of debate (see the Interpretations section). Yet it would be over-hasty to see *A Vision* and the poems associated with it as the work of a proto-Fascist. Yeats's 'system' has in it enough checks and complexities to give a satisfying sense of human and historical complexity. Moreover, his poems frequently dramatize a breaking-down of the attempt to impose systematic order on life, as 'A Dialogue of Self and Soul' reveals. Here Self refuses the Soul's attempt to achieve a mystical escape from life's impurities. Even the embrace of 'tragic gaiety' in Yeats's final works, in which he recommends an attitude to catastrophe and suffering equivalent to that experienced by the spectator of Shakespeare's greatest tragedies (see the extract from 'A General Introduction for My Work', **p. 32**), does not exclude recognition of the reality of human pain. Indeed, much of this later work admires the repeated drive towards 'civilisation' evident throughout history. In a poem such as 'Lapis Lazuli', Yeats accepts the inevitability of destruction, celebrates the human instinct to create and recommends a profound acceptance of loss and reconstruction. 'A civilisation', Yeats writes in *A Vision*, 'is a struggle to keep self-control', and much of the power of Yeats's work comes from his awareness of how costly and difficult that 'struggle is', and yet how valuable it is, too.[25] It is typical of him, and of his rewarding devotion to self-quarrelling and conflict, that his final poems, especially 'Man and the Echo' and 'The Circus Animals' Desertion', affectingly weigh in the balance the value of his own creative career.

24 Ibid., p. 141.
25 Ibid., p. 268.

Chronology

Bullet points are used to indicate events in Yeats's life and career; asterisks are used to indicate other relevant contextual events (largely historical and literary).

1865
- William Butler Yeats born in Sandymount Avenue, Dublin, on 13 June to John Butler Yeats and Susan Yeats (née Pollexfen)

1866
* December, birth of Maud Gonne

1867
- July, family moves to London, near Regent's Park, after J. B. Yeats abandons law in favour of painting
* Marx, *Das Kapital*

1872
- Yeats with his grandparents (the Pollexfens) in Sligo (and for the next two years)

1877
- Yeats attends the Godolphin School, Hammersmith (until 1881)

1881
- Family returns to Ireland (Howth); Yeats attends school in Dublin

1884
- Yeats attends Metropolitan School of Art, Dublin

1885
- Publishes his first poems in *Dublin University Review*; meets John O'Leary, who had returned from political exile in Paris

1886
* Nietzsche, *Ideas of Good and Evil*; First Home Rule Bill defeated in Commons

1887
• Mother suffers two strokes

1888
• September, edits *Fairy and Folk Tales of the Irish Peasantry*; family move to Bedford Park in London; joins the Esoteric Section of the Theosophical Society

1889
• January, publishes *The Wanderings of Oisin and Other Poems*; in London meets Maud Gonne for the first time and falls in love with her

1890
• Co-founds the Rhymers' Club; March, joins the Hermetic Order of the Golden Dawn in London

1891
• March, edits *Representative Irish Tales*; September, organises with John O'Leary a meeting of a Young Ireland League; October, proposes marriage unsuccessfully to Maud Gonne (and again in 1894, 1899, 1900 and 1901)
* Wilde, *The Portrait of Dorian Gray*; October, death of Parnell

1892
• August, publishes *The Countess Kathleen and Various Legends and Lyrics*; January, helps to found the Irish Literary Society in London; May, founds the National Literary Society in Dublin

1893
• February, co-edits *The Works of William Blake* (3 vols)
* September, Home Rule Bill passed in the House of Commons, defeated in the House of Lords

1895
• October, publishes *Poems*; from October, shares rooms with Arthur Symons for a few months
* Wilde, *The Importance of Being Ernest*; May, Wilde sentenced to two years in prison

1896
• Starts affair with Olivia Shakespear (lasts until 1897)

1897

- April, publishes *The Secret Rose*; stays with Lady Gregory at Coole Park, discusses folklore and setting up a theatre, often visits in future years
- * Queen Victoria's Diamond Jubilee; riots in Dublin provoked, in part, by Maud Gonne's anti-British speeches

1898

* Boer War begins (ends in 1902)

1899

- April, publishes *The Wind among the Reeds*; May, *The Countess Cathleen* performed in Dublin
- * Publication of Arthur Symons's *The Symbolist Movement in Literature*, dedicated to Yeats.

1900

- January, Yeats's mother dies
- * Freud, *The Interpretation of Dreams*

1901

* January, death of Queen Victoria and accession of Edward VII

1903

- Publishes *In the Seven Woods*
- * January, Maud Gonne marries John MacBride

1904

- Abbey Theatre opens, with Yeats as producer-manager; December, stages *On Baile's Strand*

1907

* January, riots in response to J. M. Synge's play *The Playboy of the Western World*, which had been staged at the Abbey Theatre; December, J. B. Yeats emigrates to New York

1908

- June, renews close relationship with Maud Gonne, who had separated from John MacBride in 1905; meets Ezra Pound; has affair with Mabel Dickinson

1909

* March, death of Synge

1910

- August, awarded a Pension (150 pounds) on the Civil List

1913

- Stays at Stone Cottage, Sussex, with Ezra Pound (see Pound, *Canto LXXXIII*)
* January and July, Home Rule Bill defeated in the House of Lords; Lane Gallery dispute; September, Lock-Out of workers in Dublin; James Connolly forms Irish Citizen Army

1914

- Publishes *Responsibilities*
* 4 August, First World War begins; Home Rule Bill passed, but suspended because of the war; James Joyce's *Dubliners* published

1916

- March, publishes *Reveries over Childhood and Youth*; July to August, in Normandy with Maud Gonne – proposes marriage to her and then (in 1917) to her daughter, Iseult, in both cases unsuccessfully
* April, Easter Rising in Dublin; May, execution of the leaders, including John MacBride; December, Joyce's *A Portrait of the Artist as a Young Man* published

1917

- 20 October, marries Georgie Hyde-Lees; November, publishes *The Wild Swans at Coole*
* Russian Revolution

1918

- Publishes *Per Amica Silentia Lunae*; September, moves into Thoor Ballylee
* January, death of Robert Gregory, son of Lady Gregory

1919

- 26 February, birth of daughter, Annie Butler Yeats
* Sinn Féin wins election victory; Anglo-Irish War begins

1921

- February, publishes *Michael Robartes and the Dancer*; attacks British policy in Ireland at the Oxford Union; 22 August, birth of son, Michael Butler Yeats
* December, Anglo-Irish Treaty

1922

- February, J. B. Yeats dies in New York; October, publishes *The Trembling of the Veil*; December, nominated to Irish Senate
* Treaty ratification leads to Irish Civil War; bridge at Ballylee blown up by Republicans; Joyce's *Ulysses* and Eliot's *The Waste Land* published

1923
- November, awarded Nobel Prize for Literature
- * May, end of Civil War

1926
- January, publishes *A Vision* (dated 1925, revised edition October 1937); November, publishes *Autobiographies*; Chairman of Coinage Committee in Senate; visits St Otteran's School in Waterford (see 'Among School Children', **pp. 163–7**)

1927
- Ill with congestion of the lungs

1928
- February, publishes *The Tower*; November to May 1929, in Rapallo, Italy; July, makes last Senate speech

1929
- October, publishes *The Winding Stair*; December, seriously ill with Malta fever, a complicated bacterial fever of long duration, which was common in Malta and other places in the Mediterranean

1932
- * August, death of Lady Gregory

1933
- Publishes *The Winding Stair and Other Poems* and *Collected Poems*; July to August, involved with General O'Duffy's Blueshirts

1934
- November, publishes *Collected Plays*; April, has Steinach operation (unilateral vasectomy); September, meets and becomes close to Margot Ruddock, a young poet and actress
- * Hitler comes to power in Germany

1935
- Again seriously ill with congestion of the lungs
- * Italy invades Abyssinia

1936
- November, publishes *The Oxford Book of Modern Verse: 1892–1935*; suffers ill health
- * Abdication crisis; outbreak of the Spanish Civil War

1938
- May, publishes *New Poems*

1939

- 28 January, dies at Cap Martin, France, and is buried at Roquebrune. *Last Poems and Two Plays* published posthumously in July and *On the Boiler* in September
* Spanish Civil War ends with victory of Franco and defeat of the Republic; September, Second World War begins

1948

- Yeats's body exhumed and returned to Ireland; buried in Drumcliff churchyard, Sligo

Contemporary Documents

From **W. B. Yeats, 'The Celtic Element in Literature'** (1898), in *Essays and Introductions*, London: Macmillan, 1961, p. 184

Yeats is responding in this brief extract from the opening of section IV of his essay to Matthew Arnold's *The Celtic Element in Literature* (1867). Arnold saw the Celtic temperament as complementary to the Saxon or Germanic temperament and had asked (as paraphrased by Yeats) 'how much of the Celt must one imagine in the ideal man of genius', a question to which Yeats's opening words reply. The essay is important both for showing Yeats's admiration for the Celtic (all that is 'unbounded' and 'wild') in literature and for his emphasis on its universality. The Celtic, for Yeats, is not at odds with modern literature; rather, it is essential to its sustenance since 'literature dwindles to a mere chronicle of circumstance, or passionless fantasies, and passionless meditations, unless it is constantly flooded with the passions and beliefs of ancient times'.[1] The extract captures a view of art as 'founded on the life beyond the world' articulated in much of Yeats's earlier work, especially *The Wind among the Reeds*.

I prefer to say, how much of the ancient hunters and fishers and of the ecstatic dancers among hills and woods must one imagine in the ideal man of genius. Certainly a thirst for unbounded emotion and a wild melancholy are troublesome things in the world, and do not make its life more easy or orderly, but it may be the arts are founded on the life beyond the world, and that they must cry in the ears of our penury until the world has been consumed and become a vision.

---

1 *Essays and Introductions*, p. 185.

From **W. B. Yeats, 'Magic'** (1901), in *Essays and Introductions*, London: Macmillan, 1961, p. 28

'Magic', defined in the *Oxford English Dictionary* as the 'supposed art of influencing the course of events . . . by the occult control of nature or of spirits', was central to Yeats's understanding of reality. Cut off from Christianity by the sceptical rationalism of his father's generation, and separated from the Catholic beliefs and practices of the majority of Irish people by his Protestant background, the young poet longed to create a system of belief. The chief elements of this system, to begin with, were myths and magic. He wrote that he 'made a new religion, almost an infallible Church of poetic tradition, of a fardel of stories, and of personages, and of emotions, inseparable from their first expression'.[1] In 1892 he told John O'Leary, the Irish nationalist who influenced the poet's choice of subject matter, that 'the mystical life is the centre of all that I do & all that I think & all that I write' and that his work embodied 'the revolt of the soul against the intellect'.[2] Yeats spent much of his youth involved in occult research, spiritualism and explorations of esoteric matters. In this essay of 1901 he sets out the central tenets of his beliefs. His wording carefully leaves open the possibility that belief is less doctrinal than imaginative; if he believes in 'what I must call the evocation of spirits', he adds straightaway, 'though I do not know what they are'; 'the power of creating', he exalts, is a power of creating 'magical *illusions*' (**p. 23**; emphasis added). He anticipates here his later refusal wholly to commit himself to literal belief in the system laid out in *A Vision*, writing that he regards his 'circuits of sun and moon' in that later work as 'stylistic arrangements of experience' that 'have helped me to hold in a single thought reality and justice' (**p. 28**). This extract from section 1 of 'Magic' articulates Yeats's fascination with the existence of a 'great mind' including the memories of all minds (what in 'The Second Coming' he will call '*Spiritus Mundi*') and with the power of 'symbols' to evoke (literally 'call up', as a magician might call up spirits) the contents of this great mind.

I believe in the practice and philosophy of what we have agreed to call magic, in what I must call the evocation of spirits, though I do not know what they are, in the power of creating magical illusions, in the visions of truth in the depths of the mind when the eyes are closed; and I believe in three doctrines, which have, as I think, been handed down from early times, and been the foundations of nearly all magical practices. These doctrines are:—

(1) That the borders of our mind are ever shifting, and that many minds can flow

1   W. B. Yeats, *Autobiographies*, London: Macmillan, 1955, pp. 115–16; 'fardel' means 'bundle, a little pack'.
2   John Kelly and Eric Domville (eds), *The Collected Letters of W. B. Yeats, vol. 1, 1865–1895*, Oxford: Clarendon, 1986, p. 303.

into one another, as it were, and create or reveal a single mind, a single energy.

(2) That the borders of our memories are as shifting, and that our memories are a part of one great memory, the memory of Nature herself.

(3) That this great mind and great memory can be evoked by symbols.

I often think I would put this belief in magic from me if I could, for I have come to see or to imagine, in men and women, in houses, in handicrafts, in nearly all sights and sounds, a certain evil, a certain ugliness, that comes from the slow perishing through the centuries of a quality of mind that made this belief and its evidences common over the world.

From **W. B. Yeats, 'Anima Hominis'** (1918), in *Mythologies*, London: Macmillan, 1959, section V, pp. 331–2

'Anima Hominis' ('the Soul of Man') is a section of one of Yeats's finest and most important prose works, *Per Amica Silentia Lunae* (the title is taken from a line in Virgil's *Aeneid*, Book II, and means 'through the friendly silences of the moon'); the book's other section is entitled 'Anima Mundi' ('the Soul of the World'). 'Anima Hominis' explores the relation between the self and the mask, and is best read in conjunction with 'Ego Dominus Tuus', a poem used by Yeats as the epigraph to *Per Amica Silentia Lunae*. In this extract Yeats contrasts 'the quarrel with others' that breeds 'rhetoric' with 'the quarrel with ourselves' (**p. 25**) that results in poetry. Self-quarrelling is a fundamental feature of Yeats's understanding of poetry and the poet, and is traced in commentary on poems in the Key Poems section. Yeats's mistrust of 'rhetoric', the language deployed by those who address a crowd, links with his dislike of opinionated poetry (partly inherited from his father's dislike of 'the Victorian poetry of ideas' (see **p. 33**)). The extract illustrates his acute and eloquent self-awareness about his poetry. He captures well the blend of intensity and doubt to be found in work such as 'Easter 1916' or the Byzantium poems when he writes 'we sing amid our uncertainty' (**p. 25**). At the centre of the extract is its reference to 'The other self, the anti-self or the antithetical self' (**p. 25**). By the 'antithetical self' Yeats means a 'self' (shaped through poetic exploration) that is the opposite of the poet's ordinary personality. Indeed, he describes this self as an achievement won by those 'whose passion is reality' (**p. 25**). Such a passion opposes the 'happiness' sought by 'sentimentalists'; it is experienced as 'ecstasy' and, in its readiness to endure 'all imaginable pangs' (**p. 25**), it anticipates Yeats's theory of 'tragic joy' in his later work (see the headnote to 'The Gyres', **pp. 171–2**). The extract also expresses Yeats's view that creativity must deal with 'of all things not impossible the most difficult' (**p. 25**). Toil, arduous labour and self-quarrelling are the means of questing after 'reality'. As in much of Yeats's prose the language uses metaphors with great power; in the final sentence Yeats uses highly condensed images to convey his sense that the poet creates work of

value only when he recognizes that he has 'nothing'. Yeats's pronouns are also worth observing; he uses 'we' to imply shared knowledge of artistic experience, its necessary sacrifice and toil, 'I' to intimate its final loneliness.

We make out of the quarrel with others, rhetoric, but of the quarrel with ourselves, poetry. Unlike the rhetoricians, who get a confident voice from remembering the crowd they have won or may win, we sing amid our uncertainty; and, smitten even in the presence of the most high beauty by the knowledge of our solitude, our rhythm shudders. I think, too, that no fine poet, no matter how disordered his life, has ever, even in his mere life, had pleasure for his end. Johnson and Dowson, friends of my youth, were dissipated men, the one a drunkard, the other a drunkard and mad about women, and yet they had the gravity of men who had found life out and were awakening from the dream; and both, one in life and art and one in art and less in life, had a continual preoccupation with religion. Nor has any poet I have read of or heard of or met with been a sentimentalist. The other self, the anti-self or the antithetical self, as one may choose to name it, comes but to those who are no longer deceived, whose passion is reality. The sentimentalists are practical men who believe in money, in position, in a marriage bell,[1] and whose understanding of happiness is to be so busy whether at work or at play that all is forgotten but the momentary aim. They find their pleasure in a cup that is filled from Lethe's wharf,[2] and for the awakening, for the vision, for the revelation of reality, tradition offers us a different word—ecstasy. An old artist wrote to me of his wanderings by the quays of New York, and how he found there a woman nursing a sick child, and drew her story from her. She spoke, too, of other children who had died: a long tragic story. 'I wanted to paint her,' he wrote; 'if I denied myself any of the pain I could not believe in my own ecstasy.' We must not make a false faith by hiding from our thoughts the causes of doubt, for faith is the highest achievement of the human intellect, the only gift man can make to God, and therefore it must be offered in sincerity. Neither must we create, by hiding ugliness, a false beauty as our offering to the world. He only can create the greatest imaginable beauty who has endured all imaginable pangs, for only when we have seen and foreseen what we dread shall we be rewarded by that dazzling, unforeseen, wing-footed wanderer. We could not find him if he were not in some sense of our being, and yet of our being but as water with fire, a noise with silence. He is of all things not impossible the most difficult, for that only which comes easily can never be a portion of our being; 'soon got, soon gone,' as the proverb says. I shall find the dark grow luminous, the void fruitful when I understand I have nothing, that the ringers in the tower have appointed for the hymen of the soul a passing bell.[3]

1   True to their convention-bound nature, such men believe in marriage.
2   Water from Lethe, a river in the underworld, brought forgetfulness to a person who drank it.
3   By contrast with the 'practical men' of the world who believe in the social conventions symbolized by 'a marriage bell', the poet must concentrate on what is scarcely attainable; the soul will achieve its 'hymen' or marriage when it forsakes the gratifications of this world, a forsaking symbolized by the 'passing bell' or death-knell.

From **W. B. Yeats, 'Anima Hominis'** (1918), in *Mythologies*, London: Macmillan, 1959, section VI, pp. 333–4

> In this extract from the same work Yeats expresses his critique of modern culture as flawed by its belief in notions of 'sincerity and self-realisation' **(p. 26)**. Against such notions, he sets the idea of willed heroism, the 'consciously dramatic' **(p. 27)** assumption of a mask. The passage is crucial for understanding Yeats's view of selfhood as bound up with the 'theatrical' playing of a part. Without such role-play, 'we cannot', the passage asserts, 'impose a discipline upon ourselves though we may accept one from others'. For Yeats, creative freedom is not a question of spontaneity; 'being oneself', as the phrase has it, is likely to involve being unconsciously imprisoned by 'others'. Instead, Yeats places his trust in the capacity to 'imagine ourselves as different from what we are' **(p. 26)**. Poem after poem stages the contest between self as it is and self as it longs to be. In support of his present belief, Yeats summons words written in 'an old diary' **(p. 26)**, as if demonstrating the unity that can be achieved by bringing together present and past selves.

Some years ago I began to believe that our culture, with its doctrine of sincerity and self-realisation, made us gentle and passive, and that the Middle Ages and the Renaissance were right to found theirs upon the imitation of Christ or of some classic hero. Saint Francis and Caesar Borgia made themselves overmastering, creative persons by turning from the mirror to meditation upon a mask.[1] When I had this thought I could see nothing else in life. I could not write the play I had planned, for all became allegorical, and though I tore up hundreds of pages in my endeavour to escape from allegory, my imagination became sterile for nearly five years and I only escaped at last when I had mocked in a comedy my own thought. I was always thinking of the element of imitation in style and in life, and of the life beyond heroic imitation. I find in an old diary: 'I think all happiness depends on the energy to assume the mask of some other life, on a re-birth as something not one's self, something created in a moment and perpetually renewed; in playing a game like that of a child where one loses the infinite pain of self-realisation, in a grotesque or solemn painted face put on that one may hide from the terror of judgment. . . . Perhaps all the sins and energies of the world are but the world's flight from an infinite blinding beam'; and again at an earlier date: 'If we cannot imagine ourselves as different from what we are, and try to assume that second self, we cannot impose a discipline upon ourselves though we may accept one from others. Active virtue, as distinguished from the passive acceptance of a code, is

---

1   Saint Francis of Assissi (?1181–1226); Caesar Borgia (1476–1507), an illegitimate son of Pope Alexander VI who was created a Cardinal and also acted as a military leader (employing Leonardo da Vinci as an architect and engineer), is often regarded as the type of a cruel, vicious ruler, though he is praised by Machiavelli for his command of policy in *The Prince* (1513).

therefore theatrical, consciously dramatic, the wearing of a mask. . . . Wordsworth, great poet though he be, is so often flat and heavy partly because his moral sense, being a discipline he had not created, a mere obedience, has no theatrical element. This increases his popularity with the better kind of journalists and politicians who have written books.'

From **W. B. Yeats, A Vision** (1926, 1937), London: Macmillan, 1962, pp. 8, 24–5

Catalysed by his wife's practice of automatic writing (see the first extract), Yeats's A Vision (1926, 1937) gives systematic form to his ideas about personality and history. The work sees human beings and historical epochs as involved in what, in 'Anima Hominis', Yeats calls a 'blind struggle in the network of the stars' (see **p. 2**): that is, people and cultures belong to phases or eras whose characteristics are determined, and yet they frequently struggle to be the opposite of what is dictated by the predominant features of their phase or era. In the first excerpt, from the Introduction, Yeats describes the origins of A Vision and suggests that one way in which the underlying system was important for him as a poet was that it gave him 'metaphors for poetry' (**p. 27**).

In the second passage, Yeats addresses a question often raised: what kind of credence did he give the system he created in A Vision? His answer is that at times he did experience something close to literal belief but that, with hindsight, the work is comparable to other modernist constructions of reality. Above all, it has allowed him to fuse 'reality' (the raw multiplicity of living) with 'justice' (the desire to find or impose order).

On the afternoon of October 24th, 1917, four days after my marriage, my wife surprised me by attempting automatic writing. What came in disjointed sentences, in almost illegible writing, was so exciting, sometimes so profound, that I persuaded her to give an hour or two day after day to the unknown writer, and after some half-dozen such hours offered to spend what remained of life explaining and piecing together those scattered sentences. 'No,' was the answer, 'we have come to give you metaphors for poetry.'

[. . .]

Some will ask whether I believe in the actual existence of my circuits of sun and moon [. . .] To such a question I can but answer that sometimes, overwhelmed by miracle as all men must be when in the midst of it, I have taken such periods [the supposedly historical eras into which A Vision divides history] literally, my reason has soon recovered; and now that the system stands out clearly in my imagination I regard them as stylistic arrangements of experience comparable to the cubes in

the drawing of Wyndham Lewis and to the ovoids in the sculpture of Brancusi.[1] They have helped me to hold in a single thought reality and justice.

From **W. B. Yeats, Introduction to *The Oxford Book of Modern Verse: 1892–1935***, Oxford: Clarendon, 1936, section IX, pp. xxi–xxii

Yeats published his anthology, the *Oxford Book of Modern Verse*, in 1936. The book was highly idiosyncratic in his choices (it included many poems by Yeats's friends) and exclusions (no space was found for Wilfred Owen and other poets of the First World War on the grounds that 'passive suffering is not a theme for poetry').[1] The excerpt below gives Yeats's judgement on T. S. Eliot, whom Yeats powerfully misreads as more 'satirist' 'than poet' (**p. 29**). For Yeats, Eliot is a modern-day Pope who has turned his back on Romanticism and its legacy. This is a misunderstanding easier to imagine in context since Eliot's critical prose expressed many reservations about Romantic poetry, but it slights the musical power to haunt that co-exists with wry irony in Eliot's early work. Significantly Yeats exempts from criticism stanzas from the close of 'Sweeney among the Nightingales' that have something in common with his own account, in 'Leda and the Swan', of 'Agamemnon dead' (l. 11). For his part, Eliot grew to admire Yeats greatly, but his puzzlement concerning the older poet is clear in a review of 1919 in which he remarks that 'Mr Yeats's mind is a mind in some way independent of experience; and anything that occurs in that mind is of equal importance'.[2]

Eliot has produced his great effect upon his generation because he has described men and women that get out of bed or into it from mere habit; in describing this life that has lost heart his own art seems grey, cold, dry. He is an Alexander Pope, working without apparent imagination, producing his effects by a rejection of all rhythms and metaphors used by the more popular romantics rather than by the discovery of his own, this rejection giving his work an unexaggerated plainness that has the effect of novelty. He has the rhythmical flatness of *The Essay on Man*—despite Miss Sitwell's advocacy I see Pope as Blake and Keats saw him[3]—later, in *The Waste Land*, amid much that is moving in symbol and imagery there is much monotony of accent:

---

1   Wyndham Lewis (1882–1957), a leading artist, friend of Ezra Pound and founder with Pound of Vorticism, a movement that sought to represent energy in condensed artistic forms; Constantin Brancusi (1876–1956), a Romanian sculptor whose work reveals a search for simplified forms.

1   'Introduction' to *The Oxford Book of Modern Verse*, p. xxxiv.
2   Quoted in A. Norman Jeffares (ed.), *W. B. Yeats: The Critical Heritage*, London: Routledge & Kegan Paul, 1977, p. 231.
3   Dame Edith Sitwell (1887–1964), poet; wrote a study of Alexander Pope (1930). Yeats would have regarded Blake's whole poetic career as antagonistic to the supposedly rationalist matter and manner of Pope's poetry. For Keats's early dismissive view of Pope and Augustan poetry, see 'Sleep and Poetry', ll. 185–7.

When lovely woman stoops to folly and
Paces about her room again, alone,
She smooths her hair with automatic hand,
And puts a record on the gramophone.

I was affected, as I am by these lines, when I saw for the first time a painting by
Manet. I longed for the vivid colour and light of Rousseau and Courbet, I could
not endure the grey middle-tint—and even to-day Manet gives me an incomplete
pleasure; he had left the procession.[4] Nor can I put the Eliot of these poems
among those that descend from Shakespeare and the translators of the Bible. I
think of him as satirist rather than poet. Once only does that early work speak in
the great manner:

The host with someone indistinct
Converses at the door apart,
The nightingales are singing near
The Convent of the Sacred Heart,

And sang within the bloody wood
When Agamemnon cried aloud,
And let their liquid siftings fall
To stain the stiff dishonoured shroud.

From **W. B. Yeats, Introduction to *The Oxford Book of Modern Verse: 1892–1935***, Oxford: Clarendon, 1936, section X, pp. xxiii–xxiv, xxiv–xxv

In this extract Yeats distils his opinions about the American poet Ezra Pound,
who worked as Yeats's secretary for a while. They shared a cottage in Sussex
(Stone Cottage) for a number of winters, and enjoyed a close if sometimes edgy
friendship. The passage is of value for showing the subtlety of Yeats's critical
manner and his intimate understanding of the modernist movement with which
he is rightly associated yet from which he stood apart. The comments on *The
Cantos* are of interest for an understanding of Yeats's *A Vision*. Whereas Yeats
sought to give a pattern to the flux of history, Pound, on the older poet's
reading, finds 'nothing to check the flow' (**p. 30**). Pound is made a figure in
Yeats's gallery of types, a poet who is the living embodiment of a divided self,
exhibiting 'deliberate nobility' and yet haunted by its 'direct opposite' (**p. 30**).

Ezra Pound has made flux his theme; plot, characterization, logical discourse,
seem to him abstractions unsuitable to a man of his generation. He is mid-way in
an immense poem in *vers libre* called for the moment *The Cantos* [. . .] Like other
readers I discover at present merely exquisite or grotesque fragments. He hopes to

---

4   Edouard Manet (1832–83); Henri Rousseau (1844–1910); Gustave Courbet (1819–77): all French
    painters.

give the impression that all is living, that there are no edges, no convexities, nothing to check the flow; but can such a poem have a mathematical structure? Can impressions that are in part visual, in part metrical, be related like the notes of a symphony; has the author been carried beyond reason by a theoretical conception? His belief in his own conception is so great that since the appearance of the first Canto I have tried to suspend judgment.

When I consider his work as a whole I find more style than form; at moments more style, more deliberate nobility and the means to convey it than in any contemporary poet known to me, but it is constantly interrupted, broken, twisted into nothing by its direct opposite, nervous obsession, nightmare, stammering confusion; he is an economist, poet, politician, raging at malignants with inexplicable characters and motives, grotesque figures out of a child's book of beasts. This loss of self-control, common among uneducated revolutionists, is rare—Shelley had it in some degree—among men of Ezra Pound's culture and erudition. Style and its opposite can alternate, but form must be full, sphere-like, single. Even where there is no interruption he is often content, if certain verses and lines have style, to leave unbridged transitions, unexplained ejaculations, that make his meaning unintelligible.

From **W. B. Yeats, 'A General Introduction for My Work'** (1937), in *Essays and Introductions*, London: Macmillan, 1961, pp. 509, 522–3

> The first extract below brings to a focus Yeats's complex understanding of the self. It is clear to him that 'A poet writes always of his personal life', but that 'he is never the bundle of accident and incoherence that sits down to breakfast' (**p. 30**). The poet needs 'mythologies' and 'traditional romance' on which to draw; he is more like a character in a play than his everyday self, and 'we adore him', Yeats writes, 'because nature has grown intelligible' (**pp. 30, 31**). Virtually a prose poem in itself and exulting in Yeats's riddling sense of the closeness yet difference between man and poet, the passage conveys his belief in poetry as a remaking of the self into 'something intended, complete' (**pp. 30–1**).

[I. THE FIRST PRINCIPLE]

A poet writes always of his personal life, in his finest work out of its tragedy, whatever it be, remorse, lost love, or mere loneliness; he never speaks directly as to someone at the breakfast table, there is always a phantasmagoria. Dante and Milton had mythologies, Shakespeare the characters of English history or of traditional romance; even when the poet seems most himself, when he is Raleigh and gives potentates the lie, or Shelley 'a nerve o'er which do creep the else unfelt oppressions of this earth', or Byron when 'the soul wears out the breast' as 'the sword outwears its sheath', he is never the bundle of accident and incoherence that sits down to breakfast; he has been reborn as an idea, something intended,

complete.[1] A novelist might describe his accidence, his incoherence, he must not; he is more type than man, more passion than type. He is Lear, Romeo, Oedipus, Tiresias; he has stepped out of a play, and even the woman he loves is Rosalind, Cleopatra, never The Dark Lady. He is part of his own phantasmagoria and we adore him because nature has grown intelligible, and by so doing a part of our creative power.

[. . .]

> The second extract, from the same essay, explains and enacts Yeats's opinions about 'style and attitude'. For him, style is a preservative; it prevents the poet from lapsing into mere subjective egotism. Style, modelled on traditional forms (though continually made new by the individual artist), serves, on Yeats's account, to ensure that emotion does not 'rot' – hence Yeats's lack of interest in 'free verse' and his aphoristic assertion that 'Ancient salt is best packing' **(p. 32)**. The passage is remarkable for its acting out of Yeats's preferred 'style and attitude'. The prose mimics a man growing heated at babble about 'originality', until he erupts in a series of self-definitions that end in 'nothing': 'I am a crowd, I am a lonely man, I am nothing' **(p. 32)**. In the extract Yeats evokes with much skill his admiration for Shakespearean tragedy as the very essence of the style and attitude he recommends; the extract concludes with a reference by Yeats to the end of his poem 'The Fisherman' **(pp. 125–7)**.

[III. STYLE AND ATTITUDE]

[. . .] The translators of the Bible, Sir Thomas Browne,[2] certain translators from the Greek when translators still bothered about rhythm, created a form midway between prose and verse that seems natural to impersonal meditation; but all that is personal soon rots; it must be packed in ice or salt. Once when I was in delirium from pneumonia I dictated a letter to George Moore[3] telling him to eat salt because it was a symbol of eternity; the delirium passed, I had no memory of that letter, but I must have meant what I now mean. If I wrote of personal love or sorrow in free verse, or in any rhythm that left it unchanged, amid all its accidence, I would be full of self-contempt because of my egotism and indiscretion, and foresee the boredom of my reader. I must choose a traditional stanza, even what I alter must seem traditional. I commit my emotion to shepherds, herdsmen, camel-drivers, learned men, Milton's or Shelley's Platonist, that tower Palmer

1 References are to Sir Walter Raleigh, 'The Lie', l. 18, Shelley, *Julian and Maddalo*, ll. 449–50 and Byron, 'So, we'll go no more a-roving', ll. 6, 5.
2 Sir Thomas Browne (1605–82), prose writer noted for his elaborate rhythm and sonorous diction.
3 George Moore (1852–1923), Irish novelist and close acquaintance of Yeats, whom he satirizes in his fictionalized autobiography *Hail and Farewell* (1911).

drew.[4] Talk to me of originality and I will turn on you with rage. I am a crowd, I am a lonely man, I am nothing. Ancient salt is best packing. The heroes of Shakespeare convey to us through their looks, or through the metaphorical patterns of their speech, the sudden enlargement of their vision, their ecstasy at the approach of death: 'She should have died hereafter', 'Of many thousand kisses, the poor last', 'Absent thee from felicity awhile'. They have become God or Mother Goddess, the pelican, 'My baby at my breast', but all must be cold; no actress has ever sobbed when she played Cleopatra, even the shallow brain of a producer has never thought of such a thing.[5] The supernatural is present, cold winds blow across our hands, upon our faces, the thermometer falls, and because of that cold we are hated by journalists and groundlings. There may be in this or that detail painful tragedy, but in the whole work none. I have heard Lady Gregory say, rejecting some play in the modern manner sent to the Abbey Theatre, 'Tragedy must be a joy to the man who dies'. Nor is it any different with lyrics, songs, narrative poems; neither scholars nor the populace have sung or read anything generation after generation because of its pain. The maid of honour whose tragedy they sing must be lifted out of history with timeless pattern, she is one of the four Maries,[6] the rhythm is old and familiar, imagination must dance, must be carried beyond feeling into the aboriginal ice. Is ice the correct word? I once boasted, copying the phrase from a letter of my father's, that I would write a poem 'cold and passionate as the dawn'.

From **W. B. Yeats, *Reveries over Childhood and Youth*** (first published in 1916), in *Autobiographies*, London: Macmillan, 1955, pp. 64–6

As the end of the previous extract illustrates, J. B. Yeats exercised much influence over his son. The father was liberal, rationalist and artistic; he at once inspired his son's love of the imagination and provoked antagonism in him because of his rejection of religious belief. The following passage alludes to the father's reading of Shelley's *Prometheus Unbound*. Yeats observes that he preferred the earlier acts to the last, a sign of his father's lack of sympathy with the ideal and visionary in poetry. He also draws attention to his father's enjoyment of the human dimension of literature, of literature as coming out of speech even as it formed an 'idealization' of it. Yeats writes about him with a blend of heightened observation and detached intensity as he draws his father into his own 'phantasmagoria'. The father's preferences are bound together by a fascination with literature at 'its most passionate moment' (**p. 33**), a fascination shared by his son.

---

4   Alludes to a favourite image of the poet as thinker set apart from the madding crowd, which Yeats found in Milton's *Il Penseroso*, ll. 85–96 and Shelley's character, Prince Athanase; the sentence also alludes to the painter Samuel Palmer (1805–81) and his illustration 'The Lonely Tower'.

5   Quotations are from *Macbeth*, 5. 5. 16; *Antony and Cleopatra*, 4. 16. 21; *Hamlet*, 5. 2. 289; *Antony and Cleopatra*, 5. 2. 300.

6   An allusion to the 'four Maries' in a traditional song, 'The Queen's Maries', associated with Mary, Queen of Scots.

My father's influence upon my thoughts was at its height. We went to Dublin by train every morning, breakfasting in his studio. He had taken a large room with a beautiful eighteenth-century mantelpiece in a York Street tenement-house, and at breakfast he read passages from the poets, and always from the play or poem at its most passionate moment. He never read me a passage because of its speculative interest, and indeed did not care at all for poetry where there was generalization or abstraction however impassioned. He would read out the first speeches of the *Prometheus Unbound*, but never the ecstatic lyricism of that famous fourth act; and another day the scene where Coriolanus comes to the house of Aufidius and tells the impudent servants that his home is under the canopy. I have seen *Coriolanus* played a number of times since then, and read it more than once, but that scene is more vivid than the rest, and it is my father's voice that I hear and not Irving's or Benson's.[1] He did not care even for a fine lyric passage unless he felt some actual man behind its elaboration of beauty, and he was always looking for the lineaments of some desirable, familiar life [. . .] All must be an idealization of speech, and at some moment of passionate action or somnambulistic reverie. I remember his saying that all contemplative men were in a conspiracy to overrate their state of life, and that all writers were of them, excepting the great poets. Looking backwards, it seems to me that I saw his mind in fragments, which had always hidden connections I only now begin to discover. He disliked the Victorian poetry of ideas, and Wordsworth but for certain passages or whole poems. He said one morning over his breakfast that he had discovered in the shape of the head of a Wordsworthian scholar, an old and greatly respected clergyman whose portrait he was painting, all the animal instincts of a prize-fighter. He despised the formal beauty of Raphael, that calm which is not an ordered passion but an hypocrisy, and attacked Raphael's life for its love of pleasure and its self-indulgence.[2] In literature he was always Pre-Raphaelite, and carried into literature principles that, while the Academy was still unbroken, had made the first attack upon academic form.

He no longer read me anything for its story, and all our discussion was of style.

From **W. B. Yeats, *Four Years, 1887–1891*** (first published in 1921), in *Autobiographies*, London: Macmillan, 1955, p. 171

In this excerpt Yeats revisits the topic of the self and the anti-self. Here he suggests that he is ignorant of both, before offering a surmise about what lay behind his admiration for the solitary. It is, he guesses, because he is by nature 'gregarious' that he loves 'proud and lonely things' **(p. 34)**. He draws a comparison between himself and Shelley, a Romantic poet whose work he

---

1 Sir Henry Irving (1838–1905), reputed to be the finest English actor of his day; Sir Frank Benson (1858–1939), actor.
2 Raphael (1483–1520); painter of the Italian Renaissance, famous for the grace and ease of his compositions, and for their fidelity to a Neoplatonic ideal of beauty.

responded to profoundly if at times ambivalently.[1] In his final sentence Yeats alludes to Prince Athansae from the poem that he would have known by that name (it is now referred to as *Athanase*) and to Ahasuerus, the mysterious prophet-figure from *Hellas*. The gendered distinctions of the passage are noteworthy. Yeats's sense of self is founded on a feeling of difference from, and yet dependence on, the women who support and help him.

[. . .] I know very little about myself and much less of that anti-self: probably the woman who cooks my dinner or the woman who sweeps out my study knows more than I. It is perhaps because Nature made me a gregarious man, going hither and thither looking for conversation, and ready to deny from fear or favour his dearest conviction, that I love proud and lonely things. When I was a child and went daily to the sexton's daughter for writing lessons, I found one poem in her School Reader that delighted me beyond all others: a fragment of some metrical translation from Aristophanes wherein the birds sing scorn upon mankind.[2] In later years my mind gave itself to gregarious Shelley's dream of a young man, his hair blanched with sorrow, studying philosophy in some lonely tower, or of his old man, master of all human knowledge, hidden from human sight in some shell-strewn cavern on the Mediterranean shore. [. . .]

From letter from **Maud Gonne to W. B. Yeats**, 8 November 1916, about 'Easter 1916', in Anna MacBride White and A. Norman Jeffares (eds), *Always Your Friend: The Gonne–Yeats Letters 1893–1938*, London: Pimlico, 1993, pp. 384–5

In this letter sent from Paris, Maud Gonne shows herself to be unimpressed by Yeats's 'Easter 1916', disliking its complexities of tone. The letter helps us understand Yeats's difficult cultural position: among the most famous modern poets, he is found to be insufficiently 'sincere' and inadequately patriotic by the woman who inspired so much of his poetry. Articulating her own impassioned nationalism in the letter, and refusing to allow any doubts about the value of the sacrifice made by MacDonagh, Pearse, Connolly and MacBride (her estranged husband), Gonne lands some shrewd hits in the letter. She suggests that Yeats has failed in his attempt 'To write for my own race' ('The Fisherman', l. 11, **p. 126**), and accuses him of 'unintelligible' entanglement in his own private system of thought. Yeats himself aims a not dissimilar criticism at himself at the close of 'Meditations in Time of Civil War' (**p. 155**); yet it is clear that his greatness as a poet derives from his capacity to permit the self-quarrelling that Gonne seeks to outlaw.

---

1 See George Bornstein, *Yeats and Shelley*, Chicago, Ill.: University of Chicago Press, 1970.
2 *Birds*, written by the Greek comic dramatist Aristophanes, was a play produced in 414 BC. In one chorus, the birds assert, 'A treacherous thing always in every way/Is human nature', ed. and trans. Jeffrey Henderson, Cambridge, Mass.: Harvard University Press, 2000, p. 79. Yeats's passage (first published in 1921) anticipates his bird's scorn for mankind in 'Byzantium'.

My dear Willie

No I don't like your poem, it isn't worthy of you & above all it isn't worthy of the subject – Though it reflects your present state of mind perhaps, it isn't quite sincere enough for you who have studied philosophy & know something of history know quite well that sacrifice has never yet turned a heart to stone though it has immortalised many & through it alone mankind can rise to God – You recognise this in the line which was the original inspiration of your poem 'A terrible Beauty is born' but you let your present mood mar & confuse it till even some of the verses become unintelligible to many. Even Iseult reading it didn't understand your thought till I explained your [?retribution] theory of constant change & becoming in the flux of things –

But you could never say that MacDonagh & Pearse & Conally [Connolly] were sterile fixed minds, each served Ireland, which was their share of the world, the part they were in contact with, with varied faculties & vivid energy! those three were men of genius, with large comprehensive & speculative & active brains the others of whom we know less were probably less remarkable men, but still I think they must have been men with a stronger grasp on Reality a stronger spiritual life than most of those we meet. As for my husband he has entered Eternity by the great door of sacrifice which Christ opened & has therefore atoned for all so that praying for him I can also ask for his prayers & 'A terrible beauty is born'[1]

There are beautiful lines in your poem, as there are in all you write but it is not a great WHOLE, a living thing which our race would treasure & repeat, such as a poet like you might have given to your nation & which would have avenged our material failure by its spiritual beauty –

You will be angry perhaps that I write so frankly what I feel, but I am always frank with my friends & though our ideals are wide apart we are still friends. [. . .]

Alwys [sic] your friend

Maud Gonne

---

1   Quotes the refrain used at key moments, including the last line, of 'Easter 1916'.

2

Interpretations

2

Interpretations

Critical History

Yeats's poems have always provoked admiration, debate and, not infrequently, qualified or negative responses. In this survey of criticism I shall indicate major critical preoccupations and comment on the extracts included in this section (the extracts are discussed in more detail in relevant headnotes). The extracts are arranged in chronological order.

In the Early Critical Reception chapter of this Sourcebook a few brief extracts indicate some perceptive contemporary responses to Yeats's work as it appeared. His friend the poet Lionel Johnson notes Yeats's Irish themes and praises his 'haunting music' (**p. 47**). Arthur Symons, another friend and poet, underlines the importance of Yeats's use of symbols and Irish mythology. Writing about *The Tower* Austin Clarke finely observes how Yeats's poems immerse themselves in the 'commotion' of historical events, yet retain an imaginative freedom (**p. 48**). In so doing Clarke anticipates a point to which Louise Bogan, in a piece published in 1938, draws attention: 'What impresses us most strongly in Yeats's late work is that here a whole personality is involved' (**p. 48**). Bogan's article shows an attempt to consider the implications of Yeats's career that is evident, too, in groundbreaking work by Edmund Wilson in his chapter on Yeats in *Axel's Castle* (1931). Wilson's chapter is still among the best introductions to the poetry. It discusses the grafting, in Yeats, of the Symbolist tradition on to national concerns, and it traces the development from the aestheticism of the early work, itself aware that 'the fascination of fairyland' is 'inimical to life in the real world', to a poetry that faces 'life's hard conditions'.[1] It offers shrewd comments on Yeats's divorce 'from the general enlightened thought of his day' and his construction of a system of his own, a system that Wilson describes with admirable clarity.[2] Wilson is sceptical about this system, and, indeed, points out the strain of scepticism in Yeats,[3]

1 Edmund Wilson, *Axel's Castle: A Study in the Imaginative Literature of 1870–1930* (1931), London: Fontana, 1961, pp. 28–30, 34, 35.
2 Ibid., pp. 45, 46–51.
3 Ibid., pp. 52–4.

but he argues that 'Yeats's sense of reality to-day is inferior to that of no man alive'.[4]

All these commentators bring out salient features of Yeats's work: its artistic subtlety; the significance of its Irish themes; the richness of its development; its ability to respond to history without sacrificing the complexity of the poet's 'personality'. A fifth contemporary response included here (**p. 49**), that of F. R. Leavis to *Last Poems and Plays*, illustrates how Yeats has always been the target of hostile and negative criticism, too; evaluative issues – is the late work narrower, coarser and less subtle than earlier poems? – are alive here, and elsewhere. It is a sign of Yeats's power to engage the reader that he should induce strong responses. Leavis's sense of imaginative diminishment in the later work is picked up, in qualified ways, by subsequent critics such as Harold Bloom, made 'uncomfortable' by aspects of the tone of the last poems.[5]

Yeats and the Occult

' "A Vision," when we try to read it, makes us impatient with Yeats';[6] so Edmund Wilson asserts. Certainly much ink has been spilt over the nature of Yeats's interest in the occult. When W. H. Auden wrote in his elegy, 'In Memory of W. B. Yeats' (1939), 'You were silly like us', he was disguising the fact that, for many readers, Yeats was extraordinarily different in his readiness to pursue esoteric and spiritualist sources of knowledge. This readiness culminates in his work *A Vision* (1926, 1937), in which he sets out his system of thought concerning people, historical cycles and life after death (see Contextual Overview, **pp. 13–15** for an account of the work). The question of whether the poetry needs to be read in the light of his ideas has fascinated and vexed critics. An early attempt by Cleanth Brooks (in 1939) to explicate 'Byzantium' in relation to *A Vision* induced the following response from the American poet and critic Allen Tate: 'Yeats's special qualities will instigate special studies of great ingenuity, but the more direct and more difficult problem of the poetry itself will probably be delayed.'[7] Brooks, on the contrary, believed that Yeats's system gave him a coherent and complex world-view, and had for him 'the authority and meaning of a religion'.[8]

Much fine criticism elucidates *A Vision* and its relationship with Yeats's work.

4   Ibid., p. 53.
5   Harold Bloom, *Yeats*, New York: Oxford University Press, 1970, p. 435. See also Jonathan Allison's 'The Attack on Yeats', *South Atlantic Review*, 55:4, 1990, pp. 61–73, reprinted in *W. B. Yeats: Critical Assessments*, ed. David Pierce, 4 vols, Mountfield, near Robertsbridge: Helm Information, 2000, vol. 4, pp. 421–32, for an account of the attack by some distinguished Irish critics on 'Yeats's canonical position' (p. 421).
6   *Axel's Castle*, p. 50.
7   Allen Tate, 'Yeats's Romanticism', *Southern Review*, 7:3, 1942; quoted in Elizabeth Cullingford (ed.), *Yeats: Poems, 1919–1935*, Basingstoke: Macmillan, 1984, p. 88.
8   Cleanth Brooks, *Modern Poetry and the Tradition*, Chapel Hill, NC, 1939; 2nd edn, 1965; quoted in Cullingford (ed.), *Yeats: Poems, 1919–1935*, p. 65.

A valuable survey of critical attitudes is provided by David Pierce.[9] Relevant sections of Ellmann's classic study *Yeats: The Man and the Masks* (1948, 1979) are still rewarding. Ellmann tackles the question all readers of Yeats find themselves articulating: 'Did Yeats believe in esoteric Yeatsianism?' Pointing to the mixture of faith and scepticism in Yeats's pronouncements, he asserts, 'It cannot be answered simply.' He does, however, propose that Yeats's ideas may have been more important to him than to his readers, part of the process by which Yeats becomes 'not merely a poet, but the symbol of a poet', and he remarks of 'The Second Coming' that 'an awareness of the system was more useful for writing than it is for reading the poem'.[10] This view tallies with Tate's wish to focus on 'the poetry itself', and with the views of many critics and readers of the poetry. Among other stimulating discussions is the chapter 'A *Vision*: The Great Wheel' in Harold Bloom's *Yeats*, which reads the work as itself 'a considerable if flawed major poem' and finds many parallels between it and Blake's epics and Shelley's *Prometheus Unbound*.[11] Northrop Frye has a searching chapter (1965) on *A Vision* in which he questions the work's capacity to do justice to 'some of Yeats's more profound insights'.[12] More recently, Terence Brown offers a perceptive account of *A Vision* that stresses how the work 'seems to have satisfied some deep need of [Yeats's] nature for pattern and structure in reality' and 'allowed the poet to engage with the drama of self and world with an imaginative certitude'.[13]

Development, Ireland, Poetic and Cultural Legacy

Virtually all commentators have noted the remarkable nature of Yeats's poetic development, involving continuity and change, and the importance and complexity of his Irishness. The classic early studies of his development are T. S. Eliot's lecture of 1940 and Louis MacNeice's critical study *The Poetry of W. B. Yeats* (1941). Eliot finds the later Yeats to be the kind of poet 'who, out of intense and personal experience, is able to express a general truth; retaining all the particularity of his experience, to make of it a general symbol'.[14] Louis MacNeice offers a searching yet celebratory account of the poetry, throwing out insights and suggestions that other writers will take up; he asks, for instance, whether Yeats

9 David Pierce, 'Yeats and His Beliefs', in *W. B. Yeats: A Guide through the Critical Maze*, Bristol: The Bristol Classical Press, 1989.
10 Richard Ellmann, *Yeats: The Man and the Masks* (1948), Oxford: Oxford University Press, 1979, pp. 230, 238, 233.
11 Harold Bloom, *Yeats*, New York: Oxford University Press, 1970, p. 211.
12 Northrop Frye, 'The Rising of the Moon: A Study of *A Vision*', in Denis Donoghue and J. R, Mulryne (eds), *An Honoured Guest: New Essays on W. B. Yeats*, London: Edward Arnold, 1965; quoted in David Pierce (ed.), *W. B. Yeats: Critical Assessments*, vol. 3, p. 191.
13 Terence Brown, *The Life of W. B. Yeats* (1999), Oxford: Blackwell, 2001, p. 308.
14 T. S. Eliot, 'Yeats', in Frank Kermode (ed.), *Selected Prose of T. S. Eliot*, London: Faber and Faber, 1975, p. 251.

'sometimes faked his passion because he so much wanted to be passionate', but concludes that his subject, 'as a poet, is characterized by integrity'.[15]

Much later, another Irish poet, Seamus Heaney, will return to similar concerns in his essay 'Yeats as an Example?', which finds 'the finally exemplary moments' in Yeats to be those when the poet's characteristically 'powerful artistic control is vulnerable to the pain or pathos of life itself'.[16] Like Eliot, Heaney finds Yeats to be a major poet of middle-age, an author continually evolving ways of holding artistic control open to experience.[17] Heaney is one of many poets who have responded to Yeats's injunction 'Irish poets, learn your trade' ('Under Ben Bulben', V. 1), and significant writing on Yeats has appeared by practitioners and critics reflecting on his legacy. Some of the richest responses come from poets writing in the Yeatsian shadow: Tom Paulin dislikes Yeats's 'crazy political notions' and 'domineering sexism' but praises 'the uniquely wonderful cadencing of the poems'.[18] In the same symposium, Seamus Heaney speaks memorably of the writing as a 'deed of poetry' and defends the 'unconstrained quality of the work', its 'danger'.[19]

Other critics, including Edna Longley, Neil Corcoran and Peter McDonald, have examined the cultural and artistic legacy of the poetry.[20] In ' "Defending Ireland's Soul" ', for example, Longley reviews ways in which 'Yeats, and a few of his Protestant literary successors, negotiate their marginalisation at the hands of Irishness as a Nationalist construct'.[21] Longley is too good a critic to be ensnared by the sectarianism her phrasing echoes and combats, but her phrasing shows how Yeats continues to loom large in turbulent cultural battles. Corcoran and McDonald reaffirm Yeats's formalist skills as a poet and recognize the poetry's awareness of all that challenges formal order.

Suggestive studies of Yeats's development include Frank Kermode's account in *Romantic Image* (1957) of Yeats's hostility to discursive language and trust in images such as that of the dancer to transcend and heal the split between art and life.[22] In *The Romantic Survival* (1957) (excerpted on **pp. 54–5**) John Bayley surveys the poetic career in order to bring out Yeats's dealings with his Romantic inheritance.[23] Like the Romantics, Yeats places the self at the centre of his work;

15 Louis MacNeice, *The Poetry of W. B. Yeats* (1941), London: Faber and Faber, 1967, p. 196.
16 Seamus Heaney, *Preoccupations: Selected Prose 1968–1978*, London: Faber and Faber, 1980, p. 109.
17 Ibid., p. 111.
18 In 'A Yeats Symposium', *The Guardian Review*, 27 January 1989, pp. 25–6; quoted in David Pierce (ed.), *W. B. Yeats: Critical Assessments*, vol. 4, p. 369.
19 Ibid., p. 370.
20 See Edna Longley in many places, including ' "Defending Ireland's Soul": Protestant Writers and Irish Nationalism after Independence', in her *The Living Stream: Literature and Revisionism in Ireland*, Newcastle upon Tyne: Bloodaxe, 1994; Neil Corcoran, 'Architectures of Yeats: Perspectives on *The Winding Stair*', in his *Poets of Modern Ireland: Text, Context, Intertext*, Cardiff: University of Wales Press, 1999; and Peter McDonald, 'Yeats and Remorse', *Proceedings of the British Academy* 94 (1998), pp. 173–206, and 'Yeats's Poetic Structures', *English* 48 (Spring 1999), pp. 17–32.
21 ' "Defending Ireland's Soul" ', p. 131.
22 Frank Kermode, *Romantic Image*, London: Routledge and Kegan Paul, 1957.
23 John Bayley, *The Romantic Survival: A Study in Poetic Evolution* (1957), London: Constable, 1969.

but he gives to the theme of self-making unique and rhetorically persuasive deliberateness. In Bayley's view, 'Yeats is certainly the last Romantic to believe implicitly in the power of poetry' (p. 54); he explains the poetry's power in terms of Yeats's development of a style that balances calculation and passionate assertion.

Yeats's concerns with Ireland, including his growing re-attachment to his Anglo-Irish roots, are discussed by many critics. Notable contextual work in recent years includes Declan Kiberd's *Inventing Ireland* (1995),[24] which sees Yeats as working in a transitional political period of immense complexity, during which the idea of a new Irish nation was actively being imagined by writers. Kiberd's reading of 'Leda and the Swan' (pp. 83–4) is an example of criticism informed by post-colonial theory (it associates the poem with the Irish Civil War and its aftermath), but is keen less to argue a thesis than to intimate different ways of reading a by now classic poem. Roy Foster's detailed biography, *W. B. Yeats: A Life* illustrates how a desire to meditate on the scope of Yeats's career, while taking on board the insights of decades of research, enriches study of the poetry. Foster points out that Yeats 'came to fame as the poet of the new Ireland, asserting its identity', but that he 'was also a product of the *ancien régime*: Victorian, Protestant, Ascendancy Ireland'.[25] Such a context is relevant for understanding what Foster calls Yeats's 'quarrels with himself and others over the shape-changing phenomenon of Irish nationalism'.[26]

Fascism, Right-Wing Politics, Post-Colonialism, Feminism

Attention to Yeats's politics and cultural identity has produced significant work from various angles. Yeats's right-wing views were the target of controversy during his lifetime. In the aftermath of his death Auden mounted a mock-trial of the poet in his essay 'The Public v. the Late Mr. William Butler Yeats' (1940). His 'Counsel for the Defence', given the second and final word, argues that 'the virtues that the deceased praised in the peasantry and the aristocracy, and the vices he blamed in the commercial classes, were real virtues and vices'.[27] He concedes that Yeats's ideas may have been 'false or undemocratic', but he asserts that the poet moved towards a 'true democratic style'.[28] Auden's witty, thoughtful piece has done much to shape subsequent debate. Seminal for more recent criticism is Conor Cruise O'Brien's ' "Passion and Cunning": An Essay on the Politics of W. B. Yeats'. O'Brien's brilliant essay stresses the abiding relevance to Yeats's

---

24 Declan Kiberd, *Inventing Ireland: The Literature of the Modern Nation* (1995), London: Vintage, 1996.
25 R. F. Foster, *W. B. Yeats: A Life: I: The Apprentice Mage 1865–1914*, Oxford: Oxford University Press, 1997, p. xxviii.
26 Ibid., p. xxix.
27 Edward Mendelson (ed.), *The English Auden*, London: Faber and Faber, 1977, p. 393.
28 Ibid.

politics of 'the Anglo-Irish predicament';[29] it finds in Yeats a mixture of 'pride' and 'prudence';[30] and it locates in the later Yeats a blend of 'Anglophobe Irish nationalism and . . . authoritarianism'.[31] O'Brien distinguishes between the man, a fascist sympathizer on the critic's account, and the poet, telepathically attuned to the violence and horror of the age through which he was living.

The most impressive answer to O'Brien's essay is offered by Elizabeth Cullingford in her book-length study *Yeats, Ireland and Fascism* (1981), extracted on **pp. 75–6.** Cullingford accepts O'Brien's description of Yeats's 'Anglophobe Irish nationalism', which she calls 'Fenianism' (**p. 75**), but she does not agree with his view of Yeats as a proto-Fascist, offering carefully measured qualifications (see the relevant headnote for further discussion, **pp. 74–5**). Edward Said is a further defender of Yeats's politics, hailing him in a pamphlet of 1988 as a writer in pursuit of decolonization, despite the fact that he 'stopped short of imagining the full political liberation he might have aspired towards'.[32] Timothy Webb also writes sympathetically about Yeats's ambivalent relationship with the English, and his 'sustained attempt to maintain his political and intellectual independence, to be the master of his own discourse'.[33] A critic who has offered a searching yet sympathetic critique of Yeats's brand of nationalism is Seamus Deane. In his *A Short History of Irish Literature* (1986) Deane is alive to the creative potential of conflict in Yeats, to the way in which in 'all the great poems of the 1920s, we meet time and again magnificent rhetorical structures based upon antinomies [. . .] which gain definition from one another without ever reaching, or seriously seeking, reconciliation'.[34]

Relations with women, notably Maud Gonne, were central to Yeats's writing; so, too, were his meditations on the role of women, as in 'A Prayer for My Daughter'. Often these reflections are complex, even contradictory. In 'A Prayer for My Daughter', the poet wishes for his daughter all that is 'accustomed, cere-monious' (l. 74), allotting her a traditional role in embodying and sustaining the Anglo-Irish aristocratic ideal. Yet, he wishes her, too, to know a spiritual auton-omy and independence. A number of critics have recognized that Yeats's cultural reflections have at their core a fair degree of sexual politics, and are incompletely understood without that recognition. Terry Eagleton points out that, in Yeats, 'the feminine would seem at once to symbolise the desired social order and to

---

29 Conor Cruise O'Brien, ' "Passion and Cunning": An Essay on the Politics of W. B. Yeats', in A. Norman Jeffares and K. G. W. Cross (eds), *In Excited Reverie: A Centenary Tribute to William Butler Yeats 1865–1939*, London: Macmillan, p. 211.
30 Ibid., p. 214.
31 Ibid., p. 270.
32 Edward W. Said, *Nationalism, Colonialism and Literature: Yeats and Decolonization*, A Field Day Pamphlet, 15, Derry, 1988; quoted in David Pierce, *W. B. Yeats: Critical Assessments*, vol. 4, p. 363.
33 Timothy Webb, 'Yeats and the English', in Joseph McMinn *et al.* (eds), *The Internationalism of Irish Literature and Drama*, Gerrards Cross: Colin Smythe, 1992; quoted in David Pierce, *W. B. Yeats: Critical Assessments*, vol. 4, p. 518.
34 Seamus Deane, *A Short History of Irish Literature*, London: Heinemann, 1986, p. 158 ('anti-nomies', a word favoured by Yeats, means 'contradictions' or 'opposites'). See also the chapter on Yeats in the same author's *Celtic Revivals*, London: Faber and Faber, 1985.

subvert it'.[35] Elizabeth Cullingford, in *Gender and History in Yeats's Love Poetry* (1993), seeks to show how questions of gender and history bear on Yeats's love poems. So, in the extract printed on **pp. 76–80**, she argues that Yeats's representation of the female dancer in 'Among School Children' (**pp. 163–7**) 'emerges from his oppositional dialogue' (**p. 80**) with the post-Civil-War Ireland that had come into being, a Free State dominated by the Church.[36] In *Yeats's Nations* (1996) Marjorie Howes brings together, in the words of her book's subtitle, 'Gender, Class, and Irishness' (extracted on **pp. 84–5**) in order to uncover 'different kinds of ambivalence' at work in Yeats's poetry.[37]

Close Reading, Formalism, Deconstruction, Intertextuality

There is an impressive tradition, in Yeatsian criticism, of close reading of the poetry, and detailed commentary on the poetic *oeuvre*, as valuable works by A. Norman Jeffares and John Unterecker bear witness.[38] Other critics, notably Jon Stallworthy and Curtis B. Bradford, have explored the 'sedentary toil' ('Ego Dominus Tuus', **pp. 129–32**, l. 65) that led, in processes of revision carefully traced by these critics, to the creation of Yeats's masterpieces.[39] The extract from Stallworthy printed below (**pp. 55–62**) demonstrates such processes at work in the composition of 'The Second Coming'.

Among the very best work on Yeats has been criticism that looks at and celebrates, where appropriate, his artistic achievement. Harold Bloom's *Yeats* (1970) is an example of evaluative close reading (he is unafraid of negative judgements) and a work that anticipates his later absorption (in works beginning with *The Anxiety of Influence*, 1973) in questions of influence and intertextuality. The extract printed on **pp. 70–1** discusses 'The Secret Rose' (**pp. 109–11**), which is linked to poems by Blake and Shelley. Denis Donoghue, taking his cue from the poet's own self-descriptions, stresses the consciously dramatic nature of Yeats's imagination, as is illustrated by the extract printed below that examines 'The Secret Rose' and 'Adam's Curse' (**pp. 72–4**).[40] In a much more recent book (excerpted on **pp. 86–7**), Daniel Albright has also sought his bearings from Yeats's poetics, or theory of poetry, and gives an account of Yeats's symbols in the

35 Terry Eagleton, 'Politics and Sexuality in W. B. Yeats', *The Crane Bag*, 9:2, 1988, pp. 138–42; quoted in David Pierce (ed.), *W. B. Yeats: Critical Assessments*, vol. 4, p. 216.
36 Elizabeth Cullingford, *Gender and History in Yeats's Love Poetry*, Cambridge: Cambridge University Press, 1993.
37 Marjorie Howes, *Yeats's Nations: Gender, Class, and Irishness*, Cambridge: Cambridge University Press, 1996, p. 4.
38 A. Norman Jeffares, *A New Commentary on the Poems of W. B. Yeats*, Basingstoke: Macmillan, 1984; John Unterecker, *A Reader's Guide to William Butler Yeats*, London: Thames & Hudson, 1959.
39 Jon Stallworthy, *Between the Lines: Yeats's Poetry in the Making*, Oxford: Clarendon, 1963; Jon Stallworthy, *Vision and Revision in Yeats's 'Last Poems'*, Oxford: Clarendon, 1969; Curtis B. Bradford, *Yeats at Work*, Carbondale, Ill.: Southern Illinois University Press, 1965.
40 Denis Donoghue, *Yeats*, London: Fontana/Collins, 1971.

light of a distinction that the poet makes between 'intellectual' and 'emotional' symbols.[41] Helen Vendler, among the finest close readers of poetry of her generation, focuses on the minute particulars of Yeats's achievement in her 'Technique in the Earlier Poems of Yeats'.[42] The excerpt (pp. 88–9) from my own study of poetic self-consciousness examines the cunning self-awareness pervading the late, seemingly desolate, poem 'The Circus Animals' Desertion'.[43] The fascination with Yeats's tones in my piece builds on the shrewd discussion by Richard Ellmann of Yeats's 'affirmative capability' (excerpted on pp. 51–4)[44] and links with J. R. Mulryne's fuller discussion of the tragic tonalities in later Yeats, also excerpted below (pp. 67–9).[45] In other extracts included in the present volume, C. K. Stead and M. L. Rosenthal offer analyses (pp. 62–6, 81–3) of 'Easter 1916' and 'Nineteen Hundred and Nineteen' (pp. 155–61), respectively, that seek to be responsive to the imaginative life and artistry of the poems, and to stress, in Stead's case, Yeats's ability to blend a poetry of argument and of symbol.[46]

Deconstruction, with its passion for teasing out underlying contradictions, has caught up with a poet who thrives on self-quarrelling while longing for what he called Unity of Being. Impressive examples include Paul de Man's 'Image and Emblem in Yeats', which suggests that Yeats deconstructs the capacity of his images to convey reconciliation by showing them to be artificially manipulated emblems, and Edward Larrissy's Yeats the Poet: The Measures of Difference (1994), a work that brings together deconstruction and cultural studies to explore Yeats's self-consciousness about difference, whether linguistic or historical.[47]

Critical work on Yeats has proliferated in the last few decades, to illuminating ends. The diversity of approaches represented in the following pages will, it is hoped, prove stimulating and intimate the possibility of fresh and independent ways of thinking about a formidable body of poetry.

41 Daniel Albright, Quantum Poetics: Yeats, Pound, Eliot, and the Science of Modernism, Cambridge: Cambridge University Press, 1997.
42 Helen Vendler, 'Technique in the Earlier Poems of Yeats', in Warwick Gould (ed.), Yeats Annual, 8, Basingstoke: Macmillan, 1991, pp. 3–20.
43 Michael O'Neill, Romanticism and the Self-Conscious Poem, Oxford: Oxford University Press, 1997.
44 Richard Ellmann, The Identity of Yeats, London: Macmillan, 1954.
45 J. R. Mulryne, 'The Last Poems', in Denis Donoghue and J. R. Mulryne (eds.), An Honoured Guest: New Essays on W. B. Yeats, London: Edward Arnold, 1965.
46 C. K. Stead, The New Poetic, London: Hutchinson, 1964; M. L. Rosenthal, Running to Paradise: Yeats's Poetic Art, New York and Oxford: Oxford University Press, 1994.
47 Paul de Man, 'Image and Emblem in Yeats', in his The Rhetoric of Romanticism, New York: Columbia University Press, 1984; Edward Larrissy, Yeats the Poet: The Measures of Difference, Hemel Hempstead: Harvester Wheatsheaf, 1994.

Early Critical Reception

From **Lionel Johnson's review of *The Countess Kathleen and Various Legends and Lyrics*,** *The Academy,* 42:1065, 1 October 1892

> This extract from an early review by Lionel Johnson, a well-known poet, friend of Yeats and a fellow member of the Rhymers' Club, indicates how Yeats's early poems were seen by many readers as characterised by a concern for 'ideal beauty' and 'ideal wisdom', ideals associated with the poet's construction of Ireland, and as revealing 'a subtle strain of music in their whole quality of thoughts and images'.

They [the Legends and Lyrics] conclude with a poem ['To Ireland in the Coming Times'], in which Mr Yeats makes his profession of faith and loyalty towards Ireland, and justifies the tone of his poems, their 'druid' quality, their care for an ideal beauty of love and an ideal wisdom of truth [. . ..] In these poems, the immediate charm is their haunting music, which depends not upon any rich wealth of words, but upon a subtle strain of music in their whole quality of thoughts and images, some incommunicable beauty, felt in the simplest words and verses.

From **Arthur Symons's review of *The Wind among the Reeds*,** *The Saturday Review,* 6 May 1899

> Arthur Symons (1865–1945), poet and critic, was a close friend of Yeats (sharing rooms with him in 1896) and fellow member of the Rhymers' Club. In this extract he writes perceptively about Yeats's Symbolist poetry in *The Wind among the Reeds*; indeed, the terms of his praise chime closely with Yeats's own frequently articulated desire to be 'profoundly personal' in his poetry, yet, by means of 'symbol' and 'Irish mythology', to get beyond the 'merely personal' and participate in a 'universal consciousness'.

The conception of lyric poetry which Mr. Yeats has perfected in this volume [. . .] may be clearly defined [. . .] A lyric [. . .] is an embodied ecstasy, and an ecstasy so profoundly personal that it loses the accidental qualities of personality, and becomes a part of the universal consciousness. Itself, in its first, merely personal stage, a symbol, it can be expressed only by symbol; and Mr. Yeats has chosen his symbolism out of Irish mythology, which gives him the advantage of an elaborate poetic background, new to modern poetry.

From **Austin Clarke's review of The Tower**, Times Literary Supplement, 1 March 1928

In this extract from his review of The Tower, the Irish poet Austin Clarke (1896–1974) gives a succinct account of the conflict between personal and public that gives life to the volume. Alert to the poetry's awareness of its status as art, Clarke suggests perceptively that, in the volume, the 'imagination' retains its freedom and capacity for 'symbolic' transformation of experience.

Upon these poems, despite their isolation, their manifestation of pride as refuge, other realities obtrude as suddenly as the armed young man who arrived at Thoor Ballylee to blow up the bridge, as Mr. Yeats tells us in a note, 'saying at last, "Goodnight, thank you," as though we had given them the bridge.' [. . .] Personal discontents and the commotion of Irish public times mingle, indeed, in these verses, satirical or lyrical; but happily the imagination, despite its own inhibitions, remains as free and symbolic.

From **Louise Bogan's article on Yeats**, Atlantic Monthly, CLXI, 5 May 1938

In this extract Louise Bogan seeks to account for Yeats's development, the subject of much critical investigation – and praise. How can one explain the transformation of Yeats from the poet of the early work, who was, in Bogan's words, 'a Romantic exile', to the poet who 'advanced into the world he once shunned'? For Bogan the explanation has to do with Yeats's capacity in his later work to convey a sense that 'a whole personality is involved'.

If we grant naturalness, sincerity, and vigor to Yeats's late style, we still have not approached its secret. [. . .] What impresses us most strongly in Yeats's late work is that here a whole personality is involved. A complex temperament (capable of anger and harshness, as well as of tenderness), and a powerful intellect, came through; and every part of the nature is released, developed, and rounded in the later books. The early Yeats was, in many ways, a youth of his time: a Romantic exile seeking, away from reality, the landscape of his dreams [. . .] Yeats advanced into the world he once shunned, but in dealing with it he did not yield to

its standards. That difficult balance, almost impossible to strike, between the artist's austerity and 'the reveries of the common heart' – between the proud passions, the proud intellect, and consuming action – Yeats finally attained and held to.

From **F. R. Leavis's review of *Last Poems and Plays***, *Scrutiny* 8:4, March 1940

This extract illustrates how, from the beginning, Yeats has been a poet who has provoked hostile as well as admiring comment. F. R. Leavis, unabashedly committed to evaluative criticism, expresses here his disappointment with the last poems. For Leavis, there is a falling-off after the poetry of *The Tower*, a volume that, in a poem such as 'Sailing to Byzantium', expresses a 'complex tension' as it balances the claims of different 'positives'. This falling-off, apparent in Leavis's reading of 'Byzantium', is increasingly evident, so the critic asserts, in subsequent work and especially in his last poems.

This is a saddening volume. That isn't merely because it illustrates once more that slackening of tension which is so apparent in Yeats's work of the past decade – the last. [. . .] what makes this volume painful reading is that in it which reminds one of a point about 'Byzantium' [compared unfavourably by Leavis with 'Sailing to Byzantium'] not yet made. The inferiority of that poem relates to the absence from it of the positives between which the complex tension of 'Sailing to Byzantium' is organized [. . .] [I]nstead of the 'monuments of unaging intellect', which are felt as a positive presence in 'Sailing to Byzantium', we find the ironic potentialities implicit in 'artifice of eternity' developed into an intensity of bitterness and an agonized sense of frustrate impotence [. . .] The bitterness prevails in *Last Poems and Plays*, and takes very unpleasant forms [. . .]

Modern Criticism

Louis MacNeice on character and style in Yeats, from *The Poetry of W. B. Yeats* (1941), London: Oxford University Press, 1967, pp. 110, 110–11

Louis MacNeice (1907–63), a major poetic heir of Yeats, offers what is still among the most penetrating and luminous criticism of the poetry. He takes issue with much in Yeats, yet he expresses his admiration for the work. In the following extract, MacNeice writes out of the concern he shared with other poets of his generation (notably W. H. Auden, Stephen Spender and C. Day Lewis) with the challenge posed by Marxist thought. He interprets Yeats's fascination with the heroic as kin to Shakespeare's and as ignoring 'Marxist conditioning', that is, the belief that even heroic individuals are shaped by socio-economic forces. Whether Yeats or Shakespeare are so indifferent to conditioning is questionable; but MacNeice pinpoints a crucial element in Yeats's tragic vision, the drive towards 'simplification' or the revelation of some unalterable, unyielding essence of human emotion. The passage links this drive with the way Yeats's mature style works, its captivating blend of 'Rhythm and rhetoric'. It should be read in conjunction with Yeats's own account of the 'tragic' in the extract from 'A General Introduction for My Work' **(pp. 31–2)**.

Yeats in his poems treated Synge or Major Robert Gregory in the same way that Shakespeare treated his tragic heroes; the hero is conceded full individuality, his Marxist conditioning is ignored. This means simplification, means – in Shakespeare and in Yeats – the elimination from the tragic figure of all psychology except some simple trends, it means the explanation of a man not by his daily life but by one or two great moments; thus we get the paradox that in Shakespeare death is so often the great moment of life [. . .]

In keeping with this simplified world of more than life-size figures [. . .] is Yeats's peculiar grand manner. This is not, like that of Shakespeare or Milton, florid and redundant. It appears often to be governed by the principles of prose (it is significant that in his later years Yeats would often first write a poem in prose

and then versify it). [. . .] Yeats [. . .] bluffs the reader into giving him his attention. [. . .] In his rôle of the poet as whole man Yeats now uses all the tricks, combining them cunningly, not overdoing any one; [. . .] using mainly the words of prose he is always prepared [. . .] to slash in colour, to heighten. His most consistent weapon is rhythm. Rhythm and rhetoric in wedlock produce a poetry unique in his time [. . .]

Richard Ellmann on Yeats's 'affirmative capability', from *The Identity of Yeats*, London: Macmillan, 1954, pp. 238–41, 241–2

Richard Ellmann's two books on Yeats – *Yeats: The Man and the Masks* and *The Identity of Yeats* – are remarkable for their sympathetic inwardness with Yeats's life and thought. In this extract he explains what he calls Yeats's 'affirmative capability'. The phrase deliberately plays a variation on John Keats's famous admiration for 'negative capability', the ability to remain in a state of doubt without searching for premature resolution.[1] Ellmann views Yeats as preferring 'the more solid fare of affirmation' (**p. 51**). He quotes a long, fascinating journal entry of January 1929 in which Yeats contrasts his outlook with that of Ezra Pound. In common with the eighteenth-century Scottish philosopher David Hume, Pound had been urging a thoroughgoing scepticism about human knowledge. Yeats shares Pound's dislike of 'the word belief', but he places his trust in affirmation, feeling the imperative need to 'kill scepticism in myself' (**p. 52**), a need that drives him to find support in tradition. Ellmann reminds us of the complexity of Yeats's 'affirmative capability': it shuns yet needs scepticism as 'one of the obstacles which the poet masters' (**p. 54**). As Ellmann puts it, in terms that underline the intimacy between scepticism and affirmation in Yeats's work, 'It [scepticism] is the wind resistance which makes flight possible' (**p. 54**).

[. . .] To explain and confirm his practice Yeats evolved a hypothesis which is closer to defining the situation in which the modern poet finds himself than negative capability. It might be described as *affirmative capability*, for it begins with the poet's difficulties but emphasizes his resolutions of them. Rejecting Keats's cry for 'a life of Sensations rather than of Thoughts', Yeats considered it the poet's duty to invade the province of the intellect as well as of the emotions. Neither the intellect nor the emotions can be satisfied to remain in 'uncertainties, mysteries, and doubts'; they demand the more solid fare of affirmations.

Yeats expressed himself on this crucial matter in a journal entry of January 1929. He had been talking about it at Rapallo with Ezra Pound, and Pound had apparently urged, with Hume, that even causation cannot be proved, since we can only be sure of a sequence, and that scepticism is therefore the only possible

1 John Keats, *Letters*, ed. Hyder E. Rollins, 2 vols, Cambridge, Mass.: Harvard University Press, 1958, 1. 192–3.

attitude for a responsible poet. Yeats felt that scepticism constricted the mind as much as pliant submission:

> Ezra Pound bases his scepticism upon the statement, that we know nothing but sequences. 'If I touch the button the electric lamp will light up — all our knowledge is like that.' But this statement, which is true of science, which implies an object beyond the mind and therefore unknown, is not true of any kind of philosophy. Some Church father said, 'We can never think nor know anything of the Gospel'; some Arian,[2] 'I know God as He is known to Himself'. The Church father had like Ezra a transcendent object of thought; his arose out of self-surrender, Ezra's out of search for complete undisturbed self-possession. In Eliot, and perhaps in [Wyndham] Lewis, bred in the same scepticism, there is a tendency to exchange search for submission. Blake denounced both nature and God considered external like Nature as mystery; he was enraged with Wordsworth for passing Jehovah 'unafraid',[3] not because Jehovah is mystery but because the passage from potential to actual man can only come in terror. 'I have been always an insect in the roots of the grass' — my form of it perhaps.[4]

As the cure for scepticism he does not propose belief:

> I agree with Ezra in his dislike of the word belief. Belief implies an unknown object, a covenant attested with a name or signed with blood, and being more emotional than intellectual may pride itself on lack of proof. *But if I affirm that such and such is so, the more complete the affirmation, the more complete the proof, and even when incomplete, it remains valid within some limit. I must kill scepticism in myself, except in so far as it is mere acknowledgement of a limit*, gradually, in so far as politeness permits, rid my style of turns of phrase that employ it. Even the politeness should be ejected when charm takes its place as in poetry. *I have felt when re-writing every poem — 'The Sorrow of Love' for instance — that by assuming a self of past years, as remote from that of today as some dramatic creation, I touched a stronger passion, a greater confidence than I possess, or ever did possess.* Ezra when he re-creates Propertius or some Chinese poet escapes his scepticism.[5] *The one reason for putting our actual situation into our art is that the struggle for complete affirmation may be, often must be, that art's chief poignancy.* I

---

2   i.e. a follower of Arius, a famous heretic in the early Church.
3   Alludes to Blake's response in his marginalia to Wordsworth's Prospectus at the start of *The Excursion*.
4   Ellmann's footnote refers us to Yeats's comment at the end of the introduction to the first edition of *A Vision*: 'I murmured, as I have countless times, "I have been a part of it always, and there is maybe no escape, forgetting and returning life after life like an insect in the roots of the grass." But murmured it without terror, in exultation almost', quoted in *The Identity of Yeats*, p. 162n.
5   Alludes to Ezra Pound's poem *Homage to Sextus Propertius* (1917).

must, though [the] world shriek at me, admit no act beyond my power, nor thing beyond my knowledge, yet because my divinity is far off I blanch and tremble. [Emphases are Ellmann's.]

He is caught between the meaningless beliefs which the mob continually casts up before him, and the struggle to affirm on his own, individuality being a vital test of the affirmation's quality. The struggle is the more desperate because its sanction, his divinity — the sphere or world of completeness — is far-off and known only slightly. In this situation the poet receives help from tradition, which provides roots when scepticism parades its rootlessness as modernity:

We, even more than Eliot, require tradition and though it may include much that is his, *it is not a belief or submission, but exposition of intellectual needs.* I recall a passage in some Hermetic writer[6] on the increased power that a God feels on getting into a statue. I feel as neither Eliot nor Ezra do *the need of old forms, old situations that, as when I recreate some early poem of my own, I may escape from scepticism.* For years past I have associated the first unique [?] impulse to any kind of lyric poetry that has the quality of a ballad ('The Tower', for instance) with an imagination of myself awaiting in some small seaside inn the hour of embarking upon some eighteenth or seventeenth century merchant ship, a scene perhaps read of in boyhood, that returns with simpler rhythms and emotions. Nor do I think that I differ from others except in so far as my preoccupation with poetry makes me different. The men sitting opposite me, in the Rapallo restaurant where some days ago the sound of a fiddle made me remember the old situation, are to my eyes modern but only a perverted art makes them modern to themselves. *The 'modern man' is a term invented by modern poetry to dignify our scepticism.* [Emphases are Ellmann's.]

Old forms and situations give the poet dignity and reassurance. His individuality is not anarchic, but is founded on the re-enactment of an ideal. His mind cannot bear what is raw and sanctionless; it must anastomose [cross-connect] with the past.

Yeats's journal entry is so closely packed that it must be amplified. In his youth he had defended his thematic and conceptual variations from poem to poem on the grounds that he was depicting a series of moods or states of mind. He now extended this notion by demanding an art of affirmations, by which he meant positive statements which were the active expression of a man, distinguished from beliefs or ideas which were outside structures to which the man submitted himself. [. . .]

His attitude towards scepticism is not entirely defined, but he was working

---

6   i.e. a writer in the Hermetic tradition (an esoteric approach to spiritual matters) whose central texts
     are included in the Corpus Hermeticum, a body of writings translated by G. R. S. Mead in 1906.

towards some such generalization as this: in so far as scepticism prevents positive statement, it is a danger to art. Such scepticism feeds parasitically upon the beliefs of others, and cannot satisfy the mind. But in so far as scepticism is one of the obstacles which the poet masters in the course of his attempt to transcend the limits of his incompleteness, it may render his positiveness, wrung from him partly in spite of himself, more poignant, and more noble because marked with the scars of battle. It is the wind resistance which makes flight possible. In poems which scepticism has affected, the specific affirmation is often of less central consequence than the struggle with the incompleteness of the human situation; the poet labours to speak his whole mind, yet — such are his human limitations — even his most fervent utterances will reflect the incompleteness he cannot wholly overcome.

John Bayley on Yeats and the Mask, from *The Romantic Survival: A Study in Poetic Evolution* (1957), London: Constable, 1969, pp. 101–2, 102, 103

John Bayley reads Yeats as a latter-day Romantic poet, concerned (like Words-worth) with the self and the question, 'how was that self to be kept interesting, to be kept both apart from life and engaged in it?'[1] In the following discussion he looks at the cool manipulativeness that underlies some of the poetry's most affecting moments and sees Yeats as a poet who is never so much in control as when he asserts the loss of control. This does not lead Bayley to convict Yeats of insincerity, but rather to admire him for the consummate artistry with which he deploys the notion of the Mask.

The sense of discouragement, and the dream image that always accompanies in Yeats a temporary questioning of endeavour, is extremely moving.[2] The choice is made, and it seems more than a temporary one; the Mask appears to be laid aside for a moment and the real Yeats to appear, subject to an envy and dejection in which any of his readers can share. But this is not really the case. 'The real Yeats' is a misleading phrase, for the appearance of hesitation is itself a Mask, a kind of behaviour that has been meticulously studied in the genesis of the poem. What we can observe is how completely Yeats has turned the experience to his own account [. . .]

One of the assumptions of the Mask is that poetry and life are indivisible, that ways of behaving in life are the same as ways of writing in poetry, and that therefore art may and should have a deep effect on action [. . .] Yeats is certainly the last Romantic to believe implicitly in the power of poetry, whether he believed in the power of magic or not [. . .] It is difficult for us not to feel a certain incredulity at

1   *The Romantic Survival*, p. 82.
2   Bayley has just quoted the last two stanzas of 'The Road at my Door', section V of 'Meditations in Time of Civil War' (**pp. 152–3**), in which Yeats turns away, 'caught / In the cold snows of a dream', from soliders fighting on both sides of the Civil War.

Yeats's distress about the effect his words may have had,[3] but there is no doubt that the distress is genuine, and it shows how great and how poetically valuable was his self-confidence. The Mask of the conscience-stricken poet is not absurd when Yeats wears it.

Jon Stallworthy on 'The Second Coming', from Between the Lines: Yeats's Poetry in the Making, Oxford: Clarendon Press, 1963, pp. 17–24

In two major critical studies (Between the Lines (1963) and Vision and Revision in Yeats's 'Last Poems' (1969)), Jon Stallworthy has traced the development of various poems from initial draft to completed poem. He describes, in this extract, the evolution of 'The Second Coming', a poem that contains a frightening prophecy of the end of contemporary civilization and its replacement by a more violent era (see **pp. 134–5** for commentary). Stallworthy shows that the poem, to begin with, was explicitly rooted in specific historical circumstances; so, the first verse-draft refers to the German invasion of Russia before and after the Bolshevik revolution of October 1917 ('The germans are (   ) now to Russia come' (**p. 56**)). But in ensuing drafts, as Stallworthy explains in great and perceptive detail, and with illuminating reference to Yeats's thinking about world history in A Vision, as well as to the literary influences of Shelley and Blake, the poet widens and generalizes his poem's 'scope and focus' (**p. 59**). In an insight vital to grasping the drama of Yeats's apocalyptic vision, Stallworthy points out that in later draftings 'The prophet comes into the open' and that 'we are not allowed to overlook the figure of the prophet behind the prophecy' (**p. 62**). The extract shows how much can be learned about a poem by careful attention to relevant manuscript evidence.

Ellmann dates this poem January 1919,[1] although it was not published until November 1920, in *The Dial*. Manuscripts in Mrs. Yeats's possession show how large a part the world situation of 1918–19 played in its conception and growth. There are six small, loose-leaf sheets of preliminary manuscript working, and two fair copies, the earlier of which Yeats tore in half and committed to his waste-paper basket: from this Mrs. Yeats recovered it.

'The Second Coming' begins with a tantalizingly illegible prose draft. Of its twelve lines I can read in the first five:

F. 1r: *Ever more wide sweeping gyre*

Ever further hawk flies outwards

---

3 Bayley has just quoted Yeats's question in 'Man and the Echo': 'Did that play of mine send out / Certain men the English shot?'

1 [Stallworthy's note.] *The Identity of Yeats*, London: Macmillan, 1954, p. 290.

> *from the falconer's hand. surely*
>
> (   ) *fallen who*
>
> *when the mob* (   )

In the remaining six lines one word only stands out, in splendid isolation at the opening of line nine: 'Burke'. Below this passage the iambic pentametres begin:

> *intellectual gyre is* (   )
> The ~~gyres grow wider and more~~ *wide*
>   *falcon cannot hear*
> The ~~hawk can no more hear~~ *the falconer*
>
>   ~~The germans to Russia to the place~~
>
> *The germans are* (   ) *now to Russia come*
>
> *Though every day some innocent has died*
>
> (   ) *& murder*
> ~~├─────┤~~

'Wide' and 'died' on this folio, 'day'/'pay', 'falconer'/'murderer' on F. 2*r*, and 'clock'/'dock' on F. 1*v* show that the poem was originally to have been in rhyme.

An important alteration is that from 'hawk' to 'falcon'. Ellmann is right when he says:

> The image of the falcon who is out of the falconer's control should not be localized, as some have suggested, as an image of man loose from Christ; Yeats would not have cluttered the poem by referring to Christ both as falconer and as rocking cradle further on.[2]

The falcon has long been a problem. Once, however, we realize that the bird was originally a hawk, we are on familiar territory. As a boy Yeats had often 'climbed Ben Bulben's back', which he describes in *The Celtic Twilight* as 'famous for hawks', and his footnote to 'Meditations in Time of Civil War' is immediately relevant:

> I suppose that I must have put hawks into the fourth stanza because I have a ring with a hawk and a butterfly upon it, to symbolize the straight road of logic, and so of mechanism, and the crooked road of intuition: 'For wisdom is a butterfly and not a gloomy bird of prey'.—1928.[3]

It is 'The intellectual gyre' that is growing 'wider and more wide'. We are told in *A*

---

2   [Stallworthy's note.] Ellmann, *The Identity of Yeats*, 1954, p. 258.
3   [Stallworthy's note.] *The Variorum Edition of the Poetry of W. B. Yeats*, New York: Macmillan, 1957, p. 827.

Vision: 'As Christ was the *primary* (objective) revelation to an *antithetical* (subjective) age, He that is to come will be the *antithetical* revelation to a *primary* age.'[4] And again: 'When our historical era approaches . . . the beginning of a new era, the *antithetical* East will beget upon the *primary* West and the child or era so born will be *antithetical*.'[5] The 'gloomy bird of prey' has slipped its leashes, and will soon be lost to sight. In this first verse-draft Yeats follows a symbolic reference with a more topical and specific one: 'the germans are (   ) now to Russia come'. By the end of July 1917 the Russian front had crumbled in face of the enemy. In October of that year the Bolsheviks brought off their revolution, and at the Treaty of Brest-Litovsk, on 3 March 1918, Lenin had surrendered to the Germans: Finland, Esthonia [*sic*], Courland, Lithuania, and tracts of Russian Poland. The Germans had indeed come to Russia, and I think it not impossible that Yeats, with his reverence for the aristocratic virtues epitomized by Castiglione, had in mind the fate of the Russian Royal House, as he wrote: 'Though every day some innocent has died'.

The poem's second verse-draft, after some preliminary scribbles, reads:

F. 2r: ~~Broader & broader is the~~

~~Forth~~

~~ever more wide~~

day by day
The gyres sweep wider ~~by year~~
every ~~year day~~
can no more hear the falconer
The hawk, ~~flies from the falconer's hand~~
Things have begun to break & f
All ~~things are broken up &~~ *fall apart*

~~After they have got the (──────)~~

Then a line or two more of illegible jottings, followed by:

The tyrant has the anarch in his pay

And murderer to follow murderer

Written sideways, across the horizontal lines of F. 1*v* a stanza begins to take shape:

Things fall apart—at every stroke of the clock

~~*Of innocence most foully put to death*~~

---

4   [Stallworthy's note.] 1925 edition, p. 169.
5   [Stallworthy's note.] 1937 edition, p. 257.

> *have*
> ~~Old wisdom and young innocence has died~~
>
> ~~The gracious and the innocent have~~
>
> ~~Or~~ *while the mobs fawn upon the murderer*
>
> *And the judge nods before the empty dock.*

F. 3*r* suggests that Yeats was now thinking of anarchy and unrest nearer home than Russia. Again he writes across the horizontal lines:

> *All things break up—no stroke upon the clock*
>
> *But ceremonious innocence has died,*
>   ~~Yet the~~ *where*
> ~~While~~ *the mob fawns upon the murderer*
>   *And*
> ~~While~~ *the judge nods before his county dock,*
>
> ~~And there's no Burke to cry aloud no Pitt~~
>
> *And there is none to pluck them by the gown*

This last line is written in pencil. On F. 4*r* the first full draft of the poem begins:

>   *widening gyre*
> *Turning and turning in the wide gyre*
>
> *The falcon cannot hear the falconer*
>
> (———) ~~the gyres~~
>
> ~~Things fall apart—the centre has lost~~
>   ( )
> *Things fall apart—the centre cannot hold*
>   *Mere*
> ~~Vile~~ *anarchy is loose there on the world*
>   *dim tide*
> *The blood stained flood is loose & anarchy*
>
> *The ceremony of innocence is drowned.*
>   ~~intensity~~
> ~~The good are wavering & intensity~~
>   *lack*   ~~while~~
> *The best ~~lose~~ all conviction while the worst*
>
> *Are full of passionate intensity.*
>   ~~Surely the great falcon must come~~
> ~~Surely the hour of the second birth is here~~
>
> ~~We have the desert   say to (———)~~

~~*say (————)*~~
~~*The second Birth! Scarce have those*~~
words been spoken

Already German and Russian, Burke and Pitt, mob and murderer, and the judge before his dock have fallen away. The poem's scope and focus have widened. Lest particular details distract the reader's eye and limit his vision, Yeats introduces more general terms, such as 'anarchy', 'the ceremony of innocence', 'the good', and 'the worst'. Except for a hint of assonance in the first four lines, rhyme also has been abandoned, for the reason perhaps that it too might distract and limit the reader's attention. The hawk has finally become the falcon, and not only, I suspect, because the metre demanded a disyllable. Had he used hawk, readers versed in his symbolism would have been tempted to make the simple equation, hawk = logic + intellect. Once so clearly defined, a symbol is drained of much of its imaginative potency: but no sooner does he change it to the less familiar falcon, than he injects it with new energy in the form of half-realized associations. [. . .] Yeats's falcon is the pride of the intellect, and, it may be, more also. There remains, however, a difficulty. 'Surely the great falcon must come' has been crossed out, but we must consider how it came there in the first place. It would seem that for one moment at least, the poet planned to introduce the visionary second coming with 'a gloomy bird of prey'. A passage, previously quoted, from *A Vision* supports this: 'When our historical era approaches . . . the beginning of a new era, the *antithetical* East will beget upon the *primary* West and the child or era so born will be *antithetical.*' It is well known that Yeats saw history as a pattern of recurrent cycles. For him, Leda and the swan that was Zeus had inaugurated one such cycle; Virgin and the dove that was the Holy Ghost had inaugurated another. In the line which he later cancelled, he was saying, I suggest, that the predatory falcon would inaugurate this third cycle. He would then have cancelled it because his symbols were becoming confused. The falcon represents the outgoing power, out of which a new antithetical power must be born: as such it cannot fulfil a new annunciation.

F. 5r continues the first full draft:

Surely some revelation is at hand

~~*We have the desert (————)*~~
~~*must leap*~~
~~*The cradle at Bethlehem has rocked anew*~~
the second coming is at
Surely ~~*the hour of the second birth has struck*~~
Scarcely are these words
coming   have   spoken
The second ~~*Birth. Scarce have the words been spoken*~~
and new intensity rent as it were cloth
~~*Before the dark was cut as with a knife*~~
lost

> And a ~~stark~~ image out of spiritus mundi
>
> Troubles my sight. ~~A waste of sand~~
>   —A waste of desert sand
> A shape with lion's body & with (   )
>   and the head of a man ~~breast & head~~
> ~~Move with a slow slouching step~~
>   A gaze
> ~~An eye~~ blank and pitiless as the sun
>
> ~~Slouches~~   thighs
>
> Moves its slow ~~feet~~ while all about its head
>
> ~~An angry crowd of desert b~~
>   ~~Run~~
> ~~Fall~~ shadows of the ~~desert birds they~~
>   indigant desert birds

On this sheet again we see the poet weeding out particular detail: the over-localized striking of the hour of the second coming, the 'knife' and 'cloth' which diminish the image of the darkness torn, 'An eye' altered to 'A gaze', and the — perhaps too human — 'feet' altered to 'thighs'. Ellmann is, I think, on the right track when he says that Yeats 'refers to the image as a "shape", and intends the indeterminate label to increase its portentousness, (and) he makes clear that it is, or is like, the Egyptian sphinx, which is male (unlike the Greek sphinx)'. Yeats, in his *Autobiographies*, tells how as a young man, 'there rose before me mental images that I could not control: a desert and a black Titan raising himself up by his two hands from the middle of a heap of ancient ruins'.[6] This suggests a sub-conscious recollection of Shelley's 'Ozymandias':

> . . . Two vast and trunkless legs of stone
> Stand in the desert. . . . Near them, on the sand,
> Half sunk, a shattered visage lies. . . .

Weeks detects a further Shellean source of 'The Second Coming' in 'Prometheus Unbound' (i. lines 625–8):[7]

> The good want power, but to weep barren tears.
> The powerful goodness want; worse need for them.
> The wise want love; and those who love want wisdom;
> And all best things are thus confused to ill.

Yeats himself says in a note to *Wheels and Butterflies*, that from about 1903 he

---

6 [Stallworthy's note.] p. 185.
7 [Stallworthy's note.] D. Weeks, 'Image and Idea in Yeats's "The Second Coming"', *Publications of the Modern Language Association of America*, lxiii, pp. 281–92.

was always imagining 'at my left side just out of the range of sight, a brazen winged beast that I associated with laughing, ecstatic destruction ... afterwards described in my poem "The Second Coming" '.[8]

F. 6r concludes the first full draft:
> The darkness drops again but now I know

Four lines of illegible scribble, then:

> That   of ~~its~~ stony
> ~~For~~ twenty centuries a stony sleep
>
> ~~Were vexed & all but broken by the second~~
>   Were vexed
> ~~Were vexed~~ to night mare by a rocking cradle
>
> ~~And now at last, (——————)~~
>
> ~~It slouches towards Bethlehem to be born~~
>
> It has set out for Bethlehem to be born
>   ~~that~~
> ~~And now at last—knowing its hour come round~~
>
> It has set out for Bethlehem to be born
>   ~~wild thing~~—its hour come round at last
> And what ~~at last~~—knowing the hour ~~come round~~
>   rough beast
> ~~Is slouching~~ towards Bethlehem to be born
>
> Slouches towards Bethlehem to be born[9]

Inexorably we watch Yeats's pen pursuing the poem's magnificent and sinister conclusion.

The two manuscript fair-copies of 'The Second Coming' are the same as for the first printing, except for punctuation and also in what appears to be the later of the two, it is not 'thirty' but 'twenty centuries of stony sleep'. Miss M. Rudd reveals the phrase 'stony sleep' to have been borrowed (no doubt unconsciously) from Blake's lines in 'The First Book of Urizen':[10]

> Ages and ages roll'd over him
> In stony sleep ages roll'd over him.

At the second printing Yeats changed the iambic pattern of line 13 for the striking, dune-like undulation of 'somewhere in sands of the desert'.

8 [Stallworthy's note.] 1934, p. 103.
9 [Stallworthy's note.] On F. 6v is a manuscript draft of 'Michael Robartes and the Dancer', beginning: 'Lady turn from all opinions'.
10 [Stallworthy's note.] M. Rudd, *Divided Image: A Study of William Blake and W. B. Yeats*, London: Routledge and Kegan Paul, 1953, p. 119.

Considering now the completed poem as an artistic whole, we find that most common Yeatsian pattern of an objective first movement passing into a more subjective second movement. There is a natural division between lines 8 and 9, like that dividing the octave of a Petrarchan sonnet from the sestet. Incantatory repetition prepares us for the change:

> Surely some revelation is at hand;
> Surely the Second Coming is at hand.
> The Second Coming!

The prophet comes into the open: 'a vast image . . . Troubles my sight:'. Having described the image he sums up:

> but now I know
> That twenty centuries of stony sleep
> Were vexed to nightmare by a rocking cradle,

Just as Yeats never wrote a love poem that does not treat of lover as well as of beloved, we are not allowed to overlook the figure of the prophet behind the prophecy.

C. K. Stead on 'Easter 1916', from *The New Poetic*, London: Hutchinson, 1964, pp. 35–9

In this extract, C. K. Stead offers a reading of 'Easter 1916', a poem about the Easter Rising of 1916 (commentary on **pp. 132–4**), as a poem in which ' "Life" and "Art" interact and merge into a single image' (**p. 63**). Stead discusses Yeats's complex view of the nationalists: if they have 'transcended the mutable world' evoked in the third section, they have done so 'only by the destruction of normal human values' (**p. 64**). Of particular interest is the analogy Stead draws between the nationalists and the poet: just as the 'revolutionaries gave up life', so he must give up 'his personality', the man who told mocking jokes about the nationalists, who believed that he lived in a comic world, 'where motley is worn' (**p. 65**). By surrendering personality, Yeats is able to 'achieve the mask of tragedy' (**p. 65**). Stead refers to an important distinction between comedy and tragedy made by the poet, in which, on Stead's paraphrase, Yeats sees tragedy as pursuing 'something universal' and comedy as accentuating 'individual character' (**p. 63**). The extract, part of a larger discussion of 'the new poetic' in twentieth-century poetry in English, praises the poem as combining elements of symbolism and argument, and as able 'to assimilate a complex political event into the framework of a poem without [. . .] loss of its human character in abstraction' (**p. 66**).

[. . .] 'Easter 1916', written to commemorate the 1916 rising against the British occupation of Ireland, is one of the finest of Yeats's public poems. It is a complete

poem which, more than illustrating Yeats's achievement of objectivity by means of the dramatic 'mask', uses the terms of drama in order to stylize and objectify the world of political fact which is its subject. In the writing of this poem literary problems have become, for Yeats, analogues for the problems of living: 'Life' and 'Art' interact and merge into a single image.

The first three sections of the poem look backward to a 'comic' world that has been left behind – a world of restless individuality, of mutability, subject to death and regeneration. The fourth section points forward to a world of tragic stasis, achieved by those killed in the rising. Thus the movement of the poem – from the temporal to the timeless – and the intermediate position of Yeats's persona in that movement, make the poem a forerunner of the more famous 'Sailing to Byzantium'.

The opening lines of the poem present the 'comic' Dublin scene before the Easter rising:

> I have met them at close of day
> Coming with vivid faces
> From counter or desk among grey
> Eighteenth-century houses.
> I have passed with a nod of the head
> Or polite meaningless words,
> Or have lingered awhile and said
> Polite meaningless words, . . .

These, whom Yeats met 'at close of day', are the Irish patriots, shaped in the world of modern commerce ('from counter or desk') which came into being with 'grey eighteenth-century' reason. Dublin is part of the civilization that followed when 'the merchant and the clerk / Breathed on the world with timid breath' ['At Galway Races'] – a fragmented society, where 'polite meaningless words' serve in place of collective spiritual enterprise. 'Doubtless because fragments broke into ever smaller fragments', Yeats writes in his *Autobiographies* (p. 192), 'we saw one another in a light of bitter comedy.' The 'vivid faces' of the patriots could never, it seemed, assume the static mask of tragedy. So the persona of this poem recalls his certainty

> . . . that they and I
> But lived where motley is worn:

But we are warned:

> . . .
> All changed, changed utterly:
> A terrible beauty is born.

Comedy, Yeats suggests in an essay, accentuates personality, individual character; tragedy eliminates it in favour of something universal: 'Tragedy must always be a

drowning and breaking of the dykes that separate man from man, and ... it is
upon these dykes comedy keeps house.'[1]

The second section of the poem sketches the personalities of some of the
nationalists before their destruction in the Easter rising. One, beautiful when
young, had spoiled her beauty in the fervour of political agitation; another was a
poet and schoolteacher; a third had shown sensitivity and intellectual daring; a
fourth had seemed only 'a drunken vainglorious lout'. But the 'dykes that separate man from man' have now been broken. Each has

> ... resigned his part
> In the casual comedy ...
> Transformed utterly:
> A terrible beauty is born.[2]

So far the change seems all achievement: the petty modern comedy has given way
to tragic beauty. But this is also a '*terrible* beauty', beauty bought only at the
expense of life:

> Hearts with one purpose alone
> Through summer and winter seem
> Enchanted to a stone
> To trouble the living stream.
> The horse that comes from the road,
> The rider, the birds that range
> From cloud to tumbling cloud,
> Minute by minute they change;
> A shadow of cloud on the stream
> Changes minute by minute;
> A horse hoof slides on the brim,
> And a horse plashes within it;
> The long-legged moor-hens dive,
> And hens to moor-cocks call;
> Minute by minute they live:
> The stone's in the midst of all.

This third section is a general image of the world subject to time and death
('minute by minute they live') – an image which implies another, kindlier way of
seeing the Dublin street before the rising. The nationalists have transcended the
mutable world, but only by the destruction of normal human values, by a single-
mindedness that turns the heart to stone. The movement of this section imparts

1   [Stead's note.] *Essays and Introductions*, London, p. 241.
2   [Stead's note.] Cf. *Autobiographies*, p. 195: 'I had seen Ireland in my own time turn from the
    bragging rhetoric and gregarious humour of O'Connell's generation and school, and offer herself
    to the solitary and proud Parnell as to her anti-self, buskin followed hard on sock ...'

the joy of life, which throws a new light on the 'terrible beauty', emphasizing terror over beauty. The events are thus presented with an ambiguity which does justice to their complexity.

'Nations, races, and individual men', Yeats tell us

> are unified by an image, or bundle of related images, symbolical or evocative of the state of mind which is, of all states of mind not impossible, the most difficult to that man, race or nation; because only the greatest obstacle that can be contemplated without despair rouses the will to full intensity.[3]

The 'most difficult' image which the nationalists have contemplated 'without despair' is that of a united, independent Ireland. But there is another way of looking at their aspirations:

> We had fed the heart on fantasies,
> The heart's grown brutal from the fare;
> . . .   ['Meditations in Time of Civil War']

Approval and disapproval, delight and disappointment, lie behind the poem. Out of the tensions in Yeats's own mind a complex image is generated. We know from what Maud Gonne has written that Yeats hated in her the passionate intensity that turned the heart to stone.

> Standing by the seashore in Normandy in September 1916 he read me that poem ['Easter 1916']; he had worked on it all the night before, and he implored me to forget the stone and its inner fire for the flashing, changing joy of life.[4]

But it was Yeats as a man who urged her to abandon her patriotic intensity. As a poet his task was more difficult; to make an image that would encompass the event, transcending mere 'opinion' – his own, and that of others. To achieve this he must transcend himself, giving up his personality as the revolutionaries gave up life, in order to achieve the mask of tragedy. At this level the writing of the poem becomes an analogue for the event which is its subject. Yeats is caught up in the play, and must move with it. He can no longer take pleasure in 'a mocking tale or a gibe' at the nationalists' expense, for he is no longer 'where motley is worn'. Nor can he pass judgement: 'That is heaven's part.' 'Our part' is only that of chorus—

> . . . our part
> To murmur name upon name,
> As a mother names her child

3   [Stead's note.] Ibid., p. 194.
4   [Stead's note.] *Scattering Branches: Tributes to the Memory of W. B. Yeats*, ed. Stephen Gwynn, London, 1940, pp. 31–2.

When sleep at last has come
On limbs that had run wild.

At whatever human expense, a new symbol of heroism has been created. For good or ill

MacDonagh and MacBride
And Connolly and Pearse
Now and in time to be,
Wherever green is worn,
Are changed, changed utterly:

The Irish mind carries a new symbol, and Irish literature a new poem: there is a new stone resisting the flow of the stream. Such an achievement constitutes a defeat over the mutable world. The personalities of principal actors and chorus – of all those whose interaction created the play – are irrelevant to the effect. The world is, for the moment in which the event is contemplated, 'transformed utterly'.

Yeats stands alone among English-speaking poets of this century in his ability to assimilate a complex political event into the framework of a poem without distortion of the event or loss of its human character in abstraction.

J. R. Mulryne on 'Lapis Lazuli', from 'The Last Poems' in Denis Donoghue and J. R. Mulryne (eds), An Honoured Guest: New Essays on W. B. Yeats, London: Edward Arnold, 1965, pp. 134–7

This extract from J. R. Mulryne's essay on Yeats's Last Poems begins with an explanation of Yeats's views of tragedy. Whereas C. K. Stead in his piece on 'Easter 1916' (p. 62–6) lays emphasis on tragedy as being bound up, for Yeats, with the impersonal, Mulryne points out that, in the later work, the tragic is intimately connected to the display of 'some abundant but uncomplicated personal energy' (p. 67). He also underlines the importance of the notion of 'tragic joy' in later Yeats; this joy is a form of exultation roused by confrontation with suffering and mortality, and means, at one extreme, that 'For the true tragic hero . . . there will be no mourning' (p. 67). The evocation of tragic joy is a sign of poetic 'power' for later Yeats, as Mulryne demonstrates in his account of 'Lapis Lazuli', a poem that meditates, by way of a carving made from lapis lazuli, a precious stone, on the role of art in the face of suffering (commentary on the poem can be found on pp. 173–5). On his reading, the poem demonstrates the experience of tragic joy in the face of immediate and recurrent loss and catastrophe. The poet, through his knowledge and stance, is freed from 'the world of cyclical accident' to which the 'hysterical women' of the poem's opening line are bound (p. 68). Artists of all kinds spearhead the rebuilding by 'each new "gay" civilisation' of 'its own focal images' (p. 69). Yeats mimics the

'imaginative possession' necessary for such rebuilding in his response to the carving in lapis lazuli, departing from what he can observe to what he can 'delight' in conjuring up. Again, the poem's drama centres on the poet's consciousness.

Yeats's somewhat personal views of tragedy ask explanation. In common with other literary forms, tragedy is properly given over to 'action' not to 'thought': 'masterpieces, whether of the stage or study, excel in their action, their visibility; who can forget Odysseus, Don Quixote, Hamlet, Lear, Faust, all figures in a peep-show';[1] tragedy is, to put it simply, the locus of personality. Not of intricate psychology; the tragic heroes are a gallery of figures who exhibit, like the figures, the personal archetypes, of *Last Poems*, some abundant but uncomplicated personal energy. To identify with them, as author or spectator, is to discover joy, the familiar reward: 'Some Frenchman has said that farce is the struggle against a ridiculous object, comedy against a movable object, tragedy against an immovable; and because the will, or energy, is greatest in tragedy, tragedy is the more noble; but I add that "will or energy is eternal delight", and when its limit is reached it may become a pure aimless joy, though the man, the shade [the inferior Heracles?] still mourns his lost object.'[2] For the true tragic hero – the real Heracles – there will be no mourning: 'There may be in this or that detail painful tragedy, but in the whole work none. I have heard Lady Gregory say, rejecting some play in the modern manner sent to the Abbey Theatre, "Tragedy must be a joy to the man who dies!" '[3] The implications of joy are specified: 'The heroes of Shakespeare convey to us through their looks, or through the metaphorical patterns of their speech, the sudden enlargement of their vision, their ecstasy at the approach of death.'[4] The metaphor is reversible: 'ecstasy is a kind of death';[5] to conflate, confuse, the two experiences is the outcome of Yeats's heady logic; death will be ecstasy, apocalypse – not an enemy – to the man who conceives of life as tragedy. Meditating on such a fittingly tragic death, that of Hamlet, Yeats tells us: 'This idea of death suggests to me Blake's design . . . of the soul and body embracing.'[6] We are back at the language appropriate to 'The Statues', where body and soul embrace in knowledge of the sculptor's work. To remake one's death in the tragic idiom is to discover an ecstasy closely allied to the joy attaching to imaginative possession of the sculpted figure, the joy known to Rocky Face. The writing of poetry, imaginative conquest, becomes subversive of the last reality.

1   [Mulryne's note.] Yeats, *On the Boiler*, Dublin: Cuala Press, 1939, p. 13.
2   [Mulryne's note.] Ibid., p. 35. [Editor's note.] Mulryne alludes to the final sentence of *A Vision* (1937), in which Yeats asks, 'Shall we follow the image of Heracles that walks through the darkness bow in hand, or mount to that other Heracles, man, not image [. . .]?', *A Vision*, p. 302.
3   [Mulryne's note.] *Essays and Introductions*, London: Macmillan, 1961, p. 522.
4   [Mulryne's note.] Ibid., pp. 522–3.
5   [Mulryne's note.] Ibid., p. 71.
6   [Mulryne's note.] *The Letters of W. B. Yeats*, ed. Allan Wade, London: Hart-Davis, p. 917.

The *personae* of tragedy, with whom the poet may identify, are frequent in *Last Poems*. Yeats elects to 're-make' himself as Timon and Lear ('An Acre of Grass'); Hamlet and Lear, Ophelia and Cordelia 'perform their tragic play' in 'Lapis Lazuli'; Hamlet is named in 'The Statues'. None of these characters had made previous appearances in the lyric verse. In 'Hound Voice' there is a reminiscence of *Lear*;[7] the madness of 'Why should not Old Men be Mad?' again remembers Lear.[8] Cuchulain, as tragic hero, is present in 'The Statues', 'Crazy Jane on the Mountain', 'The Circus Animals' Desertion', 'Cuchulain Comforted'; Parnell, hero of three poems, is described in prose as 'a tragedian';[9] Margot Ruddock, the unnamed heroine of 'A Crazed Girl', was 'a frustrated tragic genius' who found herself in the ecstasy of her frenzied dance upon the shore.[10] All serve within the economy of *Last Poems* as examples of tragic dying, or tragic ecstasy, by imaginative knowledge of whom Yeats may re-make his own death.

'Lapis Lazuli' is the considerable poem in which Yeats specifies the intimate connection between tragic joy and the poet's discovered power. The first two verses effect a redemption of the word 'gay'; contemptuously pronounced by the 'hysterical women' – bound as they are to the world of cyclical accident – it becomes in verse two synonymous with tragic joy, the joy of liberation. Unlike the despised actors of 'The Old Stone Cross', the actors of this poem understand 'what unearthly stuff / Rounds a mighty scene'; by successful interpretation of their roles they achieve ecstasy and apocalyptic knowledge: 'Heaven blazing into the head.' The abrupt syntax, connectives altogether pared away, mimics the immediacy and the power of the discovered knowledge. 'Tragedy wrought to its uttermost' brings about the ecstatic confusion of death the prose describes. But the poet's especial craft has yet to be linked with this victory, his joy, 'gaiety', justified. Like 'A Bronze Head' and 'The Statues', 'Lapis Lazuli' took its origin from the contemplation of a sculpted image; a letter to Dorothy Wellesley speaks of 'a great piece [of lapis lazuli] carved by some Chinese sculptor . . . Ascetic, pupil, hard stone, eternal theme of the sensual east. The heroic cry in the midst of despair. But no, I am wrong, the east has its solutions always and therefore knows nothing of tragedy. It is we, not the east, that must raise the heroic cry.'[11] The logic moves confidently between sculpted image, tragedy and the 'heroic cry' of poetry; 'Lapis Lazuli' offers an imaginative collocation of the same order. Section

---

7   [Mulryne's note.] Cf. 'The woman that I picked spoke sweet and low' ['Hound Voice', 1. 8] with *Lear* v iii (of Cordelia): 'Her voice was ever soft / Gentle and low'.

8   [Mulryne's note.] Behind Lear stands that 'silent and fierce old man' William Pollexfen, another of the book's personal archetypes. See Yeats, *Autobiographies*, London: Macmillan, 1955, p. 9.

9   [Mulryne's note.] See *The Variorum Edition of the Poems of W. B. Yeats*, ed. Peter Allt and Russell K. Aspach, New York: Macmillan, 1957, p. 835; the contrast is with 'the great comedian' O'Connell [editor's note: that is, Daniel O'Connell (1775–1847), whose inspirational leadership was a major reason for the granting by the British of Catholic Emancipation in 1829. Yeats saw O'Connell as thriving on contact with large crowds, and thus a 'comedian'; by contrast, Parnell seemed to Yeats a lonely, tragic hero].

10   [Mulryne's note.] See Yeats's introduction (p. ix) to her *The Lemon Tree* (1937).

11   [Mulryne's note.] *Letters on Poetry from W. B. Yeats to Dorothy Wellesley*, ed. Dorothy Wellesley, London: Oxford University Press, 1964, p. 8.

three contains properties that directly recall 'The Statues'; Callimachus 'handled marble as if it were bronze' (the characteristic materials), but his images that shaped the thought of a civilisation were destroyed by time's action; as in 'The Statues' each new 'gay' civilisation must rebuild its own focal images. The remaining sections recall 'A Bronze Head' and 'To Dorothy Wellesley'. They enact the imaginative possession of the sculpted image, to bring the poet 'gaiety', as Dorothy Wellesley possessed her environment to win her own apocalyptic vision. The short fourth section presents the lapis lazuli carving as it appears to an objective scrutiny; the final section mimics an encroaching act of imaginative possession. At first the stone of the carving remains actual; its 'Every discoloration . . . accidental crack or dent' merely 'seems' water-course or avalanche; but even here the process of re-making is incipient. Then details are added ('doubtless'), details not even registered on the stone by 'accidental' usage; plum and cherry-branch flower at the poet's command. The next phrase brings confession:

I
Delight to imagine them seated there;

The act of imaginative possession is complete. And on its completion the image is made to contradict its marble repose; the scene the last lines depict is one of animation, of request and compliance, music and glittering eyes. The outcome is inevitable; the poem comes to rest declaring the poet's achievement, through imaginative exertion, of his apocalyptic reward: the last word is 'gay'.

Harold Bloom on *The Wind among the Reeds* and 'The Secret Rose', from *Yeats,* New York: Oxford University Press, 1970, pp. 130–2

Harold Bloom's study of Yeats looks ahead to the same critic's highly influential exploration of 'influence' in works such as *The Anxiety of Influence* (1973). For Bloom, a great poet may be one who powerfully misreads precursor poets. Yeats's identity is shaped, according to Bloom, out of his complex response to High Romanticism, especially the poetry of Blake and Shelley. In this extract, Bloom explores Yeats's late Romanticism in *The Wind among the Reeds*. In a passage preceding the extract, Bloom relates the volume to the Symbolist movement, particularly the work of Stephane Mallarmé, and points out the importance of the role played by Arthur Symons. In articles and his book *The Symbolist Movement in Literature* (1899), Symons, a minor poet, friend of Yeats and a sensitive critic, introduced French Symbolism to many English-speaking readers. In another passage preceding this extract, Bloom supplies a cultural context for *The Wind among the Reeds*, focusing on the volume's mood of anxiety and use of stylish finish to ward off the threat of time. In the extract, Bloom offers an account of what he calls the volume's 'finest poem' **(p. 70)**, 'The Secret Rose', a poem that celebrates the symbol of the rose, identifying it with the sum of human desire and seeing it as a portent of change (see

pp. 109–11 for text and commentary). He compares the poem's end to the close of Blake's prophetic poem *The Four Zoas*. Ultimately, though, Bloom sees this Yeatsian conclusion as best glossed by Shelley's invocation in 'Ode to the West Wind' of the wind as a force that is both destructive and creative.

[. . .] The principal virtues of *The Wind Among the Reeds* are concentrated in its finest poem, *The Secret Rose*. Yeats's own long note on this poem provides the reader with all the information necessary to identify the few arbitrary references; the real difficulties are also the poem's splendors. For the Rose prayed to in this poem is no longer the esoteric emblem of the poems in *The Rose* grouping in *The Countess Kathleen and Various Legends and Lyrics* (1892) [. . .] It remains true that nothing in the poem works against an esoteric meaning, but the poem's concerns are no longer with the Rose but with the poet and his state of consciousness. Yeats begins as though he were still writing mystical addresses, as he had five years before:

> Far-off, most secret, and inviolate Rose,
> Enfold me in my hour of hours . . .

This privileged hour is a state where questers "dwell beyond the stir / And tumult of defeated dreams," like Oisin in his long repose.[1] The questers and dreamers are named in a majestic catalogue; the Magi, Conchobar, Cuchullain and Fand, Caolte, Fergus, and then the nameless youth who quests after and finds a pastoral ideal:

> And him who sold tillage, and house, and goods,
> And sought through lands and islands numberless years,
> Until he found, with laughter and with tears,
> A woman of so shining loveliness
> That men threshed corn at midnight by a tress,
> A little stolen tress.

Yeats has no real source for this; it is his own beautiful fiction, a vignette attaining a visionary climax in a remarkable Romantic conceit, an idyll to be illustrated by Calvert or Palmer.[2] The shining pathos here is that this is the poet's own defeated dream, and with a wholly satisfactory sudden transition the poet again addresses the Secret Rose:

---

1   Oisin is the mythic hero of *The Wanderings of Oisin* (1889), a long poem by Yeats; in the poem he spends 300 years in fairyland with Niamh, an immortal figure, including a visit to an enchanted island devoted to 'repose' (see the first stanza of section 2 of 'The Circus Animals' Desertion', a late poem that refers to *The Wanderings of Oisin*).
2   Edward Calvert (1799–1883) and Samuel Palmer (1805–81), both English painters.

<blockquote>
I, too, await,

The hour of thy great wind of love and hate.
When shall the stars be blown about the sky,
Like the sparks blown out of a smithy, and die?
Surely thine hour has come, thy great wind blows,
Far-off, most secret, and inviolate Rose?
</blockquote>

It is a great passage by any standards, and ends the poem greatly, and surprisingly, with the opening line now transformed into a genuinely open question. The passage suggests both the great wind of creation and destruction in Shelley's ode,[3] and the violent imagery of the opening of *Night the Ninth, Being the Last Judgment* of Blake's *The Four Zoas*, while prophesying also the smithies of the Emperor in Byzantium. [. . .]

But, though he echoes Blake, Yeats ends the poem more in Shelley's skeptical if fierce spirit. "Destroyer and creator" Shelley names the wind, and he ends his ode with a subtle and open question.[4] So, here at the end of *The Secret Rose*, Yeats ends also, and the "surely" that begins the penultimate line is already more of a question than an assertion, or is perhaps balanced unevenly between the two. Like Shelley, Yeats wants and does not want the great wind to rise. Something in the poet is more willing to understand an impulse always present in him, though usually an undersong at best. The Rose is best kept far-off, most secret, and inviolate, for if the hour of hours gives at last the sought love and creation, it must give also unsought hate and destruction, the end of nature and of human nature.

Denis Donoghue on 'The Secret Rose' and 'Adam's Curse', from *Yeats*, London: Fontana/Collins, 1971, pp. 36–9

Denis Donoghue's *Yeats* is still among the very best introductions to the poetry. Like Bloom, Donoghue dwells on the nature of Yeats's achievement. He emphasizes the dramatic quality of the poetry, its ability to convey tension-ridden moods and feelings. Like Bloom, Donoghue is not uncritical of Yeats, detecting in him a sporadic tendency to be histrionic rather than dramatic. In this extract, however, his tone is admiring: he praises 'The Secret Rose' for 'the verve with which [Yeats] declares himself member of a great company' (**p. 72**) (reinforcing Bloom's sense of Yeats as a poet who consciously derived from 'a great tradition in poetry'[1] and the later, more conversationally inflected 'Adam's Curse' (a poem about love and poetry; see **pp. 111–13** for text and commentary) for 'the poise which it sustains between fact and value' (**p. 73**). For

---

3   'Ode to the West Wind' (published 1820).
4   'Ode to the West Wind', ll. 14 and 69–70, respectively; Shelley actually refers to the wind as 'Destroyer and preserver'.

---

1   Harold Bloom, *Yeats*, p. 471.

Donoghue, the poem emerges from a clash between the 'primary' (life as it is, composed of ageing, hard work, and disappointment) and the 'antithetical' (life as it is dreamed to be, a world of beauty and imagination). Yeats may concede sorrow and defeat at the poem's close, but 'such poetry', according to Donoghue, is 'a form of power' because of its 'dignity of tone' (**p. 74**). The insight is valuable, and can be applied to much of Yeats's work that continually discovers in poetry itself a compensation for the defeats of experience.

The poem ['The Secret Rose'] begins as if its chief object were to receive Cuchulain and the other heroes into the Order of the Golden Dawn: hence the hieratic tone, the movement of figures as in a tapestry. The procession continues, descending from gods to men, and Yeats develops another part of the priestly role, prepares the next revelation: "I too await / The hour of thy great wind of love and hate." The note of pride comes from Yeats's association with the Rose, now invoked as the spirit of poetry. Adept of the imagination in a heroic context, he is composing an Ode to the Poetical Character.[2] The context is exalted, but it does not reduce the poet to shame or silence, he is a hero in his role if not in demonstrable achievement. I read the poem as an exemplary moment in Yeats's career because of the verve with which he declares himself member of a great company; that he carries it off can hardly be disputed. He has gained by pride of role what he could not have achieved by mere pride of station. Yeats is claiming kinship with the Muse on the basis of a great role accepted rather than a great work accomplished; he is a poet, different from the Muse only in degree. A Romantic poet who deals with such matters is bound to take them gravely, and it is well that he should: if the auspices are good, he gains, if nothing else, a new air of authority. Some poets deem themselves sufficient authority, but Yeats is of the other fellowship; of those poets who must join the visionary company and declare themselves in good standing with the Muse before they can gather their talents about them. Such poets need to become 'the Poet' before they can do anything worthy. Many of Yeats's early verses move in this direction, but 'The Secret Rose' is the first occasion on which, by speaking to the Muse as a poet speaks to the spirit of poetry, he adds a new string to his Aeolian lyre.[3] The string, which we recognise in the tone of pride, cannot be found by examining a certain bundle of accident and incoherence, it is a work of pure imagination.

The string is sounded again in 'Adam's Curse', though the dominant tone is elegiac rather than proud. A poet, who has loved his beloved for years and still loves her but now hopelessly and knowing his hopelessness, speaks to her and her sister, "that beautiful mild woman, your close friend". The themes are love, beauty and poetry, so we think of some Platonic academy and of fine discourse, except that the poet's conversation is poignant rather than speculative. The time is the end of summer, its emblems the waning moon, the shell of wisdom and

---

2   Alludes to a poem of the same title by the eighteenth-century poet William Collins.
3   An instrument placed in a window over which the wind could blow, creating music; associated with poetic, especially Romantic, inspiration; see Coleridge's 'The Eolian Lyre' (1795).

prophecy, its rhythm a dying fall. The structure of the poem embodies its feeling; beginning with forms, speeches, tokens of a brave start, but ending abruptly, when these poor things have failed, and silence is all that remains. 'In Memory of Major Robert Gregory' is a comparable occasion, so far as structure goes. If moral power is certified by speech, lapse into silence marks its loss and perhaps the poet's acceptance of that loss or his bewilderment in defeat.

Such poems do not merely come to an end. In 'Adam's Curse' what is enacted is the acceptance of defeat, the failure of a man's love, in the first instance, and then the failure of the entire terminology which that love sustained—in this case, the force of everything in life which Yeats praised as subjective and antithetical. For the moment, these powers have failed, defeated by the primary world, objectivity, the tyranny of fact. Adam's curse: in Genesis God said to Adam, "cursed is the ground for thy sake, in toil shalt thou eat of it all the days of thy life". In the primary world it is the better part of prudence to bear the curse of Adam as genially as we can: the comforter gave this counsel in Yeats's beautiful poem, 'The Folly of Being Comforted'. 'Adam's Curse' does not sponsor patience, but it moves to a condition in which the poor opposing spirit is worn out; the victory of time and objectivity is evidently complete. Meanwhile the conversation proceeds, setting up a rhetorical conflict between primary and antithetical terms. In beauty, the antithetical element is the beloved's "great nobleness", as Yeats described it in 'The Folly of Being Comforted', "the fire that stirs about her, when she stirs". The equivalent in poetry is imagination, the inner fire, secret discipline. Poets and beautiful women are in league against "the noisy set / Of bankers, schoolmasters, and clergymen / The martyrs call the world". But poets and beautiful women are subjective spirits, and for them the time is out of phase, they are faces belaboured by time. In 'No Second Troy' Maud Gonne's beauty is "a kind / That is not natural in an age like this, / Being high and solitary and most stern". As for imagination, it courts difficulty and is often defeated by its love: what is ruined, in 'The Fascination of What's Difficult', is "spontaneous joy and natural content", and the imagination is compelled to "shiver under the lash, strain, sweat and jolt". The pain cannot be eased until Yeats defines a sense of experience which does not depend upon finalities of victory or defeat; and until he devises a corresponding idiom. The values which cry aloud in 'Adam's Curse' are not assuaged until they are taken up in the different contexts of 'A Prayer for My Daughter' and later poems. To be specific: these feelings are not released until the word "labour", epitome of Adam's curse, is transformed into the blossoming and dancing labour of 'Among School Children'.

But it is not enough to say that the poet in 'Adam's Curse' accepts defeat, or persuades himself to accept it; he does not hang his head. The poem is remarkable for the poise which it sustains between fact and value. If the world's verdict endorses fact, the reader is left in no doubt where value resides. Defeat is not registered as heroic or glorious, but as beautiful, the moral question is answered in aesthetic terms, and Yeats is a master of that resource. Poetry and love meet in the beautiful, which explains why of the three presences in the conversation Maud is contained in silence. Poet and friend have to make a case, but Maud's beauty is itself a declaration of independence. The poignancy of the poem,

especially when we read it with 'The Secret Rose' not entirely forgotten, is that in the earlier poem Yeats got whatever he needed from the symbols at hand, and he had merely to find his power in them; but in 'Adam's Curse' the symbols cannot help, beyond providing an appropriate decor for his sorrow. Yeats's mastery in the later poem is a remarkable achievement of style, and its proof is composure, the dignity of tone with which time's cruelty is received. It is proper to speak of such poetry as a form of power, even where the official theme is the defeat of that power. The poet is not obliged to report that his values prevail, as a practical matter, in the objective world. In his first poems Yeats knew that he had this power, but he did not know what to do with it, beyond releasing it now in one way, now in another. His progress as a poet had to wait for the discovery that there was at least one way of converting divisions to poetic use, making chance amenable to that degree of choice.

Elizabeth Butler Cullingford on Yeats and fascism, from *Yeats, Ireland and Fascism*, London: Macmillan, 1981, pp. 219–20, 220, 221

Yeats and fascism is a stormy and controversial topic. Undoubtedly right-wing ideas appealed to the later Yeats. He writes at times (especially in the calculated rant of *On the Boiler* (1939)) as though he favours an authoritarian mode of government; he seems opposed to the formlessness, as he saw it, of democracy; and he espouses a cult of the hero. At the same time, he emphasizes the brutality as much as the glamour of power; he sides with the beggar and the peasant; and he explores the human imperfections that often lie behind would-be heroic attitudes. He flirts, as many others in the period did, with eugenics, the supposed 'science' of improving human beings by ensuring only those with desired genetic characteristics should breed; and yet the human being remains as mysterious and complex as ever in his later work. In her book *Yeats, Ireland and Fascism*, Elizabeth Cullingford trains a cool and judicious eye on the question of Yeats's supposed fascism. In the following samples of her discussion she points to the 'anti-English' strain in Yeats's thinking about contemporary political issues, and uses his 'Fenianism' (Irish nationalism) to explain his sympathy with anti-English fascism. Yeats was interested in the so-called 'Blueshirts', a fascist organisation led by one General O'Duffy, and indeed, Yeats composed some marching songs for the Blueshirts; before O'Duffy became their leader, Yeats writes, 'I find myself constantly urging the despotic rule of the educated classes as the only end to our troubles . . . Our chosen colour is blue, and blue shirts are marching about all over the country'.[1] But Cullingford convincingly detects in Yeats's views a consistent desire for Ireland to be free from the influence of more powerful nations, and to this extent fundamentally anti-fascist. For her, Yeats's attitude to international events – the rise of Mussolini,

---

1   *The Letters of W. B. Yeats*, ed. Allan Wade, London: Hart-Davis, pp. 811–12.

say, the Italian dictator, or the Spanish Civil War (1936–9) fought between left-wing Republicans and right-wing pro-Catholic forces under General Franco – is governed by his hopes and fears for Ireland. The coming to power in 1932 of Fianna Fáil, led by Eamon de Valera (one of the leaders of the Easter Rising and opposed to the 1921 Treaty) led to renewed tension between Britain and Ireland. De Valera demanded abolition of the oath of allegiance to the British crown, and refused to pay land annuities. It was in 1937 that Ireland finally asserted her complete independence from Britan.

Cullingford alludes to this context in her account. For her, Yeats's dislike of Franco stems in part from his hatred of what he saw as pro-Catholic bigotry in Ireland, and signals the end of his interest in fascism. In a passage not quoted she brings out Yeats's dislike of political position-taking and his humanitarian expression of sympathy for the beleaguered Spanish Republic. The discussion perceptively returns Yeats to his historical and cultural contexts.

Yeats maintained a critical attitude to fascism from the beginning of 1934 until his death in 1939. Yet [Conor Cruise] O'Brien says that as late as 1938 Yeats still hoped that Ireland 'would be a sort of satellite of a Fascist-dominated Europe'.[2] He also suggests that the virulence of *On the Boiler* may have something to do with the fascist triumph at Munich, implying that had Yeats lived to see the Second World War, he would have been on the German side. But O'Brien sees as pro-German what is in fact anti-English. Ireland was in dispute with England over the Constitution and the Land Annuities, and the economic war had brought financial chaos. The political chaos caused by the Blueshirts had stemmed from the Civil War, and Yeats found it easy to blame the English even for that. Fanaticism bred in Ireland through centuries of English oppression could not swiftly be eradicated; the Curse of Cromwell had not yet been expunged.[3] [. . .] Finally, Yeats saw the power of the Empire, backed by capitalism, still dominating India and the other colonies. Ireland had almost escaped, but she might be bribed or bludgeoned into allying herself with Great Britain in international wars. Yeats feared such an alliance above all else, and part of his stridency in *On the Boiler* resulted from his desire to stimulate anti-English feeling in Ireland. Yeats was therefore prevented from condemning the fascist countries more forthrightly by his longstanding hatred of their major rival. As in the First World War, to be anti-English did not necessarily imply sympathy for Germany. [. . .]

Critics assume that Yeats exaggerated his Fenianism to excuse his fascism, ignoring the genuineness of his past Fenian record and the intensity of Fenian

2   [Cullingford's note.] ' "Passion and Cunning": An Essay on the Politics of W. B. Yeats', in *In Excited Reverie*, eds A. Norman Jeffares and K. W. G. Cross, London and New York: St Martin's Press, 1965, p. 272.

3   'The Curse of Cromwell', the title of a late poem by Yeats, alludes to the devastating effect of Oliver Cromwell's intervention in Irish affairs, when after the execution of Charles I he spent the best part of a year in Ireland, sacking Drogheda and Wexford, confiscating land and subsequently imposing new English settlers.

emotion in his last years. At first Yeats viewed the Spanish struggle in terms of the power balance in Europe, from the point of view of an Irishman who had no desire to be sucked back into the ambit of the British Empire. To suggest that he therefore hoped to be a satellite of the Axis instead is nonsense. Yeats did not want Ireland to be anybody's satellite: the fate of Abyssinia provided a warning of what small nations might expect at fascist hands.

As the Spanish war continued the situation in Ireland deteriorated to such an extent that Yeats no longer dared even to consider a Franco victory. He praised De Valera's courage in forbidding fascist volunteers, fearing that 'if the Spanish war goes on, or if [it] ceases and O'Duffy's volunteers return heroes, my "pagan" institutions, the Theatre, the Academy, will be fighting for their lives against combined Catholic and Gaelic bigotry'.[4] Thus the Irish situation, which had helped to interest him in Mussolini, determined him conclusively against Franco.

Elizabeth Butler Cullingford on 'Among School Children', from *Gender and History in Yeats's Love Poetry*, 1993, Syracuse, NY: Syracuse University Press, 1996, pp. 198–201

There has been much critical interest in 'gender' and 'history' in Yeats's poetry. In this extract from *Gender and History in Yeats's Love Poetry*, Elizabeth Cullingford brings together the two terms as she reads Yeats's 'Among School Children', a poem that reflects on youth and age as the poet visits a school (see **pp. 163–7** for text and commentary). Cullingford's argument is that in the poem's famous conclusion Yeats's series of apostrophes constitutes the poet as someone who must be spoken to by the presences and images, 'the self-born mockers of man's enterprise', who seem initially to embody a cruelly unattainable perfection. By insisting that these presences attend to him as a physical speaker, Yeats is able to make himself 'a spokesman for others: the school children of Ireland' (**p. 77**), for whom he wishes a fulfilling education that balances the claims of soul and body, a happiness that recalls William Morris's anti-capitalist emphasis on the human right to enjoy 'play, pleasure, and the satisfaction of bodily appetite' (**p. 79**). At the poem's close, 'the individualist "I"', Cullingford points out, turns into 'the collective "we"' (**p. 80**). The poem engages, then, directly with issues of education that were Yeats's responsibility as a Senator. It is pervaded, too, by the poet's 'oppositional dialogue with the voices of Catholic Ireland'. The dancer at the end, read by some as a 'faintly sinister female symbol left over from the nineties', is also expressive of a 'contemporary social combativeness' (**p. 80**). Her representation (as Cullingford notes wittily, she 'is certainly not performing a "healthy" Irish reel', **p. 80**) opposes an ascetic view of female sexuality.

---

4   [Cullingford's note.] *The Letters of W.B. Yeats*, ed. Allan Wade, London: Hart-Davis, 1954, p. 885.

In describing how ascetic art inspired by "the Platonizing theology of Byzantium" was replaced in the Renaissance by "an art of the body" Yeats contrasted "a pinched, flat-breasted" Byzantine Virgin with the "voluptuous" women of Titian's *Sacred and Profane Love*. Still pursuing his debate with Gonne about the beneficial effects of sexual fulfillment on the artist, and remembering her denigration of Raphael as one who bowed down to sex until it killed him, he wrote, "The next three centuries changed the likeness of the Virgin from that of a sour ascetic to that of a woman so natural nobody complained when Andrea del Sarto chose for his model his wife, or Raphael his mistress, and represented her with all the patience of his 'sexual passion' ".[1] In "Among School Children" Yeats moved from Plato's sour asceticism towards his own "art of the body."

Yet he could not originally summon the energy to challenge Plato's "Presences." In earlier drafts the poem ended after stanza seven in a mood of despondency appropriate to Yeats's gloomy initial notes, which emphasize that children can never fulfill their teachers' hopes, and that all life is a preparation for something that never happens.[2] Yeats transformed the ending of his poem by deciding to apostrophize the "self-born mockers of man's enterprise." He rhetorically defies the heartbreak enforced by Platonic idealism in love and religion by employing a trope that foregrounds his own poetic and bodily presence in the poem. Culler calls apostrophe

> a device which the poetic voice uses to establish with an object a relationship which helps to constitute him. The object is treated as a subject, an *I* which implies a certain type of *you* in its turn. One who successfully invokes nature is one to whom nature might, in turn, speak. He makes himself poet, visionary. Thus, invocation is a figure of vocation . . . The poet makes himself a poetic presence through an image of voice, and nothing figures voice better than the pure O of undifferentiated voicing.[3]

In concluding his poem with five apostrophes Yeats constitutes himself as someone to whom an answer must be returned. Since voice implies a body to speak from, Yeats's apostrophes are the formal equivalent of materiality: the signifier as pure sound. The Presences from whom he demands an answer are not, as in most Romantic apostrophes, material beings. They are supernatural Platonic forms: the religious icons of Catholic Ireland, the secular icons of lovers and mothers.

Yeats's apostrophes locate him not only as the speaking subject of the poem, but also as a spokesman for others: the school children of Ireland, Gonne's special care, whose bodies need food, warmth, and cleanliness before they can begin to acquire wisdom. Arguing in the Senate that "we ought to be able to give the child

---

1 [Cullingford's note.] *Unpublished Prose by W. B. Yeats*, vol. 2, ed. John P. Frayne and Colton Johnson, London: Macmillan, pp. 478–9.
2 [Cullingford's note.] Thomas Parkinson, *W. B. Yeats: The Later Poetry*, Berkeley: University of California Press, pp. 93–4, 104–05.
3 [Cullingford's note.] Jonathan Culler, *Pursuit of Signs*, London: Routledge & Kegan Paul, 1981, p. 142.

of the poor as good an education as we give to the child of the rich",[4] Yeats upheld the rights of the voiceless and underprivileged. It is often assumed that by the last stanza of the poem Yeats has "transcended" the local and particular historical incident out of which it arose. On the contrary, we are never closer to the prosaic material details of the School Attendance Bill, and to Yeats's experiences (both good and bad) as a school inspector, than in the lines

> Labour is blossoming or dancing where
> The body is not bruised to pleasure soul,
> Nor beauty born out of its own despair,
> Nor blear-eyed wisdom out of midnight oil.

This evocation of unalienated labor and joyful learning can be read both as an impossible Utopia and as a plea for a humane and decent system of primary education. Yeats was certain that "for a child to spend all day in school with a stupid, ill-trained man under an ill-planned system, is less good for that child than that the child should be running through the fields and learning nothing".[5] Amid the general "bitterness" (Yeats's word) of *The Tower*,[6] "Among School Children" offers a Romantic image of happiness and liberation comparable to the image of the child (a Wordsworthian child escaped momentarily from the prison house of learning) "running through the fields."

Yeats saw himself primarily as a tragic artist, but at moments he longed to be otherwise. Calling William Morris "The Happiest of the Poets," he once claimed that, despite the fact that he could not value Morris's verse very highly, "I would choose to live his life, poetry and all, rather than my own or any other man's".[7] In 1927 he reflected to Gonne about the change in his political beliefs:

> In some ways you & I have changed places. When I knew you first you were anti-Drefusard all for authoritative government ... and I was Drefusard & more or less vaguely communist under the influence of William Morris.[8] Today if I lived in France I would probably join your old party – though with some reservations – & call myself a French nationalist. You I imagine would join the communists.[9]

When he worked for the good of others, however, Yeats instinctively readopted

---

4   [Cullingford's note.] *The Senate Speeches of W. B. Yeats*, ed. Donald R. Pearce, London: Faber and Faber, 1961, p. 111.

5   [Cullingford's note.] Ibid., p. 110.

6   [Cullingford's note.] *The Letters of W. B. Yeats*, ed. Allan Wade, London: Hart-Davis, 1954, p. 742.

7   [Cullingford's note.] *Autobiographies*, London: Macmillan, 1955. p. 141.

8   Alludes to the Dreyfus Affair, when Captain Alfred Dreyfus, a Jewish officer on the French general staff, was falsely accused in 1894 of spying for Germany. The resulting furore split France in two: on the one side were the anti-Dreyfusards, the conservative parties; on the other side were the Dreyfusards, the progressive forces who rallied to Dreyfus's cause. The charges were finally dropped.

9   [Cullingford's note.] *Always Your Friend: The Gonne–Yeats Letters 1893–1938*, ed. with intros Anna MacBride White and A. Norman Jeffares, London: Pimlico, 1993, p. 437.

Morris's Utopian frame of mind. In one of the pamphlets that turned the young Yeats "vaguely communist," Morris had asserted the human right to bodily integrity:

> To feel mere life a pleasure; to enjoy the moving one's limbs and exercising one's bodily powers; to play, as it were, with sun and wind and rain; to rejoice in satisfying the due bodily appetites of a human animal without fear of degradation or sense of wrong-doing: yes, and therewithal to be well-formed, straight-limbed, strongly knit, expressive of countenance – to be, in a word, beautiful – that also I claim. If we cannot have this claim satisfied, we are but poor creatures after all; and I claim it in the teeth of those terrible doctrines of asceticism, which, born of the despair of the oppressed and degraded, have been for so many years used as instruments for the continuation of that oppression and degradation.[10]

Only in the fallen world of capitalism must one labor to be beautiful: for Morris beauty is a right which socialism will restore. In play, pleasure, and the satisfaction of bodily appetite it will blossom naturally. Remembering Morris as he wrote "The Trembling of the Veil" in 1922, Yeats praised his revolutionary vision: "He imagined . . . new conditions of making and doing".[11] Following Morris, Yeats bases his new conditions of making and doing, blossoming and dancing, on physical perfection, rather than on the images of bodily torture offered by the Catholic iconography. His Christ was not the Crucified One, but that "Unity of Being Dante compared to a perfectly proportioned human body".[12] Returning to "Adam's Curse," Yeats redefines in "Among School Children" the "labour" that constituted for poets and beautiful women the consequences of the Fall. In *A Vision* he wrote that at Phase Fifteen, the phase of greatest perfection, "The ascetic, who had a thousand years before attained his transfiguration upon the golden ground of Byzantine mosaic, had turned not into an athlete but into that unlabouring form the athlete dreamed of: the second Adam had become the first".[13] The second Adam, the crucified Christ whose image inspires the asceticism of nuns, is replaced by the bodily beauty of Michaelangelo's "half-awakened Adam" ['Under Ben Bulben', IV. 11], an "unlabouring," unfallen Adam as yet uncursed by the need to earn his bread by the sweat of his brow. Asserting that "labour" is blossoming or dancing, Yeats replicates the Utopian ethos of Morris's *News from Nowhere*, in which work brings joy to the laborers. Eve, cursed by God with labor pains and subordination to her husband, is metaphorically liberated from "the pang of . . . birth" ['Among School Children', l. 39] (perhaps Yeats has contraception in mind) and from the labor of being beautiful.

The last stanza affirms the unalienated bodies of tree and dancer. Two

---

10 [Cullingford's note.] *The Collected Works of William Morris*, 24 vols, London: Longman, 1910–15, vol. 23, p. 17.
11 [Cullingford's note.] *Autobiographies*, p. 143.
12 [Cullingford's note.] *Essays and Introductions*, London: Macmillan, 1961, p. 518.
13 [Cullingford's note.] Yeats, *A Vision* (1937), London: Macmillan, 1962, pp. 291–2.

apostrophes combine with two rhetorical questions to produce a heightened coda in which the individualist "I" is replaced by the collective "we":

> O chestnut-tree, great-rooted blossomer,
> Are you the leaf, the blossom or the bole?
> O body swayed to music, O brightening glance,
> How can we know the dancer from the dance?

Yeats's choice of the dancer as a non-ascetic image of bodily sanity, grace, and wholeness is partly a product of his oppositional dialogue with the voices of Catholic Ireland. While Kermode reads her as an icon of the decadent tradition, a faintly sinister female symbol left over from the nineties,[14] Yeats's dancer also manifests a contemporary social combativeness. The Irish bishops were obsessed by "foreign corrupting dances," which were not "the clean, healthy, National Irish dances . . . [but] importations from the vilest dens of London, Paris and New York – direct and unmistakable incitements to evil thoughts, evil desires, and grossest acts of impurity."[15] Yeats's dancer, body sensuously "swayed to music," is certainly not performing a "healthy" Irish reel.

M. L. Rosenthal on 'Nineteen Hundred and Nineteen', from *Running to Paradise: Yeats's Poetic Art*, New York and Oxford: Oxford University Press, 1994, pp. 242–4

M. L. Rosenthal's *Running to Paradise* is especially valuable for the skill with which it carries out its attempt to offer 'an essay in evaluative poetic criticism' and for its trenchant restatement of belief in 'artistic quality', a notion under challenge in recent decades, as the author notes. Yeats offers, so Rosenthal claims, an example of the difficult 'pleasure' that we go to art to find. Yeats does not minimize what is harsh or ugly about experience, but in the act of finding words for experience his poetry is a revitalizing force. As Rosenthal puts it, alluding to a phrase from Yeats's 'Meru', 'Without denying "the desolation of reality," art mobilizes our psychic energies against yielding to it'.[1] 'Nineteen Hundred and Nineteen' is a good example, a sequence of poems about the collapse into chaos signalled by the Anglo-Irish guerrilla war (see **pp. 155–61** for the text and commentary). In many ways bleak in its outlook, and indeed in its overt reference to art, the poem is also imaginatively compelling; it gives us the artistic satisfaction of a rare and crafted state of awareness. Rosenthal implies the nature of this satisfaction by attending in this excerpt to the craft and vision

---

14 [Cullingford's note.] Frank Kermode, *Romantic Image*, London: Routledge & Kegan Paul, 1957, pp. 60–5.
15 [Cullingford's note.] *Irish Catholic Register*, 1925, pp. 562–3.

---

1 *Running to Paradise*, pp. xv, xi, xiii.

evident in the sixth and final poem of 'Nineteen Hundred and Nineteen'. He sees this sixth poem as evoking 'the essential feeling of the whole double sequence' (**p. 81**) (that is, 'Meditations in Time of Civil War' and 'Nineteen Hundred and Nineteen'), and looks at the quasi-cinematic effects used by Yeats. He touches deftly on the twin feelings summoned in Yeats's poetry by his images of power: attraction as well as fear. The 'chaos' depicted is, according to Rosenthal, 'fearful, yet partly seductive' (**p. 81**), and he links the poetry's suggestiveness to its formal properties, the final poem achieving swiftness through the use of long sentences and three six-line stanzas, each rhymed like a Petrarchan sonnet's sestet, 'that are jammed together in a single verse-unit' (**p. 82**).

The self-castigating ironies of the fourth and fifth poems, directed against "our" weasel-like behavior and shallow mockery of our betters in time of crisis, come naturally in the wake of Poem III. They humanize the sensibility at work. We hear the voice of a fellow citizen sick of the world in which he too has played a demeaning part.

And then, in Poem VI of "Nineteen Hundred and Nineteen," a final prophetic vision takes over. The first five lines summon up the essential feeling of the whole double sequence in a new image of fearful, yet partly seductive, chaos:

> Violence upon the roads: violence of horses;
> Some few have handsome riders, are garlanded
> On delicate sensitive ear or tossing mane,
> But wearied running round and round in their courses
> All break and vanish, and evil gathers head.

This poem moves cinematically, with its opening lines providing an overview (and, if this were an actual film, with appropriate music). Then the camera closes in on the riders, the legendary Sidhe of ominous beauty and power who had long intrigued Yeats's imagination:

> Herodias' daughters have returned again,
> A sudden blast of dusty wind and after
> Thunder of feet, tumult of images,
> Their purpose in the labyrinth of the wind;
> And should some crazy hand dare touch a daughter
> All turn with amorous cries, or angry cries,
> According to the wind, for all are blind.

In a note on the Sidhe in *The Wind Among the Reeds*, Yeats had described them as

> the gods of ancient Ireland . . . or the people of the Faery Hills [who] still ride the country as of old. Sidhe is also Gaelic for wind. They journey in

whirling wind, the winds that were called the dance of the daughters of Herodias in the Middle Ages, Herodias doubtless taking the place of some old goddess.

We may readily add the obvious folk-association with Herodias and her dancing daughter Salome—scheming women responsible for the beheading of John the Baptist. In any case, the poem's closeup of the blind, tumultuous "daughters of Herodias," now "amorous," now "angry," shows them as the very embodiment of sinister confusion amid the age's "blast of dusty wind."

And then the camera moves to an entirely different symbol, a lurching apparition—like the Sphinx in "The Second Coming," with its "gaze blank and pitiless as the sun." The new apparition, although also devoid of mercy and intellect, has a human form and is therefore an even more terrifying portent. The Sphinx that appeared to the poet's imagination was a warning of a monstrous world waiting to be born. The new figure is simply gross power in action:

> But now wind drops, dust settles; thereupon
> There lurches past, his great eyes without thought
> Under the shadow of stupid straw-pale locks,
> That insolent fiend Robert Artisson
> To whom the love-lorn Lady Kyteler brought
> Bronzed peacock feathers, red combs of her cocks.

The opening line of Poem VI—"Violence upon the roads: violence of horses"—connects directly with the central preoccupation of the double sequence: the Civil War. Apart from that line and a more abstract half-line ("and evil gathers head"), the rest of the poem retreats to "the half-read wisdom of daemonic images" the despairing poet turned to at the end of the "Meditations." Here they are the images of the Sidhe and of Robert Artisson, the supposed incubus whose sexual attentions Alice Kyteler, condemned as a witch in 1324, was accused of buying with her gifts. The poem has raced, without stanza breaks, from the violence of current guerrilla warfare, to the realm of stormy, dangerous female desire and anger, and then to its counterpart, male ruthlessness in its stupidest, most insolent form.

Attraction to the "rough beast" of power as well as fear of it, whether it be military and political power or sexual power, has revealed itself in the unfolding of the double sequence. One remembers the poet's secret "envy" of the fighting men who come by his tower and go off again to play their part in the country's destiny. Perhaps, too, an altered light has been thrown on his earlier poems of willing yet unhappy subjection to the power of his "phoenix." All this is not to deny that the expressed revulsion against the bloodshed, let alone the atrocities, of the civil war is the dominant feeling and motivation of the sequences. But they also carry the admission of the psychological complexities accompanying that revulsion. The swift movement of Poem VI is remarkable. It is made up of two long sentences and, prosodically, of three six-line stanzas, each rhyming *abcabc*, that are jammed together in a single verse-unit. In the final six lines it hardly stops

for breath: one end-stop and one caesura altogether. And it is packed with images and verbs of whirling action that give it the cinematic character mentioned earlier. The psychological associations involved, essential to the discoveries the sequences have been making, could not be "explained" poetically without this sort of pre-sentative rush of successive visions.

Declan Kiberd on 'Leda and the Swan', from *Inventing Ireland: The Literature of the Modern Nation* (1995), London: Vintage, 1996, pp. 314–15

Declan Kiberd's *Inventing Ireland* is concerned with the way 'Ireland' is imagined into existence during a period of great upheaval that saw the emergence of a new post-colonial state in the Republic. The following reading of 'Leda and the Swan', a sonnet about the sexual ravishment of Leda by Jove in the form of a swan (see **pp. 161–3** for the text and commentary), views the poem as allegorical of Yeats's divided feelings about the establishment of a new Ireland after the Treaty partitioning the island, and the subsequent civil war fought between those who accepted the Treaty and those who did not. Like many recent commentators, Kiberd makes much of Yeats's Anglo-Irishness, his split identity and allegiances. The reading has its own inventiveness, as Kiberd is aware, consciously offering a suggestive rather than definitive account of the poem. But the suggestiveness is considerable.

At the most obvious level, the poem identifies the swan with the supernatural authority and power of the creative imagination; and so the broken wall and burning roof are less significant as historic facts than as immortal elements of a poet's epic narrative. Art and image are 'engendered' there. At a deeper level, however, these references to one war remind us that Yeats was writing in the year of another: 1923, italicized at the foot of the sonnet. This leads to the possibility of interpreting the swan as the invading English occupier and the girl as a ravished Ireland. The girl is more expert in 'feeling', the swan in 'knowledge'. She is a mere mortal, whereas he comes from an imperial eternity. The debate about her alleged consent recalls vividly those common clichés to the effect that the Irish were col-onizable because they secretly wished others to take command of their lives. The poem might then be read as a study of the calamitous effects of the original rape of Ireland and of the equally precipitate British withdrawal. The final question would then be asking: when the Irish took over power from the departing occu-pier, did they also assume the centuries-honed skills of self-government and con-trol (or 'knowledge')? The 'indifferent beak' might then be Yeats's judgement on the callous and irresponsible suddenness of an unplanned and ill-prepared British withdrawal. The 'Anglo' side of Yeats [. . .] must have felt the precipitate nature of the withdrawal a hard betrayal [. . .] The 'Irish' side of Yeats was just plain angry, an anger palpable in the bitter, bleak monosyllables of the close.

The poem was to have been about one kind of politics, the Russian Revolution

and its aftermath, but Yeats explained in a commentary that the lyric he eventually wrote was different: bird and lady took possession of the scene, and he claimed that all politics went out of the poem. If politics went out [see headnote, p. 162], it returned again in the cited date and in the civil war imagery [. . .] 'Leda and the Swan' may indeed be another account of the artistic or even the readerly process: but in teasing out those themes, it has much besides to say on the crisis of a newly independent people.

Marjorie Howes on 'Ancestral Houses' and 'My House', sections I and II of 'Meditations in Time of Civil War', from *Yeats's Nations: Gender, Class, and Irishness*, Cambridge: Cambridge University Press, 1996, pp. 124–5

Like Declan Kiberd, Marjorie Howes lays emphasis on Yeats's conflict-ridden sense of national identity, especially his Anglo-Irishness, and relates his cultural divisions to further conflicts to do with gender and class. In his Big House poems (poems, that is, about the large houses built by and symbolizing the Protestant ruling class in Ireland), Yeats, according to Howes, does not simply assert the values of an aristocratic culture; rather, he insists, as she puts it, that 'the continuity of the nation' can only be sustained by 'a repeated crisis of foundations that demands that each generation begins anew amid isolation and adversity'.[1] In the following, Howes discusses the first two poems in 'Meditations in Time of Civil War', a sequence of poems that include reflections on the fate of the Protestant aristocracy and on Yeats's own attempts to assert continuity and value through the poetry he was writing in his Norman tower at Thoor Ballylee (see **pp. 147–55** for text and commentary).

'Ancestral Houses' first figures this cruel and contradictory origin for the cultured beauty of the aristocracy as the relationship between the 'violent' and 'bitter' men who founded it and the 'sweetness' and 'gentleness' of the house they create:

> Some violent bitter man, some powerful man
> Called architect and artist in, that they,
> Bitter and violent men, might rear in stone
> The sweetness that all longed for night and day,
> The gentleness none there had ever known.

The questions of the final stanza reject this neat antithetical formulation, which divides violence and gentleness into separate spheres, asking, 'what if levelled lawns and gravelled ways . . . But take our greatness with our violence?' There are two possible readings of these lines, the ambiguity of which turns on the word

---

1   *Yeats's Nations*, p. 104.

'take.' Reading 'take' as 'take away' emphasizes what the founding men lose through their creation of the house, while reading 'take' as 'take on' emphasizes the suggestion that the beauty of the house is infected by the violence of its creators. Both readings accord with Yeats's representation of the Anglo-Irish as a nation in crisis. The first illustrates a national culture or community that suppresses and impoverishes the individual; the second suggests the corruption of the very foundations of the Big House. Both readings indicate the inseparability of greatness and violence, culture and crime, beauty and cruelty, and the speaker's linguistic movement from 'a rich man's flowering lawns' to 'our' greatness, bitterness, and violence implicates himself and his whole community [. . .]

The next poem in the sequence, 'My House', presents a different version of the relationship between nature, generational continuity and ancestral houses. Daniel Harris has analyzed the systematic ways in which the poem offers, point for point, an alternative to the kind of house in 'Ancestral Houses.'[2] The natural setting is resolutely unlike the rich man's fecund flowering lawns; it is an 'acre of stony ground' in which the symbolic rose will 'break in flower,' suggesting simultaneously flourishing and death. The act of founding does not institute a self-sustaining genealogy; two men have founded here. Neither one will leave behind a tradition that perpetuates itself.

Daniel Albright on symbolism in Yeats, from *Quantum Poetics: Yeats, Pound, Eliot, and the Science of Modernism*, Cambridge: Cambridge University Press, 1997, pp. 116–19

Daniel Albright writes in this extract from his *Quantum Poetics* about symbolism in Yeats, a topic central to grasping Yeats's poetic practice and vision. The symbol, or image with supra-rational powers of evocation and suggestion, is at the heart of his use of words. Albright argues that Yeats's distinction between 'emotional' and 'intellectual' symbols is of crucial importance, and that much of the drama out of which his poetry is made derives from a battle between the two kinds of symbol. For Albright, 'Emotional *symbols* multiply a temporal context, grow tentacles and clasp the brooding world; but intellectual *symbols* deny a temporal context, lift themselves out of the earth's orbit' (**p. 86**). In other words, emotional symbols attach themselves to life with all its imperfections; intellectual symbols aim at a perfection that transcends such imperfections. Emotional symbols entangle themselves in time; intellectual symbols seek to destroy time. Both kinds of symbol, especially the intellectual kind, threaten to collapse the sentence into the phrase or word. Albright sees 'A Dialogue of Self and Soul' (see **pp. 167–8** for commentary) as, among other things, a dramatization of conflict between the two different kinds of symbols: Self embraces

2   [Howes's note.] See Daniel Harris, *Yeats, Coole Park and Ballylee*, chapter 3, Baltimore and London: Johns Hopkins University Press, 1974.

the human condition; Soul seeks to leave it behind. The extract illuminates Yeats's love of the packed and compressed in poetic speech, as means of suggesting an assault on significances that lie beyond conventional language. In a striking image, Albright describes the Yeatsian sentence as like an unfurled roller-blind always about 'to clatter itself up furiously into a tight cylinder: its extension is precarious' (p. 87).

[. . .] in 1900, Yeats recognized the intimacy between the symbolic mode and our usual planet, by offering a distinction between expansive and contractive *symbols* – or, to use his terms, emotional and intellectual *symbols*:

> It is the intellect that decides where the reader shall ponder over the procession of the symbols, and if the symbols are merely emotional, he gazes from amid the accidents and destinies of the world; but if the symbols are intellectual too, he becomes himself a part of pure intellect, and he is himself mingled with the procession. If I watch a rushy pool in the moonlight, my emotion at its beauty is mixed with memories of the man that I have seen ploughing by its margin, or of the lovers I saw there a night ago; but if I look at the moon herself and remember any of her ancient names and meanings, I move among divine people, and things that have shaken off our mortality, the tower of ivory, the queen of waters.[1]

Emotional *symbols* multiply a temporal context, grow tentacles and clasp the brooding world; but intellectual *symbols* deny a temporal context, lift themselves out of the earth's orbit. (This is exactly the symbol-competition in the late poem "A Dialogue of Self and Soul" [1929] where emotional *symbols* cluster around the Self and repudiate the intellectual *symbols* clustered around the Soul.) [. . .]

[. . .] in his lyric mode, Yeats often felt, evidently, that emotional *symbols* were admixed, tainted, and that intellectual *symbols* were pure; and he wrote poems that were caught in the act of detemporalizing themselves into single intellectual *symbols*, or groups of contiguous intellectual *symbols*. For this very reason, *symbols* are frequently destructive in tenor: fire and sword retain a strong symbolic character, because each represents an assault on time, an assault on the temporal world that clogs our senses, that impedes our ascent to a realm of more intense meanings. (Time itself is imaged as an inflammable gazebo in "In Memory of Eva Gore-Booth and Con Markiewicz" [1929].) An intellectual *symbol* is, in a sense, self-attacking, insofar as it attempts to devour or burn up its own material part, its reference to the lower world. As Yeats liked to say, "beauty is an accusation", and "True art is the flame of the Last Day".[2]

It follows, then, that, in the language of *symbols*, the "word" counts more than

---

1   [Albright's note.] *Essays and Introductions*, London: Macmillan, 1961, p. 161.
2   [Albright's note.] *Essays and Introductions*, London: Macmillan, 1961, pp. 153, 140.

the sentence. The sentence – discursive, time-bound, regulated by grammar – is like an unfurled shade with a sensitive roller, always threatening, at the least touch, to clatter itself up furiously into a tight cylinder: its extension is precarious. *Spool, perne, bobbin* – such words are typical of Yeats's vocabulary, for they are *images* of a detemporalized condition in which Time has rolled itself up, contracted, congealed, into Eternity [. . .]

[. . .] At many moments of peak intensity, the sentence-structure collapses into a kind of pictorial exposition, sometimes almost verbless, sometimes offering a texture in which (as Helen Vendler has noted),[3] the verbs seem to have lost control over their objects:

> A sudden blow: the great wings beating still
> Above the staggering girl, her thighs caressed
> By the dark webs, her nape caught in his bill.
>
> ("Leda and the Swan" [1924])

> Marbles of the dancing floor
> Break bitter furies of complexity,
> Those images that yet
> Fresh images beget,
> That dolphin-torn, that gong-tormented sea.
>
> ("Byzantium" [1932])

The pictograms seem to be struggling to escape from poetic grammar, to promote themselves into self-sufficient entities [. . .]

Michael O'Neill on 'The Circus Animals' Desertion', from *Romanticism and the Self-Conscious Poem*, Oxford: Clarendon Press, 1997, pp. 255–6, 256–7

In this extract from a larger study of 'the self-conscious poem', the present editor discusses the end of Yeats's 'The Circus Animals' Desertion' as belonging to a poem that appears to turn with scorn on the central idea of 'A General Introduction for My Work', that the poet transforms himself into 'something intended, complete' in his work. The poem was written close to Yeats's death and constitutes a review of his career, concentrating on the links and gaps between Yeats's human feelings and the artistic works to which they gave rise (see **pp. 180–1** for commentary). The larger discussion from which the following extracts are taken argues that the poem is much more complicated in its moods and position than it might seem to be, and is, in its self-quarrelling, a

---

3 [Albright's note.] Yeats's *"Vision" and the Last Plays*, Cambridge, Mass.: Harvard University Press, 1963, p. 118.

typical Yeatsian poem, consisting of 'celebration' (**p. 89**) as well as self-critique. After all, for all its declarations of imaginative fatigue, the poem has, by its close, 'tapped new sources of creativity' (**p. 89**); indeed, as is pointed out in a paragraph not included, 'To end such a last-testament-like poem with a rhyme involving "start" is itself an arrestingly self-reflexive effect'.[1] What the poem can be said to 'start' is a confessional poetry in which the self and its torments dominate. Yet, in the end, Yeats sustains in the poem the intimate, unfathomable relationship between man and poet that he seems concerned to demystify.

Yeats himself remarked famously that 'We make out of the quarrel with others, rhetoric, but of the quarrel with ourselves, poetry.'[2] For an example of inauthentic rhetoric one might look at this original ending of the poem in a draft:

> O hour of triumph come and make me gay.
> If burnished chariots are put to flight
> Why brood upon old triumph; prepare to die
> Even at the approach of un-imagined night
> Man has the refuge of his gaiety,
> A dab of black enhances every white,
> Tension is but the vigour of the mind,
> Cannon the god and father of mankind.[3]

The last two lines especially have the deliberately illiberal abrasiveness typical of too many of Yeats's later poems. This posturing heroism gives way to a more persuasive image of the poet as hero, a man accepting dereliction. However, it is important to see that Yeats does lament the failure of a dream in the revised version of the final stanza. This stanza is not the first time in his work that Yeats has turned on his 'masterful images' for being achieved at too high a cost. When in 'Byzantium' 'A starlit or a moonlit dome disdains | All that man is', the final phrase protests against such disdain; the poem's images of changelessness beget fresh images that pitch the reader back into 'That dolphin-torn, that gong-tormented sea' at the poem's close: images, yes, but images that contest the right of art's imagery to reject 'The fury and the mire of human veins'. [. . .]

But the end of 'The Circus Animals' Desertion' returns to 'The malady of the quotidian' [quoted from Wallace Stevens's 'The Man Whose Pharynx Was Bad'] with a vengeance, and is strikingly akin to Stevens's 'The Man on the Dump', a poem also composed in 1938. Stevens writes, 'One sits and beats an old tin can, lard pail. | One beats and beats for that which one believes. | That's what one wants to get near. Could it after all | Be merely oneself . . .?' 'Merely oneself': the

---

1 *Romanticism and the Self-Conscious Poem*, p. 257.
2 'Anima Hominis': see **p. 25**.
3 [O'Neill's note.] Quoted from *W. B. Yeats: The Poems*, ed. and intro. Daniel Albright (1990), London: Dent, 1994, p. 807.

tone of dismay is strong, just as in Yeats there is audible reluctance, a visible grimace, in the 'must' of 'Now that my ladder's gone | I must lie down where all the ladders start | In the foul rag and bone shop of the heart'. Of course, if Yeats is being compelled to embrace a new way of writing, the way he does so is compellingly dramatic [. . .] Nor should we ignore the fact that Yeats's despised particulars—the almost spat-out 'Old kettles, old bottles, and a broken can'—take on (as they are surely meant to) a grandeur of the gutter; they are as 'masterful' a set of images as any that Yeats has created. And the poem knows this. As Michael Hamburger has remarked, 'even the despair of this ending had to be heroic and theatrical'.[4]

Much remains even as it is pitilessly recast; the muse makes a final appearance as 'that raving slut | Who keeps the till', 'raving' implying passion as well as incoherence. The 'ladders' that lead upwards towards art's dubious triumphs are not kicked aside, merely viewed from the bottom rung. Moreover, the poet lies down 'where all the ladders start' [. . .] At least one thing manufactured in the 'foul rag and bone shop of the heart' is the (metaphorical) paper on which the heart inscribes its 'foul' but authentic 'mysteries'. The very word 'heart', employed in all but one of the previous four stanzas, grows more snarlingly intricate in its suggestions. At the start the poet had to 'be satisfied with my heart', where 'heart' means something like the 'merely personal'. *The Wanderings of Oisin* presented 'Themes of the embittered heart', a phrase which, among other things, shows the ease with which 'bitterness' can become just another rhetoric. *On Baile's Strand* involved 'Heart mysteries', a phrase that turns the 'Heart' into a place which is more than 'merely personal'. 'The foul rag and bone shop of the heart' becomes—for all its hints of anguish and self-loathing—a distinctly impersonal place, and there is celebration as well as exhaustion in the final line's strongly stressed monosyllables. The poet has tapped new sources of creativity, both breaking away from tradition and renewing it.

---

4 [O'Neill's note.] *The Truth of Poetry: Tensions in Modern Poetry from Baudelaire to the 1960s* (1969), Harmondsworth: Penguin, 1972, p. 84.

3

Key Poems

Introduction

The poems chosen are taken from the range of Yeats's career. The section starts with the early work, and the emphasis in *The Wind among the Reeds* (1899) on symbolic expressions of desire and yearning. It moves on to the less high-flown poetry of *In the Seven Woods* (1904), *The Green Helmet* (1910) and *Responsibilities* (1914), in which Yeats, without sacrificing his concern with beauty and 'the old high way of love' ('Adam's Curse', l. 36), develops a vigorous speaking voice. It then shifts to the powerful masterpieces (in some cases only commentary and notes are provided) contained in volumes of Yeats's maturity, *The Wild Swans at Coole* (1917, 1919), *Michael Robartes and the Dancer* (1921), *The Tower* (1928) and *The Winding Stair* (1929, 1933), before concluding with Yeats's achievement in his final poems. Headnotes offer commentary on theme, style, tone, form (including metre and rhythm) and context, while notes explicate allusions, supply glosses and provide further critical comment. The order of the poems (or of the commentaries in cases when the text is not printed) is based on this edition's copy-text, the *Collected Poems* (1933; 2nd edn 1950), except for the commentaries on the late poems (after 'Byzantium'). The commentaries on the late poems follow the order that Yeats drew up in a list: a list that makes it clear that 'Under Ben Bulben', placed at the head of the poems in the list, 'is meant to serve as an overture, not as a recapitulation of themes'.[1] The copy-text has been chosen because it was the last collected poems by Yeats to appear in his lifetime; Yeats's notes to his poems are quoted from this edition. The likely year of composition is given when available. The relevant major volume publication is provided, as are the first journal publications, where of particular interest. Where commentaries appear without texts, line numbers are provided in the headnotes for quotations from the poems.

Readers of Yeats's poems should know that there has been much debate about their editing. The following headnotes and notes occasionally touch on these issues, pointing out, for example, that *Crossways* and *The Rose* were never

---

1   See Curtis Bradford, 'On Yeats's *Last Poems*', in Jon Stallworthy (ed.), *Yeats's Last Poems*, London: Macmillan, 1968, pp. 93–4, 77.

published as separate volumes, but as titles used in *Poems* (1895) for groupings of earlier poems. The editorial problems surrounding Yeats, partly caused by the poet's habit of incessant revision, centre on whether the ordering and copy-texts for the poems should derive from his *Collected Poems* (1933), in which, for the first time, Yeats's longer, more narrative poems were placed out of chronological order after the lyrical volumes, or whether they should derive from a multi-volume Edition de Luxe, planned and set up in type in the 1930s, but never finding its way into print. There is further debate about the late poems, about their order and whether it is appropriate to prefer earlier periodical printings in some cases to their first appearance in volume form. The interested reader should consult Richard J. Finneran's 'Text and Interpretation in the Poems of W. B. Yeats'[2] and Warwick Gould's 'The Definitive Edition: A History of the Final Arrangements of Yeats's Work'.[3]

The reader is reminded that the high cost of reproduction fees has meant that commentary and notes only are provided in the case of thirteen poems ('Easter 1916', 'The Second Coming', 'A Prayer for My Daughter', 'A Dialogue of Self and Soul', 'Byzantium', 'The Gyres', 'Lapis Lazuli', 'Beautiful Lofty Things', 'Under Ben Bulben', 'Long-Legged Fly', 'Man and the Echo', 'The Circus Animals' Desertion' and 'Politics'). These poems are among Yeats's most famous, and texts for them can be found readily elsewhere.

---

2   In George Bornstein (ed.), *Representing Modernist Texts: Editing as Interpretation*, Ann Arbor: The University of Michigan Press, 1991, pp. 17–47.
3   Printed as Appendix 6 in A. Norman Jeffares (ed.), *Yeats's Poems* (1989), revised edn, London: Macmillan, 1991.

Key Poems

The Song of the Happy Shepherd

Composed in 1885. Published in *The Wanderings of Oisin and Other Poems* (1889) and included in *Crossways*, not a separate volume but a title Yeats gave to a section of his work in his *Poems* (1895). The poem, written in rhyming iambic octosyllabics, typifies a stance found in early Yeats: that is, an exaltation of 'Words' (or poetry and the imagination) over 'Grey Truth' (or rationalism and science). The poem conducts this defence of poetry with some sophistication. Opening with the concession that 'The woods of Arcady are dead', a line that acknowledges the futility of hankering after 'antique joy', the poem works its way to a close in which the poet seeks to reconnect himself with mythology, with 'the hapless faun,/Buried under the sleepy ground'. Yeats implies that mere nostalgia is foolish, but that the recreation of past values for the present is the poet's task. Like much of early Yeats, the poem is easy to underestimate; its diction and tones are full of the awareness that invigorates much of his work. For example, the line 'Grey Truth is now her painted toy' shrewdly suggests that a passion for 'Grey Truth' is as much a cherished illusion (or 'painted toy') as any other. Again, the claims for 'words' take on a challenging assertiveness in the lines that adapt the Biblical identification of God with the Logos (or Word) to Yeats's own post-Romantic trust in poetry: 'The wandering earth herself may be/Only a sudden flaming word'. The central image of the 'twisted, echo-harbouring shell' represents poetry, the medium through which 'words' – and 'dreams' – can be conveyed. There is some division between trust in 'dreams' (see the last line) and a more disillusioned sense that 'dreams' may be only illusions; so, the hunger for 'truth' outside 'thine own heart' may merely breed 'New dreams, new dreams'. Further evidence of division within Yeats about the capability of poetry comes from the fact this 'Song' of a 'Happy Shepherd' was followed by a poem entitled 'The Sad Shepherd'. In that poem, a song of experience after what, by contrast, appears a song of innocence, Yeats emphasizes the inadequacy of poetry.

The woods of Arcady are dead,
And over is their antique joy;
Of old the world on dreaming fed;
Grey Truth is now her painted toy;
Yet still she turns her restless head: 5
But O, sick children of the world,
Of all the many changing things
In dreary dancing past us whirled,
To the cracked tune that Chronos[1] sings,
Words alone are certain good.   10
Where are now the warring kings,
Word be-mockers? — By the Rood,[2]
Where are now the warring kings?
An idle word is now their glory,
By the stammering schoolboy said,   15
Reading some entangled story:
The kings of the old time are dead;
The wandering earth herself may be
Only a sudden flaming word,
In clanging space a moment heard,   20
Troubling the endless reverie.

Then nowise worship dusty deeds,
Nor seek, for this is also sooth,[3]
To hunger fiercely after truth,
Lest all thy toiling only breeds   25
New dreams, new dreams; there is no truth
Saving in thine own heart. Seek, then,
No learning from the starry men,
Who follow with the optic glass
The whirling ways of stars that pass—   30
Seek, then, for this is also sooth,
No word of theirs—the cold star-bane
Has cloven and rent their hearts in twain,
And dead is all their human truth.
Go gather by the humming sea   35
Some twisted, echo-harbouring shell,
And to its lips thy story tell,
And they thy comforters will be,
Rewording[4] in melodious guile
Thy fretful words a little while,   40

---

1   Time.
2   Cross.
3   True.
4   Some texts print 'Rewarding'.

Till they shall singing fade in ruth
And die a pearly brotherhood;
For words alone are certain good:
Sing, then, for this is also sooth.

I must be gone: there is a grave   45
Where daffodil and lily wave,
And I would please the hapless faun,
Buried under the sleepy ground,
With mirthful songs before the dawn.
His shouting days with mirth were crowned;   50
And still I dream he treads the lawn,
Walking ghostly in the dew,
Pierced by my glad singing through,
My songs of old earth's dreamy youth:
But ah! she dreams not now; dream thou!   55
For fair are poppies on the brow:
Dream, dream, for this is also sooth.

The Lake Isle of Innisfree

Composed in 1888. Published in the *National Observer* (1890) and in *The Count-ess Kathleen and Various Legends and Lyrics* (1892). Yeats described the genesis of this poem, among his most famous lyrics, in the following way: 'I still had the ambition, formed in Sligo in my teens, of living in imitation of Thoreau on Innisfree, a little island in Lough Gill, and when walking through Fleet Street very homesick I heard a little tinkle of water and saw a fountain in a shop-window which balanced a little ball upon its jet, and began to remember lake water. From the sudden remembrance came my poem *Innisfree*, my first lyric with anything in its rhythm of my own music.'[1] In the poem Yeats imagines going to a world of lake-water and natural beauty wholly removed from the bustle of the city's 'roadway' and 'pavements grey'; foreshadowed, however dimly, is his later deci-sion to visit Byzantium (in imagination) in 'Sailing to Byzantium'. Here the poem derives much of its beauty from the contrast between its apparent assertive-ness, 'I will arise and go now', and the peaceful, almost somnolent, drift of its movement, and from a rhythm that is poised between solemn chant and relaxed speech. The stress is on longing rather than arrival. Yeats evokes, in the lake isle, a version of Ireland that is magically remote from urban greyness yet rooted in the land, a place where the poet can have 'Nine bean-rows', the detail at once portentous and delightfully humdrum. The poem was included in *The Rose*, which was never issued as a separate volume but was the title that Yeats gave to

1   *Autobiographies*, London: Macmillan, 1955, p. 153

a section of his *Poems* (1895). yeats explained that *Crossways* was so called because in it the poet 'has tried many pathways', whereas in *The Rose* 'he has found . . . the only pathway whereon he can hope to see with his own eyes the Eternal Rose of Beauty and Peace'.

I will arise[2] and go now, and go to Innisfree,
And a small cabin build there, of clay and wattles made:
Nine bean-rows will I have there, a hive for the honey-bee,
And live alone in the bee-loud glade.

And I shall have some peace there, for peace comes dropping slow,   5
Dropping from the veils of the morning to where the cricket sings;
There midnight's all a glimmer, and noon a purple glow,
And evening full of the linnet's wings.

I will arise and go now, for always night and day
I hear lake water lapping with low sounds by the shore;   10
While I stand on the roadway, or on the pavements grey,
I hear it in the deep heart's core.[3]

The Sorrow of Love

Composed in 1891; considerably rewritten in 1924. Published in *The Countess Kathleen and Various Legends and Lyrics* (1892). Included in *The Rose*, this poem, about the impact of a woman like Helen of Troy (Maud Gonne) on the poet's view of reality, reverses in its third and final quatrain the terms of the first quatrain. In the first quatrain nature's power overwhelms the human; in the third, as a result of the woman's emergence into history, nature merely echoes human sorrow. There is, too, in the word 'compose' the suggestion that nature now arranges itself into symbols reflective of 'man's image and his cry'. The poem, much revised by Yeats, is printed in its later version; the 1895 version is supplied in the notes, to allow readers to see for themselves how Yeats revised in the interest of a harder, more knowing, above all more powerful, style. So, the 'full round moon' becomes the 'brilliant moon', 'the loud song of the ever-singing leaves' turns into 'all that famous harmony of leaves' and the earlier 'you' reappears as the impersonal and mythic 'girl'. Whether the result of such

2   Something of the Biblical solemnity of the phrase is explained by the fact that it is an echo of Luke 15:18: 'I will arise and go to my father'.
3   At once the poet's heart and a more collective repository of feelings (akin to the anima mundi of 'Magic').

The brawling of a sparrow in the eaves,
The brilliant moon and all the milky sky,
And all that famous harmony of leaves,
Had blotted out man's image and his cry.

A girl arose that had red mournful lips   5
And seemed the greatness of the world in tears,
Doomed like Odysseus[1] and the labouring ships
And proud as Priam[2] murdered with his peers;

Arose, and on the instant clamorous eaves,
A climbing moon upon an empty sky,   10
And all that lamentation[3] of the leaves,
Could but compose man's image and his cry.[4]

When You are Old

Composed in 1891 and published in *The Countess Kathleen and Various Legends and Lyrics* (1892). Included in *The Rose*, and written in quatrains made up of iambic pentameters rhyming *abba*, the poem reworks a sonnet by Pierre Ronsard (1524–85), 'Quand vous serez bien vieille'. Its even-paced, subtle

---

1   Greek hero, whose wanderings after the fall of Troy are the subject of Homer's *Odyssey*.
2   Trojan king, slain when Troy was sacked by the Greeks. Yeats gives his 'girl' attributes both of the Greeks and the Trojans.
3   As with 'that famous harmony' (l. 3), the use of 'that' is a feature of Yeats's later style, a symptom of his striving for force and urgency of utterance.
4   When printed in 1895, the poem read:

The quarrel of the sparrows in the eaves,
The full round moon and the star-laden sky,
And the loud song of the ever-singing leaves
Had hid away earth's old and weary cry.

And then you came with those red mournful lips,
And with you came the whole of the world's tears,
And all the sorrows of her labouring ships,
And all the burden of her myriad years.

And now the sparrows warring in the eaves,
The curd-pale moon, the white stars in the sky,
And the loud chanting of the unquiet leaves,
Are shaken with earth's old and weary cry.

movement encompasses sadness and assertion: sadness at the thought of the woman's loss of beauty and of her regret at the passing of love; assertion of the constancy of the lover's love and of the continuing worth of the woman's 'pilgrim soul'. The second stanza uses 'loved' in each of its four lines, calling on the reader to discriminate in favour of the way in which 'one man loved'. The poem manages successfully to combine traditional rhetoric (the personification of 'Love' hiding his face) with observed detail (the 'glowing bars' of the fire). As often, Yeats appears in the poem as a poet. Relatively unemphatic here, this poetic self-consciousness is revealed by the reference to 'this book' that the woman is urged to 'take down'.

When you are old and grey and full of sleep,
And nodding by the fire, take down this book,
And slowly read, and dream of the soft look
Your eyes had once, and of their shadows deep;

How many loved your moments of glad grace,   5
And loved your beauty with love false or true,
But one man loved the pilgrim soul in you,
And loved the sorrows of your changing face;

And bending down beside the glowing bars,
Murmur, a little sadly, how Love fled   10
And paced upon the mountains overhead
And hid his face amid a crowd of stars.

Who Goes with Fergus?

Published in *The Countess Kathleen and Various Legends and Lyrics* (1892). Included in *The Rose*, and written in two six-line stanzas of iambic octosyllabics rhyming *abcabc*, this poem was first included in Yeats's play *The Countess Kathleen*, where it is sung by the heroine's nurse to take her mistress' mind off the sorrow caused by drought and famine. Fergus was a king of Ulster, who abdicated from his throne to devote himself to peace and hunting in the woods. The lyric advocates leaving behind 'love's bitter mystery' for Fergus's realm of wood and sea; there is, though, a suggestion that it is easier to advocate than to achieve such a leaving behind. This suggestion is created by the repetition in the first line of the second stanza of the command not to 'brood', as though the impulse to brood was strong; it is created, too, by the fact that the world that Fergus rules seems not wholly to have forsaken love or erotic longing since it contains 'the white breast of the dim sea'.

Who will go drive with Fergus now,
And pierce the deep wood's woven shade,
And dance upon the level shore?
Young man, lift up your russet brow,
And lift your tender eyelids, maid,   5
And brood on hopes and fear no more.

And no more turn aside and brood[1]
Upon love's bitter mystery;
For Fergus rules the brazen cars,
And rules the shadows of the wood,   10
And the white breast of the dim sea
And all dishevelled wandering stars.

To Ireland in the Coming Times

First published in *The Countess Kathleen and Various Legends and Lyrics* (1892) under the title 'Apologia Addressed to Ireland in the Coming Days', and included in *The Rose*. In the octosyllabic couplets of this poem, Yeats defends his poetry as no less concerned 'to sweeten Ireland's wrong' than previous nationalist poets had been, poets such as Thomas Davis (1814–45), James Clarence Mangan (1803–49) and Samuel Ferguson (1810–86). Yeats's preoccupation with occult matters strengthens rather than depletes, so the poem asserts, the force of his commitment to an Ireland to be fashioned 'in the dim coming times'. Indeed, Yeats suggests that by meditating 'in measured ways' on supra-human forces that 'hurry from unmeasured mind', the poet-mage has access to Ireland's Druidic origins. He can, in turn, gain a power and knowledge that give rise to 'truth's consuming ecstasy' and render unnecessary 'love and dream'. By meditating on the heart's desire, the rose, Yeats is able, the poem claims, to find the essence of an ideal Ireland; the poem seeks to bring together the occult, the poetic, the erotic and the nationalist. Its couplets reinforce an impression of convergence, especially towards the close where Yeats rhymes the word 'rhymes' with 'dim coming times' and says, too, that he has 'cast [his] heart into [his] rhymes'. Among Yeats's most significant poetic apologias, the poem serves as a retort to dismissals of his first volumes as escapist in mood and lost in the mists of a Celtic twilight. Though the note of desire struck in the first line's use of 'would' is present as an undercurrent throughout, the poem complicates

---

1   See Blake's 'Introduction' to the *Songs of Experience*: 'Turn away no more;/Why wilt thou turn away?'

Yeats's description, in a letter of 1888, of his early poetry as a poetry of 'longing and complaint' rather than of 'knowledge and insight'.[1]

Know, that I would accounted be
True brother of a company
That sang, to sweeten Ireland's wrong,
Ballad and story, rann[2] and song;
Nor be I any less of them,   5
Because the red-rose-bordered hem
Of her,[3] whose history began
Before God made the angelic clan,
Trails all about the written page.
When Time began to rant and rage   10
The measure of her flying feet
Made Ireland's heart begin to beat;
And Time bade all his candles flare
To light a measure here and there;
And may the thoughts of Ireland brood   15
Upon a measured quietude.

Nor may I less be counted one
With Davis, Mangan, Ferguson,[4]
Because, to him who ponders well,
My rhymes more than their rhyming tell   20
Of things discovered in the deep,
Where only body's laid asleep.[5]
For the elemental creatures go
About my table to and fro,
That hurry from unmeasured mind   25
To rant and rage in flood and wind;
Yet he who treads in measured ways
May surely barter gaze for gaze.
Man ever journeys on with them
After the red-rose-bordered hem.   30

---

1   John Kelly and Eric Domville (eds), *The Collected Letters of W. B. Yeats*, vol. 1, 1865–95, Oxford: Clarendon, 1986, p. 54.
2   Verse of a poem.
3   The rose, with its manifold significances (see headnote to 'The Secret Rose', pp. 109–10).
4   Davis, leader of the Young Ireland party, wrote popular poems; Mangan, Romantic poet and essayist; Ferguson, translated Irish legends.
5   Echoes Wordsworth's *Tintern Abbey*, ll. 46–7 ('we are laid asleep / In body') and is suggestive of a mystical trance.

Ah, faeries, dancing under the moon,
A Druid land, a Druid tune![6]

While still I may, I write for you[7]
The love I lived, the dream I knew.
From our birthday, until we die,   35
Is but the winking of an eye;
And we, our singing and our love,
What measurer Time has lit above,
And all benighted things that go
About my table to and fro,   40
Are passing on to where may be,
In truth's consuming ecstasy,
No place for love and dream at all;
For God goes by with white footfall.
I cast my heart into my rhymes,   45
That you, in the dim coming times,
May know how my heart went with them
After the red-rose-bordered hem.

The Hosting of the Sidhe

Composed in 1893 and first published in the *National Observer* in that year, this is the first poem in *The Wind among the Reeds* (1899), a collection that demonstrates Yeats's preoccupation with the volume as a form in itself. *The Wind among the Reeds* is marked by a rarefied diction, a Symbolist concern with evocation, a nuanced use of rhythm, and an obsession with love, poetry, and the connection and conflict between human desire and supra-human forces. The poems ritualize experience, often through images that bring to mind the poet's study of magic. When the volume was first published, the titles of individual poems indicated the presence of three speakers: Hanrahan, Michael Robartes and Aedh (pronounced 'ay' as in 'day'), each demonstrating a different approach to love. In a note Yeats wrote: 'Hanrahan is the simplicity of an imagination too changeable to gather permanent possessions, or the adoration of the shepherds; and Michael Robartes is the pride of the imagination brooding upon the greatness of its possessions, or the adoration of the Magi; while Aedh is the myrrh and frankincense that the imagination offers continually before all that it loves.' These names were later dropped, but the divergences between their different views remain, doing much to animate the volume.

6   Ireland's origins, Yeats believed, were Druidic.
7   Appears to be 'fairies'; could also anticipate 'you' of third-to-last line (i.e. Yeats's future readers).

In 'The Hosting of the Sidhe', the 'sidhe' (pronounced 'shee'), gods of the wind in Irish mythology, emerge as being at odds with human contentment, and yet as appealing to the human longing for escape. In his note to the poem Yeats says that 'the Sidhe have much to do with the wind. They journey in whirling wind, the winds that were called the dance of the daughters of Herodias in the Middle Ages' (see the last section of 'Nineteen Hundred and Nineteen', **pp. 160–1**). The verse makes use of extra stresses to reinforce the wind-like speed of which Niamh (pronounced 'Nee+av') speaks in her italicized address. With vivid economy Yeats conveys the power of the sidhe; the reader suspends disbelief since they stand for a force that compels the poetic imagination. In the last two lines the repetition of lines 3 and 4 suggests the grip over the poet's imagination held by these legendary figures.

The host is riding from Knocknarea[1]
And over the grave of Clooth-na-Bare;[2]
Caoilte[3] tossing his burning hair,
And Niamh[4] calling *Away, come away:*
Empty your heart of its mortal dream.   5
The winds awaken, the leaves whirl round,
Our cheeks are pale, our hair is unbound,
Our breasts are heaving, our eyes are agleam,
Our arms are waving, our lips are apart;
And if any gaze on our rushing band,   10
We come between him and the deed of his hand,
We come between him and the hope of his heart.
The host is rushing 'twixt night and day,
And where is there hope or deed as fair?
Caoilte tossing his burning hair,   15
And Niamh calling *Away, come away.*

---

1 A mountain close to Sligo; 'the country people say that Maeve, still a great queen of the western Sidhe, is buried in the cairn of stones upon it' (Yeats's note to the poem).
2 Yeats's note to the poem describes her as 'the old woman of Beare' and quotes another description of this figure by him in *The Celtic Twilight* as 'seeking a lake deep enough to drown her faery life, of which she had grown weary, . . . until at last, she found the deepest water in the world in little Lough Ia, on the top of the bird mountain, in Sligo'.
3 (Pronounced 'Keel+chih'.) Friend of the legendary Fenian warrior Finn MacCool.
4 Goddess in Irish myth who brought the hero Oisin into the underworld, where he stayed for 300 years.

The Moods

First published in *The Bookman* in 1893; published in *The Wind among the Reeds* (1899). By 'moods' Yeats means feelings that exist as though outside the self, states of emotional and spiritual being that hold themselves in a condition of eternal readiness. In a short essay 'The Moods' (1895) he writes, 'Literature differs from explanatory and scientific writing in being wrought about a mood, or a community of moods, as the body is wrought about an invisible soul'.[1] The poem, rhyming *abcabca*, suggests that a mood outlives 'time', that when a mood finishes so, too, will time, mountains and woods. The *a* rhyme does much to suggest the ongoing nature of the mood.

> Time drops in decay,
> Like a candle burnt out,
> And the mountains and woods
> Have their day, have their day;
> What one in the rout   5
> Of the fire-born moods
> Has fallen away?

The Lover tells of the Rose in his Heart

First published in the *National Observer* in 1892, entitled 'The Rose in My Heart'; published in *The Wind among the Reeds* (1899). This poem, two quatrains rhyming *abab* and using long lines that depend on liberal employment of three-syllable feet for an effect of chanted lyricism, makes clear how internalized much of Yeats's earlier poetry is. The poem takes place 'in the deeps of my heart'. In the first stanza the poet protests against 'All things uncomely and broken' for 'wronging' the 'image' of the beloved, an image that still manages to blossom into 'a rose', symbol of the heart's desire and of an idealized Ireland. Cutting against the protest is the fact that the child's cry, cart's creak, and ploughman's steps urge their claims upon us. Yeats is half in love with the ordinary things he rejects, as his strong, flowing rhythms suggest. In the second stanza the poem moves away from rejection of 'unshapely things' and towards the imagining of how the poet, though wishing to set himself 'apart', would create through his art a perfected version of the real. The last line exalts 'dreams', yet recognizes that the poet is as much in love with an 'image' as with a real woman.

> All things uncomely and broken, all things worn out and old,
> The cry of a child by the roadway, the creak of a lumbering cart,

---

1   *Essays and Introductions*, London: Macmillan, 1961, p. 195.

The heavy steps of the ploughman, splashing the wintry mould,
Are wronging your image that blossoms a rose in the deeps of my heart.

The wrong of unshapely things is a wrong too great to be told;   5
I hunger to build them anew and sit on a green knoll apart,
With the earth and the sky and the water, re-made, like a casket of gold
For my dreams of your image that blossoms a rose in the deeps of my
    heart.

The Song of Wandering Aengus

First published in *The Sketch* in 1897, entitled 'A Mad Song'; published in *The Wind among the Reeds* (1899). Aengus, a Celtic equivalent to Orpheus, speaks this lyric about quest, longing and the imagining of final reconciliation of opposites. The poem brims with symbolic suggestions: the 'hazel wood' visited by the poet-speaker is a place of enchantment and metamorphosis; the 'girl' is associated with 'apple blossom'; the final imagined plucking is of the wholly metaphorical 'silver apples of the moon' and 'golden apples of the sun'. The end may conceive of achievement and synthesis, but the poem's impact derives from the haunting way it conveys change and elusiveness; diction and syntax are vital here, as when in the second stanza the enjambed lines mimic the vanishing of the girl, who 'faded through the brightening air', a line in which the verb and adjective pull in different directions. In the last stanza there is a note of resolve, a note that is affecting because the resolve concedes lack of fulfilment: 'I will find out where she has gone'. The poem is made up of active verbs that convey, on the one hand, the speaker's actions and determination, and, on the other hand, the uncapturable otherness of the 'glimmering girl'. In that we are aware, at the close, of the speaker's attempt to override the fact that he is 'old with wandering', this lyric is as much about the inability to calm the 'fire' in the 'head' as it is about some supposed triumph.

I went out to the hazel wood,
Because a fire was in my head,
And cut and peeled a hazel wand,
And hooked a berry to a thread;
And when white moths were on the wing,   5
And moth-like stars were flickering out,
I dropped the berry in a stream
And caught a little silver trout.

When I had laid it on the floor
I went to blow the fire aflame,   10
But something rustled on the floor,

And some one called me by my name:
It had become a glimmering girl
With apple blossom in her hair
Who called me by my name and ran   15
And faded through the brightening air.

Though I am old with wandering
Through hollow lands and hilly lands,
I will find out where she has gone,
And kiss her lips and take her hands;   20
And walk among long dappled grass,
And pluck till time and times are done[1]
The silver apples of the moon,
The golden apples of the sun.

The Lover mourns for the Loss of Love

First published in *The Dome* in 1898; published in *The Wind among the Reeds* (1899). Exemplifying Yeats's spare lyric art in the volume, the poem addresses the theme of the poet's unrequited love for Maud Gonne ('the old despair') and asserts the impossibility of any other woman supplanting her 'image'. Poetically, much of the work is done by the second line, 'I had a beautiful friend', where past tense and (more subtly) adjective convey the withdrawal from emotional commitment on friend's and poet's part. The friend is 'beautiful' in the Pre-Raphaelite, stylized way indicated by the first line, but the beauty (as both she and the poet realize) is no match for the hold over the poet's heart of Maud. The biographical background to the poem is likely to be the breakdown of Yeats's love affair (1896–7) with Olivia Shakespear.

Pale brows, still hands and dim hair,
I had a beautiful friend
And dreamed that the old despair
Would end in love in the end:[1]
She looked in my heart one day   5
And saw your image was there;
She has gone weeping away.

1   The line shares with other poems in *The Wind among the Reeds* a fascination with apocalypse, an end of time that is also a revelation. There is in the volume, in however occult and hermetic a form, a covert political vision, a longing for change.

1   The line's play with 'end' suggests both the poet's longing for happiness in 'love' and the remoteness of such a possibility.

A Poet to his Beloved

Composed in 1895; first published in *The Senate* in 1896; published in *The Wind among the Reeds* (1899). The poem illustrates the lyric intensity that Yeats achieves in *The Wind among the Reeds*. This intensity is, in part, the result of interwoven rhyme: the scheme is *abcacdbd*, where the *b* rhyme is the same word, the key word 'dreams'. In part, it is the result of rhythms that are solemn but not ponderous, mixing two-syllable and three-syllable feet, creating effects both of emphasis and lilt. The poet's 'rhyme' is both 'passionate' and shaped by careful art; his addressee, the 'White woman that passion has worn', is a figure of distilled imaginings. The poem suggests a connection between the poet's 'numberless dreams' and the woman's. The word 'numberless' points in the direction of an infinity of possibilities that cannot be caught in a poem's 'numbers' (the old-fashioned word for a poem's metre).

I bring you with reverent hands
The books of my numberless dreams,
White woman that passion has worn
As the tide wears the dove-grey sands,
And with heart more old than the horn   5
That is brimmed from the pale fire of time:
White woman with numberless dreams,
I bring you my passionate rhyme.

To his Heart, bidding it have no Fear

First published in *The Savoy* in 1896; published in *The Wind among the Reeds* (1899). The poet urges his 'trembling heart' to be 'still' in this seven-line lyric that employs incantatory rhythms (mainly three-syllable feet) and repetitions (such as 'starry ways' and 'starry winds'), and rhymes *abcbcac*, where the first two *c* rhymes are the same word ('flood'). The final five lines quote ancient 'wisdom' about the exclusion from '*the lonely, majestical multitude*' of one afraid of elemental, immortal energies. However, the poem's effect is to imagine precisely the trembling and exclusion that it seeks to banish.

Be you still, be you still, trembling heart;
Remember the wisdom out of the old days:
Him who trembles before the flame and the flood,
And the winds that blow through the starry ways,
Let the starry winds and the flame and the flood   5

Cover over and hide, for he has no part
With the lonely, majestical multitude.

The Valley of the Black Pig

First published in *The Savoy* in 1896; published in *The Wind among the Reeds* (1899). Yeats wrote in a note: 'All over Ireland there are prophecies of the coming rout of the enemies of Ireland, in a certain Valley of the Black Pig, and these prophecies are, no doubt, now, as they were in the Fenian days, a political force.' He goes on to see the 'Pig' as 'a type of cold and winter doing battle with the summer, or of death battling with life', in a gloss that shows him to be fully aware of the ways of reading myth to be found in James Frazer's *The Golden Bough: A Study in Comparative Religion* (1890), which he mentions. The Black Pig is the boar that killed the Irish hero, Diarmuid. The poem, consisting of eight lines, rhymed *abbacddc*, and written in alexandrines (twelve-syllable lines), imagines an Armageddon and concludes with an acceptance of the destruction decreed by the 'Master' invoked at the end. The poem is, at some level, an imagining of the collapse of imperialism ('the world's empires').

The dews drop slowly and dreams gather: unknown spears
Suddenly hurtle before my dream-awakened eyes,
And then the clash of fallen horsemen and the cries
Of unknown perishing armies beat about my ears.
We who still labour by the cromlech[1] on the shore,   5
The grey cairn on the hill, when day sinks drowned in dew,
Being weary of the world's empires, bow down to you,
Master of the still stars and of the flaming door.

The Secret Rose

First published in *The Savoy* in 1896 under the title 'O'Sullivan Rua to the Secret Rose'; published in *The Wind among the Reeds* (1899). The poem, written in couplets (iambic pentameters), distils and expands Yeats's preoccupation with the symbol of the rose in his early work. The rose represents the object of the heart's desires and functions in personal, universal and historical ways: that is, it can suggest Maud Gonne, an absolute such as Eternal Beauty, and the political

---

1 An ancient tomb.

notion of an idealized and transformed Ireland. In this poem the rose is associated with figures from the myths out of which Yeats sought to fashion a new Irish consciousness. These myths are evoked in a processional roll-call, before the poet presents himself as another figure waiting for the rose's 'great wind of love and hate', attributing to it a power to bring about necessary destruction and welcome change, rather like Shelley's West Wind. Like many poems by Yeats, 'The Secret Rose' ends with a question, leaving open the possibility that the poet is not quite ready for the 'end-of-the world' scenario that he appears to desire. See Harold Bloom's reading of the poem in the extract by him in Modern Criticism in which he argues that 'the poem's concerns are no longer with the Rose but with the poet and his state of consciousness' (p. 70).

Far-off, most secret, and inviolate Rose,
Enfold me in my hour of hours; where those
Who sought thee in the Holy Sepulchre,[1]
Or in the wine-vat, dwell beyond the stir
And tumult of defeated dreams; and deep   5
Among pale eyelids, heavy with the sleep
Men have named beauty. Thy great leaves enfold
The ancient beards, the helms of ruby and gold
Of the crowned Magi;[2] and the king[3] whose eyes
Saw the Pierced Hands and Rood of elder rise   10
In Druid vapour and make the torches dim;
Till vain frenzy awoke and he died; and him[4]
Who met Fand[5] walking among flaming dew
By a grey shore where the wind never blew,
And lost the world and Emer[6] for a kiss;   15
And him who drove the gods out of their liss,[7]
And till a hundred morns had flowered red
Feasted, and wept the barrows of his dead;
And the proud dreaming king[8] who flung the crown
And sorrow away, and calling bard and clown   20
Dwelt among wine-stained wanderers in deep woods;
And him who sold tillage,[9] and house, and goods,

1   Place where Christ was buried; in the poem Christian associations are subordinated to the symbol
    of the rose.
2   The three kings who visited Christ as a baby.
3   Conchubar who converted to Christianity, according to Yeats in his note.
4   Cuchulain.
5   A goddess who seduced Cuchulain.
6   Wife of Cuchulain.
7   Caoilte. A 'liss' is a fort.
8   Fergus.
9   Yeats says in his note to the poem that this figure was based on a folk-tale in William Larminie's
    West Irish Folk Tales about a young man who found 'an open box on the road, and a light coming
    up out of it'; he goes to serve a king, but 'In the end, the young man, and not the king marries the
    woman' (quotations from Yeats's note).

And sought through lands and islands numberless years,
Until he found, with laughter and with tears,
A woman of so shining loveliness   25
That men threshed corn at midnight by a tress,
A little stolen tress. I, too, await
The hour of thy great wind of love and hate.
When shall the stars be blown about the sky,
Like the sparks blown out of a smithy, and die?   30
Surely thine hour has come, thy great wind blows,
Far-off, most secret, and inviolate Rose?

He wishes for the Cloths of Heaven

Published in *The Wind among the Reeds* (1899). Part of the impact of this famous poem derives from its imagining of the heavens as richly 'embroidered cloths', part from the blurring into one another of different dimensions and moods: the poet may possess only 'dreams', but his implied image for them ('Tread softly') is a version of the 'cloths' he does not possess. Yeats combines longing for the variously lit poetic splendour of the opening with confession of a lack of resource, but makes that confession a kind of assertion. The poem uses no rhymes, only repeated words in the rhyme position, which creates a wave-like effect, a quality of both sameness and desire for change.

Had I the heavens' embroidered cloths,
Enwrought with golden and silver light,
The blue and the dim and the dark cloths
Of night and light and the half-light,
I would spread the cloths under your feet: 5
But I, being poor, have only my dreams;
I have spread my dreams under your feet;
Tread softly because you tread on my dreams.

Adam's Curse

Composed in 1901; first published in the *Monthly Review* in 1902; published in *In the Seven Woods* (1904). This poem is based on a conversation between Yeats, Maud Gonne and her sister, Kathleen Pilcher ('That beautiful mild woman'). Maud Gonne recalled that 'Kathleen remarked that it was hard work being beautiful which Willie turned into his poem "Adam's Curse".' The movement of its couplets, adapted to the speaking voice, makes a striking contrast with the

ritualistic solemnity of 'The Secret Rose', and shows how Yeats developed a more vigorous naturalness of speech in poems after *The Wind among the Reeds*. At the same time, the theme of failure in love is still present, especially at the end where the off-rhyme between 'grown' and 'moon' captures the final mood of disenchantment. The title refers to the fact that after the Fall, Adam had to work by the sweat of his brow (see Genesis 3:17, 19), and the poem's concern with 'labour' is repeated in later poems, especially 'Among School Children'. Here it underpins the account of how poetry is harder work than manual labour. Yeats anticipates his theories of masks and opposites when he argues that the labour of the poet must disguise itself. The poem discusses what is needed for achievement, whether in the spheres of poetry or beauty or love-making. What animates it is its awareness of failure. The crucial transition occurs in the line 'We sat grown quiet at the name of love', when a personal undercurrent rises to the poem's surface, echoing but taking deeper the poem's opening, 'We sat together at one summer's end'. For a reading that dwells on the poem as enacting 'the acceptance of defeat' and as setting up tensions dealt with in later works, see Denis Donoghue's piece in *Modern Criticism* **(pp. 71–4)**.

We sat together at one summer's end,[1]
That beautiful mild woman, your close friend,
And you and I, and talked of poetry.
I said, 'A line will take us hours maybe;[2]
Yet if it does not seem a moment's thought,[3]   5
Our stitching and unstitching has been naught.
Better go down upon your marrow-bones
And scrub a kitchen pavement, or break stones
Like an old pauper, in all kinds of weather;
For to articulate sweet sounds together   10
Is to work harder than all these, and yet
Be thought an idler by the noisy set
Of bankers, schoolmasters, and clergymen
The martyrs[4] call the world.'
                              And thereupon
That beautiful mild woman for whose sake   15
There's many a one shall find out all heartache
On finding that her voice is sweet and low
Replied, 'To be born woman is to know—

---

1   Suited to the mood of failed striving that emerges in the final paragraph.
2   Rhymed with 'poetry', the choice of word illustrates the ideal of style Yeats goes on to describe.
3   Lines 4–5 bring to mind the notion of *sprezzatura* (courtly nonchalance) celebrated by Castiglione in *The Courtier* (1528).
4   Presumably those who suffer at the hands of bourgeois culture.

Although they do not talk of it at school—
That we must labour to be beautiful.'   20

I said, 'It's certain there is no fine thing
Since Adam's fall but needs much labouring.
There have been lovers who thought love should be
So much compounded of high courtesy
That they would sigh and quote with learned looks   25
Precedents out of beautiful old books;
Yet now it seems an idle trade[5] enough.'

We sat grown quiet at the name of love;
We saw the last embers of daylight die,
And in the trembling blue-green of the sky   30
A moon,[6] worn as if it had been a shell
Washed by time's waters as they rose and fell
About the stars and broke in days and years.

I had a thought for no one's but your ears:
That you were beautiful, and that I strove   35
To love you in the old high way of love;
That it had all seemed happy, and yet we'd grown
As weary-hearted as that hollow moon.

No Second Troy

Composed in 1908; first published in *The Green Helmet and Other Poems* (1910).
The poem shows Yeats in the act of coming to terms with Maud Gonne's
nature, a nature that had caused him emotional 'misery' and that, expressed
through demagogic speech-making, had threatened to cause serious civil unrest.
As the poem progresses, though, the impulse to 'blame' (strongly present at the
start, for all the form of the initial question) passes into mythologizing and awed
acceptance. Maud is like Helen of Troy in her beauty and power; but the modern
world (and this is felt to be to its discredit) offers her passionate if potentially
destructive personality nothing worthy of it. The final question expects the
answer 'no'. The poem finds a tautness of rhythm and diction that mirrors the
'high and solitary and most stern' character attributed to its subject. Formally, it

5   Recalls the rejected version of the poet as an 'idler'; the fact that the charge of 'idleness' cannot be
    wholly repudiated suggests the poet's sense of failure.
6   The image of the moon does not imply the poet's access to esoteric wisdom as his use of symbols in
    earlier poems did; here, it serves as a focus of his feelings about the eroding effect of time, the
    passage of 'days and years'.

has the packed, explosive effect of a curtailed sonnet; it consists of three quatrains, with alternating rhymes, and is made up of four questions, the last two of which occupy only one line each.

Why should I blame her that she filled my days
With misery,[1] or that she would of late
Have taught to ignorant men most violent ways,
Or hurled the little streets upon the great,
Had they but courage equal to desire?   5
What could have made her peaceful with a mind
That nobleness made simple as a fire,
With beauty like a tightened bow, a kind
That is not natural[2] in an age like this,
Being high and solitary and most stern?   10
Why, what could she have done, being what she is?[3]
Was there another Troy for her to burn?

The Fascination of What's Difficult

First published in *The Green Helmet and Other Poems* (1910). Yeats wrote in a prose draft: 'Subject: To complain at the fascination of what's difficult [. . .] One could use the thought that the winged and unbroken colt must drag a cart of stones out of pride because it is difficult, and end by denouncing drama, accounts, public contests and all that's merely difficult.' The poem consists of thirteen lines, deliberately refusing the shape of a sonnet, and is rhymed *abbaccaddaeea*, the repeated *a* rhyme on 'difficult' driving home the poem's theme. The 'colt' of line 4 is Pegasus, the winged horse of Greek mythology, sacred to the Muses, and a symbol of poetic inspiration. The distance Yeats has travelled from *The Wind among the Reeds* is apparent in the image of the horse of poetry forced to 'sweat and jolt/As though it dragged road-metal' and in the colloquial force of 'My curse on plays'. There, Yeats alludes to his experience as producer-manager of the Abbey Theatre in Dublin; he captures the exhaustion induced by 'the day's war with every knave and dolt' and the bitter energy released by his scorn for such activity. The poem moves from a 'curse' on the grind of 'management' to another kind of swearing at the end, where the poet asserts his intention of liberating Pegasus.

---

1   The strong pause (or caesura) after the word makes the reader only too aware that the poem's 'she' did fill the speaker's days with 'misery'.
2   Maud's beauty is 'antithetical', opposed to contemporary culture's ideas of the 'natural'.
3   Though Maud's beauty may not be 'natural in an age like this' (l. 9), she is true to her own nature.

The fascination of what's difficult
Has dried the sap out of my veins, and rent
Spontaneous joy and natural content
Out of my heart. There's something ails our colt
That must, as if it had not holy blood   5
Nor on Olympus leaped from cloud to cloud,
Shiver under the lash, strain, sweat and jolt
As though it dragged road-metal. My curse on plays
That have to be set up in fifty ways,
On the day's war with every knave and dolt,   10
Theatre business, management of men.
I swear before the dawn comes round again
I'll find the stable and pull out the bolt.[1]

September 1913

First published in the *Irish Times* in September 1913 under the title 'Romance in Ireland (On Reading Much of the Correspondence against the Art Gallery)'; published in *Responsibilities* (1914), a volume that has as its epigraph, '*In dreams begin responsibility*'. 'September 1913' emerges from Yeats's involvement in topical controversies and gives savagely eloquent expression to his disaffection with the leaders of middle-class Catholic nationalism, especially the newspaper proprietor William Martin Murphy. Mobilizing the support of the Catholic Church, Murphy faced down a strike organized by James Larkin, a labour leader who sought union rights for the Dublin United Tramway Company (owned by Murphy). Yeats supported the strikers, partly through sympathy with the Irish poor, but also out of dislike for Murphy, who had opposed a scheme dear to the poet's heart. This scheme was the proposed bequest of Impressionist paintings owned by Hugh Lane, a nephew of Yeats's patron, Lady Gregory, to the city of Dublin, provided that the city would fund a gallery to house the paintings. The idea of the bequest foundered as it met strong opposition. Yeats regarded this opposition as representative of a penny-counting, religiously servile materialism. The poem contrasts such materialism with the heroic recklessness of patriotic figures from Irish history. It combines a ballad-like lament for 'Romantic Ireland' with an ironic sharpness, shown in the words that Yeats gives his opponents in the final stanza, where they are imagined ascribing, with typical small-mindedness, the patriots' fervour to love of women. Though the irony is at his opponents' expense, there is a hint that their brutal simplification may have an element of truth, and the poem has an undertow of saddened acceptance that 'Romantic' visions of Ireland are, indeed, 'dead and gone'.

---

1   Yeats plays a variation on the proverbial 'shutting the stable-door after the horse has bolted'; he is anxious that the horse should bolt.

What need you, being come to sense,[1]
But fumble in a greasy till
And add the halfpence to the pence
And prayer to shivering prayer, until
You have dried the marrow from the bone?   5
For men were born to pray and save:[2]
Romantic Ireland's dead and gone,
It's with O'Leary[3] in the grave.

Yet they were of a different kind,
The names that stilled your childish play,   10
They have gone about the world like wind,
But little time had they to pray
For whom the hangman's rope was spun,
And what, God help us, could they save?[4]
Romantic Ireland's dead and gone,   15
It's with O'Leary in the grave.

Was it for this the wild geese[5] spread
The grey wing upon every tide;
For this that all that blood was shed,
For this Edward Fitzgerald[6] died,   20
And Robert Emmet and Wolfe Tone,[7]
All that delirium of the brave?[8]
Romantic Ireland's dead and gone,
It's with O'Leary in the grave.
Yet could we turn the years again,   25
And call those exiles as they were
In all their loneliness and pain,
You'd cry, 'Some woman's yellow hair
Has maddened every mother's son':

1   Highly ironic; 'sense' is used to mean awareness of self-interest.
2   Again the tone is ironic.
3   John O'Leary (1830–1907), a Fenian (revolutionary nationalist) leader imprisoned for years, much
    admired by Yeats.
4   The need to rhyme with the refrain's rhyme-word ('grave') is used to poignant effect here as Yeats
    contrasts the inability of past heroes to 'save' (possibly implying the doomed nature of their
    heroism) with a modern generation that saves by heaping coins.
5   After the Penal Laws of 1691, which prevented many Irishmen from being commissioned in the
    British army, many Irish soldiers went abroad to serve in European armies; they were known as
    'wild geese'.
6   Irish patriot (1763–98); died during the uprising of 1798.
7   Robert Emmet (1778–1803) was executed after leading an uprising against the English; Wolfe Tone
    was an Irish patriot (1763–98) who died (probably at his own hand) after the uprising of 1798,
    which he led, failed.
8   'Delirium' is double-edged, and implies a qualifying judgement.

They weighed so lightly what they gave.   30
But let them be, they're dead and gone,
They're with O'Leary in the grave.[9]

Paudeen

Composed in September 1913; first published in *Poems Written in Discouragement* (1913); published in *Responsibilities* (1914). The poem, made up of eight
alexandrines (twelve-syllable lines) rhyming *ababcdcd*, illustrates Yeats's ability
to make poetry out of transcended emotion. He begins with scorn for the
Catholic middle-class (referred to as 'Paudeen', a derogatory form of 'Patrick'),
but he ends with a vision of the sacred value of every soul. The poem's movement is from the 'blind' stumbling of the second line to the 'luminous' revelation
in nature of the close. The final vision is private and offered almost as a random
speculation ('suddenly thereupon *I* thought'), but Yeats's rhythms make powerful his glimpse of inclusiveness ('where *all* are in God's eye') (emphases added).
In a poem concerned with 'confusion of our sound', sound effects are important
and reinforce the climbing out of one state into another, as is shown by the
repeated use of the *u* sound that runs through 'fumbling', 'stumbled', 'under',
and 'Until', before the sound sweetens into the *oo* sound of the 'u' in 'luminous'
and 'confusion'.

Indignant at the fumbling wits, the obscure spite
Of our old Paudeen in his shop, I stumbled blind
Among the stones and thorn-trees, under morning light;
Until a curlew cried and in the luminous wind
A curlew answered; and suddenly thereupon I thought   5
That on the lonely height where all are in God's eye,
There cannot be, confusion of our sound forgot,
A single soul that lacks a sweet crystalline cry.[1]

---

9   The switch from 'It's' to 'They're' means that 'Romantic Ireland' now refers to the outlook and
    deeds of particular dead heroes. By identifying 'Romantic Ireland' with particular heroes, Yeats
    leaves open the possibility that the emergence of new heroes will resurrect the lost ideal. Precisely
    such a resurrection would occur in the Easter Rising.

1   The line has the greater impact for being held back by the complex syntax that precedes it: there is
    an effect of release and clarity.

Fallen Majesty

Composed in 1912; first published in *Poetry* (Chicago) in 1912; published in *Responsibilities* (1914). Another poem written in alexandrines, which Yeats manages to use in a way that is simultaneously majestic and conversationally wry, 'Fallen Majesty' records the middle-aged poet's movingly complex response to the effect of time on Maud Gonne. Attention is drawn to his own role as poet-recorder; only through 'this hand alone', engaged in memorializing, can the fact of 'fallen majesty' be evoked. Paradoxically, the act of recording 'what's gone' allows the reader to glimpse Maud's former grandeur as though it were still present.

Although crowds gathered once if she but showed her face,
And even old men's eyes grew dim, this hand alone,
Like some last courtier at a gypsy camping-place
Babbling of fallen majesty, records what's gone.

The lineaments, a heart that laughter has made sweet,   5
These, these remain, but I record what's gone. A crowd
Will gather,[1] and not know it walks the very street
Whereon a thing once walked that seemed a burning cloud.[2]

The Cold Heaven

First published in *The Green Helmet and Other Poems* (1912 edition); published in *Responsibilities* (1914). The poem is about a vision of impassioned guilt triggered by the sight of a wintry sky. It is written in twelve alexandrines and rhyming *ababcdcdefef* (each quatrain containing a feminine rhyme). The poem opens with the word 'Suddenly', crucial to the revelation in 'Paudeen'. In 'The Cold Heaven' the adverb ushers in a storm of feelings that rages through the poem's two sentences. Overwhelmed by 'memories' of his past, the poet is 'Riddled with light'. The experience is both devastating ('riddled' as with bullets) and mysteriously illuminating ('riddled' as in posed a riddle). When Yeats says that he 'took the blame out of all sense and reason', he means two things: that he took more blame on himself than is demanded by sense and reason; and that he took the blame because of a sense of guilt that cannot be comprehended by sense and reason. This second meaning takes the poem beyond the world of 'sense' into a

---

1   Recalls, but contrasts with, the 'gathered' of line 1.
2   'Thing' has the effect of capturing the woman's refusal to be described in ordinary human terms because of her quasi-mythical beauty and force.

world of ultimate laws governing human beings. Yeats asks whether, after death, the quickening ghost (a consciously riddling phrase since 'quicken' is associated with the living) is 'sent/Out naked on the roads' 'for punishment'. Has his experience foreshadowed what happens after death, a fate decreed by 'the injustice of the skies'? The poem is a masterpiece of compression and speed as it moves from recognizable experience to occult speculation; the exclamation 'Ah!' that bridges the two sentences allows for a brief breathing space and is the signal for the dawning within the poet of his experience's possible implications. Yeats continually throws us off-balance. For example, to use the phrase 'Confusion of the death-bed over', is to see death as merely an interim 'Confusion' between lives, and yet there is no joy or exultation in that view.

Suddenly I saw the cold and rook-delighting[1] heaven
That seemed as though ice burned and was but the more ice,
And thereupon imagination and heart were driven
So wild that every casual thought of that and this
Vanished, and left but memories, that should be out of season   5
With the hot blood of youth, of love crossed long ago;
And I took all the blame out of all sense and reason,
Until I cried and trembled and rocked to and fro,
Riddled with light. Ah! when the ghost begins to quicken,
Confusion of the death-bed over, is it sent   10
Out naked on the roads, as the books say, and stricken
By the injustice of the skies for punishment?

The Wild Swans at Coole

First published in *The Little Review* in 1917; published in *The Wild Swans at Coole* (1917, 1919). The poem is set in Coole Park, County Galway, home of Lady Gregory, who served as patron and friend to Yeats. It is an elegiac poem about loss and change, and it focuses on one of Yeats's favourite images, the swan. In the first printing the order of the stanzas was 1, 2, 5, 3, 4: possibly a more pessimistic ordering since the poem initially ended with the poet's sense that 'All's changed'. In the poem the swans are 'brilliant creatures' who represent the possibility of 'Unwearied' passion, of 'hearts' that 'have not grown old'. They also suggest the notion of an order beyond the poet, and yet the 'rings' (an image of completeness) in which they 'scatter' are 'broken'. At the poem's close Yeats covertly makes the swans into permanent embodiments of feeling and

---

1   The word conveys the poet's own remoteness from 'delight'.

inspiration, who will 'Delight' other 'men's eyes' after they have deserted his. That this desertion is imagined as being noticed when 'I awake some day' suggest that the poet is currently in the grip of sleep or dream: perhaps the sleep or dream of youthful poetic fulfilment or obsession. Throughout, the poem works through understatement and implication. The mirroring of the first stanza suggests harmony, but also indicates a parallel between 'autumn beauty' and the poet's 'autumnal' emotional state, a parallel brought out in the second stanza's first line. Again, the use of the word 'still' draws us in to look closely at the poetry's moods. In the first stanza the sky is 'still', a quiet broken by the 'clamorous wings' recalled in the second stanza. The swans are 'Unwearied still' (they are not yet wearied) in the fourth stanza, and in the same stanza's last two lines, 'still' also works as an adverb, here meaning 'now as before', a use that stresses the imperviousness to time of the swans. In the very next line, the first of the final stanza, Yeats reverts to the adjectival use of the word as 'they drift on the still water'; this dance of 'still's grows mesmeric, but makes us aware that the poet's feelings are 'unstill' and that he is not what he was before, despite his careful attention to and 'counting' of the swans. The poem is written in five six-line stanzas of alternating four- and three-stress lines rhyming *abcbdd*, a scheme suited to the poem's hesitant approach towards explicit assertion.

The trees are in their autumn beauty,
The woodland paths are dry,
Under the October twilight the water
Mirrors a still sky;
Upon the brimming water among the stones   5
Are nine-and-fifty swans.[1]

The nineteenth autumn has come upon me
Since I first made my count;
I saw, before I had well finished,
All suddenly mount   10
And scatter wheeling in great broken rings
Upon their clamorous wings.

I have looked upon those brilliant creatures,
And now my heart is sore.
All's changed since I, hearing at twilight,   15
The first time on this shore,
The bell-beat of their wings above my head,
Trod with a lighter tread.

1   That the number is an odd number means that the swans, too, must experience incompletion; they cannot all paddle 'lover by lover'.

Unwearied still, lover by lover,
They paddle in the cold   20
Companionable streams or climb the air;
Their hearts have not grown old;
Passion or conquest, wander where they will,
Attend upon them still.

But now they drift on the still water,   25
Mysterious, beautiful;
Among what rushes will they build,
By what lake's edge or pool
Delight men's eyes when I awake some day
To find they have flown away?   30

In Memory of Major Robert Gregory

First published in the *English Review* in August 1918; published in *The Wild Swans at Coole* (1919 edition). This elegy was written about Lady Gregory's son, Major Robert Gregory (1881–1918), who died in action on the Italian front (shot down in error by an Italian pilot) on 23 January 1918. One of four such elegies (the others are 'An Irish Airman Foresees his Death', the bitter 'Reprisals', and 'Shepherd and Goatherd'), it seeks to celebrate the range of Gregory's activities and to represent him as a person who blended apparent opposites, unlike the friends about whom Yeats talks first of all. It is written in a stanza borrowed from the metaphysical poet Abraham Cowley, which consists of eight lines rhyming *aabbcddc*, with pentameters (five-feet lines) in lines 1, 2, 3, 5 and 8, and tetrameters (four-feet lines) in lines 4, 6 and 7; a roomy, shifting stanza suited to meditation, the rise and fall of thought and feeling. It is no accident that the poem begins by discussing intimacy (Yeats alludes to his recent setting-up of house with Georgie Hyde-Lees whom he had married in October 1917) and friendship. Yeats compares and contrasts the different talents and inclinations of his friends, building up a set of contrasts: Lionel Johnson, the Decadent poet, is seen as preferring 'learning' to 'mankind'; John Synge, though 'dying', focused on 'the living world'; George Pollexfen, 'muscular' in his youth, chose occult speculation in later years. Gregory is represented as harmoniously synthesizing apparent opposites, a modern-day Renaissance man like Sir Philip Sidney. In the midst of eulogy, however, Yeats concedes an element of overstatement. In stanza IX, for example, he asserts, 'We dreamed that a great painter had been born', where 'dreamed' contains hints of fantasy and hope. The same stanza concludes with an apparently indeterminate tense: 'he had the intensity' momentarily suggests that Gregory's intensity was such that he did publish 'all to be a world's delight', before the true meaning becomes clear: he had such intensity that he would or might have published all to be a world's delight. In

suggesting that Gregory had access to 'that stern colour and that delicate line/ That are our secret discipline', Yeats comes close to describing his own achievement in this and other poems of the period. Indeed, an unspoken contrast exists between the poet and his elegized friend. If Gregory is like someone who consumes 'The entire combustible world', the poet is more like one who burns 'damp faggots'. Gregory's potential was so great that the poet retrospectively wonders, in an emotion-filled question, 'What made us dream that he could comb grey hair?' The elegy concludes with a typical – and highly affecting – subversion of the poem's apparent course. Yeats says that he had meant to work towards some 'fitter welcome', but that his plan has broken down as a result of 'a thought/Of that late death'.

I

Now that we're almost settled in our house[1]
I'll name the friends that cannot sup with us
Beside a fire of turf in th' ancient tower,
And having talked to some late hour
Climb up the narrow winding stair[2] to bed: 5
Discoverers of forgotten truth
Or mere companions of my youth,
All, all are in my thoughts to-night being dead.

II

Always we'd have the new friend meet the old
And we are hurt if either friend seem cold,   10
And there is salt to lengthen out the smart
In the affections of our heart,
And quarrels are blown up upon that head;
But not a friend that I would bring
This night can set us quarrelling,   15
For all that come into my mind are dead.

III

Lionel Johnson[3] comes the first to mind,
That loved his learning better than mankind,
Though courteous to the worst; much falling he

1   Thoor Ballylee, the Norman tower in County Galway that Yeats bought in 1917.
2   Staircase at the centre of the house; becomes a central symbol for Yeats.
3   Scholarly poet (1867–1902) whom Yeats knew through the Rhymers' Club (founded in 1891); dissipated his talent (so Yeats thought) through alcoholism brought on by despair.

Brooded upon sanctity 20
Till all his Greek and Latin learning seemed
A long blast upon the horn that brought
A little nearer to his thought
A measureless consummation that he dreamed.

IV

And that enquiring man John Synge[4] comes next, 25
That dying chose the living world for text
And never could have rested in the tomb
But that, long travelling, he had come
Towards nightfall upon certain set apart
In a most desolate stony place, 30
Towards nightfall upon a race
Passionate and simple like his heart.

V

And then I think of old George Pollexfen,[5]
In muscular youth well known to Mayo men
For horsemanship at meets or at racecourses, 35
That could have shown how pure-bred horses
And solid men, for all their passion, live
But as the outrageous stars incline
By opposition, square and trine;[6]
Having grown sluggish and contemplative. 40

VI

They were my close companions many a year,
A portion of my mind and life, as it were,
And now their breathless faces seem to look
Out of some old picture-book;
I am accustomed to their lack of breath, 45
But not that my dear friend's dear son,

---

4 Playwright (1871–1909), whose plays, staged by the Abbey Theatre, caused controversy (especially
   The Playboy of the Western World). Yeats saw him as a major collaborator in the task of developing a specifically Irish theatre, and placed him in Phase 23 in *A Vision*, where he writes of the
   impact on Synge of the Aran Islands (the 'most desolate stony place' of stanza IV): 'He had to
   undergo an aesthetic transformation, analogous to religious conversion, before he became the
   audacious, joyous, ironical man we know', *A Vision* (1937), London: Macmillan, 1962, p. 167.
5 Yeats's uncle (1839–1910), an astrologer.
6 Astrological terms defining the angle between heavenly bodies in relation to the earth: respectively,
   180, 90 and 120 degrees.

Our Sidney and our perfect man,
Could share in that discourtesy of death.[7]

VII

For all things the delighted eye now sees
Were loved by him: the old storm-broken trees   50
That cast their shadows upon road and bridge;
The tower set on the stream's edge;
The ford where drinking cattle make a stir
Nightly, and startled by that sound
The water-hen must change her ground;   55
He might have been your heartiest welcomer.

VIII

When with the Galway foxhounds he would ride
From Castle Taylor to the Roxborough[8] side
Or Esserkelly[9] plain, few kept his pace;
At Mooneen[10] he had leaped a place   60
So perilous that half the astonished meet
Had shut their eyes; and where was it
He rode a race without a bit?
And yet his mind outran the horses' feet.

IX

We dreamed that a great painter had been born   65
To cold Clare rock and Galway rock and thorn,
To that stern colour and that delicate line
That are our secret discipline
Wherein the gazing heart doubles her might.
Soldier, scholar, horseman, he,   70
And yet he had the intensity
To have published all to be a world's delight.

---

7   Yeats employs a courtly euphemism to capture Robert Gregory's high breeding, nonchalance and
    courage.
8   The estate where Lady Gregory grew up.
9   Near Ardrahan, County Galway.
10 Near Esserkelly.

X

What other could so well have counselled us
In all lovely intricacies of a house
As he that practised or that understood   75
All work in metal or in wood,
In moulded plaster or in carven stone?
Soldier, scholar, horseman, he,
And all he did done perfectly
As though he had but that one trade alone.   80

XI

Some burn damp faggots, others may consume
The entire combustible world in one small room
As though dried straw, and if we turn about
The bare chimney is gone black out
Because the work had finished in that flare.   85
Soldier, scholar, horseman, he,
As 'twere all life's epitome.
What made us dream that he could comb grey hair?

XII

I had thought, seeing how bitter is that wind
That shakes the shutter, to have brought to mind   90
All those that manhood tried, or childhood loved
Or boyish intellect approved,
With some appropriate commentary on each;
Until imagination brought
A fitter welcome; but a thought   95
Of that late death took all my heart for speech.

The Fisherman

Composed in June 1914; first published in *Poetry* (Chicago) in 1916; published in *The Wild Swans at Coole* (1917, 1919). Written in trimeters (three-feet lines), rhyming its quatrains *abab*, the poem takes as subject the imagining of an ideal audience. Yeats conceives of his ideal reader as 'A man who does not exist, / A man who is but a dream', lines that speak eloquently of his disillusion with actual audiences. The fisherman is a figure of the people and yet, set apart in his 'grey Connemara clothes' from the 'living men that I hate', he is also akin to what Yeats calls the 'anti-self' (see Contemporary Documents, **pp. 24, 35**),

representing a 'dream' of simplicity and oneness with the land that differs wholly from the poet's tortured complexities of feeling and attitude. Yeats uses his short lines to great effect, achieving conciseness of phrase throughout, as when he speaks of his desire 'To write for my own race'. Simplification coexists with complexity in this line and elsewhere: 'my own race' must contend with the fact, spelled out in ensuing lines, that Yeats was at odds with many people in his culture because of their insolence, knavery, cheap wit and brutal treatment of 'great Art'; 'the reality' of the next line turns out to be the unlovely 'reality' of modern Ireland. The poem uses unwinding syntax and long sentences in co-ordinated tension with its short lines and bare diction. We realize, from the opening, that the poem is engaged in a re-conjuring up of a figure who has been visible to the mind's eye for some while. The use of 'maybe' in the opening and closing lines of the second verse-paragraph also signals that 'The Fisherman' is about the process and work of imagination.

Although I can see him still,
The freckled man who goes
To a grey place on a hill
In grey Connemara[1] clothes
At dawn to cast his flies,   5
It's long since I began
To call up to the eyes
This wise and simple man.
All day I'd looked in the face
What I had hoped 'twould be   10
To write for my own race
And the reality;
The living men that I hate,
The dead man[2] that I loved,
The craven man in his seat,   15
The insolent unreproved,
And no knave brought to book
Who has won a drunken cheer,
The witty man and his joke
Aimed at the commonest ear,   20
The clever man who cries
The catch-cries of the clown,
The beating down of the wise
And great Art beaten down.

Maybe a twelvemonth since   25
Suddenly I began,

---

1   A relatively desolate and unpopulated part of the west of Ireland.
2   Possibly John Millington Synge.

In scorn of this audience,
Imagining a man,
And his sun-freckled face,
And grey Connemara cloth,   30
Climbing up to a place
Where stone is dark under froth,
And the down-turn of his wrist
When the flies drop in the stream;
A man who does not exist,   35
A man who is but a dream;
And cried, 'Before I am old
I shall have written him one
Poem maybe as cold
And passionate as the dawn.'   .   40

Broken Dreams

Composed in 1915; first published in *The Little Review* in 1915; published in *The Wild Swans at Coole* (1917, 1919). Written in an artfully casual form that imitates the poet's 'rambling talk with an image of air', 'Broken Dreams' describes Maud Gonne's ageing and the poet's sense of himself as 'stubborn with his passion', seeking to lament but also to celebrate and reaffirm. Indeed, lament passes into celebration and acknowledgement of the persistence of passion. Yeats accepts loss, but he also resists it with his desperate conviction that 'in the grave all, all, shall be renewed'. Yeats is again preoccupied with his role as poet, and he comes close to defining the poem's way of working when he says, 'From dream to dream and rhyme to rhyme I have ranged'. The poem's rhymes occur as if by chance, as Yeats ranges between loss, reaffirmation, reverie and 'Vague memories, nothing but memories' (a refrain-like line repeated three times), a vagueness offset by the precision with which he recalls the redeeming imperfection of Maud's 'hands'.

There is grey in your hair.
Young men no longer suddenly catch their breath
When you are passing;
But maybe some old gaffer mutters a blessing
Because it was your prayer   5
Recovered him upon the bed of death.
For your sole sake—that all heart's ache have known,
And given to others all heart's ache,
From meagre girlhood's putting on
Burdensome beauty—for your sole sake   10
Heaven has put away the stroke of her doom,

So great her portion in that peace you make
By merely walking in a room.

Your beauty can but leave among us
Vague memories, nothing but memories.   15
A young man when the old men are done talking
Will say to an old man, 'Tell me of that lady
The poet stubborn with his passion sang us
When age might well have chilled his blood.'

Vague memories, nothing but memories,   20
But in the grave all, all, shall be renewed.
The certainty that I shall see that lady
Leaning or standing or walking
In the first loveliness of womanhood,
And with the fervour of my youthful eyes,   25
Has set me muttering like a fool.

You are more beautiful than any one,
And yet your body had a flaw:
Your small hands were not beautiful,
And I am afraid that you will run   30
And paddle to the wrist
In that mysterious, always brimming lake[1]
Where those that have obeyed the holy law[2]
Paddle and are perfect. Leave unchanged
The hands that I have kissed,   35
For old sake's sake.

The last stroke of midnight dies.
All day in the one chair
From dream to dream and rhyme to rhyme I have ranged
In rambling talk with an image of air: 40
Vague memories, nothing but memories.

---

1   A lake whose waters can make perfect, much like the river in which Thetis dipped Achilles; only his
    heel, not immersed, was vulnerable. Yeats asked Maud not to dip her hands into the lake; he prefers
    that her one imperfection should remain.
2   The phrasing suggests that Maud will be permitted to 'paddle' in the lake because she has 'obeyed
    the holy law'.

Ego Dominus Tuus

Completed in 1915; first published in *Poetry* (Chicago) in 1917; published in *The Wild Swans at Coole* (1917, 1919). This dialogue poem in blank verse is among the clearest expositions of Yeats's emerging system and reflects his thinking about the mask and anti-self in *Per Amica Silentia Lunae* (see Contemporary Documents, **pp. 25–7**). The two speakers – '*Hic*' and '*Ille*' (Latin for 'this one' and 'that one') – take opposing views. *Ille* looks for an anti-self, some form of being that is not merely the mirror of his self; 'I call', he says, 'to my own opposite, summon all / That I have handled least, least looked upon'. *Hic* 'would find myself and not an image', a view criticised by *Ille* as responsible for a modern loss of creative nerve, of 'the old nonchalance of the hand'. They debate the case of Dante; for *Hic*, Dante's art is one of self-expression; for *Ille*, Dante's art compensates in its vision of austerity, justice and exalted love for the miseries of the poet's life: it does not express Dante, but a vision 'fashioned from his opposite', and is thus an instance of the 'tragic war' that *Ille* sees as central to creativity. At the poem's heart is the diagnosis by *Ille* of the nature of 'art': said to be 'a vision of reality', opposed alike to rhetoric and sentimentality. 'Vision' reminds us that the artist must engage in shaping a way of seeing the real. The title refers to a remark made by Love to Dante in the latter's *Vita Nuova* and means, 'I, thy lord': the 'lord' for *Ille* is 'the mysterious one' of the last lines. The poem, though expository, is far more than mere exposition, as the evocativeness of the conclusion shows. It has affinities with two other 'doctrinal' poems in the 1919 edition of *The Wild Swans at Coole*, 'The Phases of the Moon' and 'The Double Vision of Michael Robartes', each of which sets out the scheme later developed in *A Vision*.

Hic. On the grey sand beside the shallow stream
Under your old wind-beaten tower, where still
A lamp burns on beside the open book
That Michael Robartes[1] left, you walk in the moon,
And, though you have passed the best of life, still trace,⠀⠀⠀⠀⠀5
Enthralled by the unconquerable delusion,
Magical shapes.

Ille.⠀⠀⠀⠀⠀⠀⠀By the help of an image
I call to my own opposite, summon all
That I have handled least, least looked upon.

Hic. And I would find myself and not an image.⠀⠀⠀⠀⠀10

1⠀⠀See headnote to 'The Hosting of the Sidhe' (**p. 103**); represents the imagination's self-confidence. Robartes is an esoteric speculator, a mage.

Ille. That is our modern hope, and by its light
We have lit upon the gentle, sensitive mind
And lost the old nonchalance of the hand;
Whether we have chosen chisel, pen or brush,
We are but critics,[2] or but half create,   15
Timid, entangled, empty and abashed,
Lacking the countenance of our friends.

Hic.   And yet
The chief imagination of Christendom,
Dante Alighieri, so utterly found himself
That he has made that hollow face of his   20
More plain to the mind's eye than any face
But that of Christ.

Ille.   And did he find himself
Or was the hunger that had made it hollow
A hunger for the apple on the bough
Most out of reach?[3] and is that spectral image   25
The man that Lapo and that Guido knew?[4]
I think he fashioned from his opposite
An image that might have been a stony face
Staring upon a Bedouin's horse-hair roof
From doored and windowed cliff, or half upturned   30
Among the coarse grass and the camel-dung.
He set his chisel to the hardest stone.
Being mocked by Guido for his lecherous life,
Derided and deriding, driven out
To climb that stair and eat that bitter bread,   35
He found the unpersuadable justice, he found
The most exalted lady[5] loved by a man.

Hic. Yet surely there are men who have made their art
Out of no tragic war, lovers of life,
Impulsive men that look for happiness   40
And sing when they have found it.

---

2   Here Yeats shares with his successor Samuel Beckett (in whose play *Waiting for Godot* 'critic' is the
    most withering term of abuse) a view of criticism as essentially non-creative. This is not to deny
    that Yeats (like Beckett) is himself a gifted critic, and, arguably, the most 'creative' lines in 'Ego
    Dominus Tuus' are forms of criticism (of Dante and Keats).
3   In 'Anima Hominis', Yeats suggest that the anti-self, contact with whom establishes creative power,
    'is of all things not impossible the most difficult, for that only which comes easily can never be a
    portion of our being' (**p. 25**).
4   Friends of Dante, Lapo Gianni and Guido Cavalcanti. Yeats would have known Shelley's 'Sonnet.
    From the Italian of Dante Alighieri to Guido Cavalcanti', which begins, 'Guido, I would that
    Lappo, thou and I'.
5   Beatrice.

Ille.   No, not sing,
For those that love the world serve it in action,
Grow rich, popular and full of influence,
And should they paint or write, still it is action:
The struggle of the fly in marmalade.   45
The rhetorician would deceive his neighbours,
The sentimentalist himself; while art
Is but a vision of reality.[6]
What portion in the world can the artist have
Who has awakened from the common dream   50
But dissipation and despair?

Hic.   And yet
No one denies to Keats love of the world;
Remember his deliberate happiness.

Ille. His art is happy, but who knows his mind?
I see a schoolboy when I think of him,   55
With face and nose pressed to a sweet-shop window,
For certainly he sank into his grave
His senses and his heart unsatisfied,
And made—being poor, ailing and ignorant,
Shut out from all the luxury of the world,   60
The coarse-bred son of a livery-stable keeper—
Luxuriant song.

Hic.   Why should you leave the lamp
Burning alone beside an open book,
And trace these characters upon the sands?
A style is found by sedentary toil   65
And by the imitation of great masters.

Ille. Because I seek an image, not a book.[7]
Those men that in their writings are most wise
Own nothing but their blind, stupefied hearts.
I call to the mysterious one who yet   70
Shall walk the wet sands by the edge of the stream
And look most like me, being indeed my double,
And prove of all imaginable things
The most unlike, being my anti-self,

---

6   Yeats is not advocating 'realism'; he is saying that an artist must pursue a vision (involving the
    enlargement of self that comes through imagining the anti-self) of what the 'real' is; the poem
    strongly implies that such a vision must be tragic.
7   *Ille* does not locate creativity in imitation of past masters, but in the quest for an image that gives
    form to the self. The line plays a variation on *Hic*'s 'I would find myself and not an image'. It is
    noticeable that *Hic* 'would find', whereas *Ille*, a continual questor, sets himself to 'seek'.

And, standing by these characters, disclose   75
All that I seek; and whisper it as though
He were afraid the birds, who cry aloud
Their momentary cries before it is dawn,
Would carry it away to blasphemous men.

Easter 1916

Composed between May and September 1916; first published in a private printing in 1916; published in the *New Statesman* in 1920, and in *Michael Robartes and
the Dancer* (1921). 'Easter 1916' commemorates the Easter Rising of 24 April
1916, when members (about 1,600) of the Irish Republican Brotherhood under
the leadership of Patrick Pearse rose against British rule of Ireland. They issued
a Proclamation setting up 'the Provisional Goverment of the Irish Republic', and
took over several major buildings in Dublin, especially the GPO. After fierce
fighting, they were defeated by the British army. Fifteen of those who took part
in the Rising were executed in May 1916. Mentioning the poem and its theme of
'terrible beauty', Yeats wrote on 11 May to Lady Gregory: 'I had no idea that any
public event could so move me – and I am very despondent about the future. At
the moment I feel all the work of years has been overturned, all the bringing
together of classes, all the freeing of Irish literature and criticism from politics.'[1]
Some commentators have seen in Yeats's refusal to publish the work immediately a self-serving canniness. But the poem is remarkable for its intelligence and
honesty. If it describes the passage from 'casual comedy' (l. 37) to 'terrible
beauty' brought about by the revolutionaries' actions, its attitude towards its
revolutionaries blends conscious mythologizing with deep reservation. The
stone-like commitment of the revolutionaries repudiates the minute-by-minute
changeableness of life evoked in the central section, and threatens to make a
sacrifice of the heart. The movement of the poem's trimeters, falling into quatrains rhyming *abab*, is powerful, but never facile or glib. The poem's rhyming is
notable for the way it sustains a troubled balance between off-rhymes and true
rhymes.

The poem is composed of four verse-paragraphs. In the first Yeats speaks of
having met the rebels and of exchanging with them 'polite meaningless words'
(ll. 6, 8), a phrase repeated to emphasize the meaninglessness of their conversation; Yeats's certainty then was that they all lived 'where motley is worn' (l. 14),
in an Ireland providing matter only for irony and derision, but now that perception, along with everything else, is 'changed, changed utterly' (l. 15), and the
paragraph concludes with the first use of the refrain-like line, 'A terrible beauty
is born' (l. 16): a line that shifts in nuance. Here it may be that the reader will

---

1   Allan Wade (ed.), *The Letters of W. B. Yeats*, London: Hart-Davis, 1954, p. 613.

stress 'beauty'. But at the end of the second paragraph one may well pick out 'terrible' (l. 40) and give both words equal weight in the poem's last line. In the second section, Yeats offers judgements on four of the Rising's leaders, and then goes on to say that they have been not only 'changed' but 'Transformed utterly' (ll. 38, 39). Experience has taken on a new and tragic form. The third section switches from overt judgement to description and metaphor; its meditation on the 'living stream' (l. 44) troubled by a 'stone' (l. 43) allows Yeats to evoke the value of the natural world as it 'Changes minute by minute' (l. 50). The passage implies that such changeableness is at odds with heroic transformation. The final section first spells out the meaning of the 'stone', seen as corresponding to a life of 'sacrifice' (l. 57) in service of a cause, such as revolutionary change. Then, working through a series of questions, the section articulates the poet's feelings of admiration and reservation, before concluding with a naming of the Rising's leaders and commemoration of their significance for Irish history. Yeats memorializes them as mythic heroes, but his poetry counts the cost of such mythic memorializing. Maud Gonne was unimpressed by the poem's vacillations, writing to Yeats, 'No I don't like your poem, it isn't worthy of you & above all it isn't worthy of the subject . . . sacrifice has never yet turned a heart to stone though it has immortalised many & through it alone mankind can rise to God' (see **p. 35**). For a reading of the poem that stresses how 'The events are [. . .] presented with an ambiguity which does justice to their complexity', see C. K. Stead's essay in Modern Criticism (**p. 65**).

Notes to the Poem

l. 14.   *motley.* Associated with a jester's particoloured dress; a symbol of folly and comedy.
l. 17.   *That woman's days.* Con Markievicz (1868–1927), née Gore-Booth; sentenced to death for her part in the Rising; her sentence was commuted to imprisonment. See Yeats's 'In Memory of Eva Gore-Booth and Con Markiewicz'.
l. 24.   *This man had kept a school.* Patrick Pearse (1879–1916) had established a boy's school.
l. 25.   *our wingèd horse.* Pegasus. Compare the later use of horse imagery ('The horse that comes from the road', l. 45), where the horse is associated with the mutable vitality of everyday life.
l. 26.   *This other.* Thomas MacDonagh (1878–1916), poet and critic.
l. 31.   *This other man.* John MacBride, who married Maud Gonne in 1901, to Yeats's dismay.
l. 34.   *some who are near my heart.* Maud Gonne and her daughter, Iseult.
l. 38.   *been changed.* It is as though MacBride and the others have been worked on by a tragic destiny over which they had only limited control.
l. 68.   *England may keep faith.* England might fulfil its promise, made in 1913 but

suspended in 1914 with the outbreak of the First World War, to pass a Bill granting Ireland Home Rule.

II. 72–3.   And what . . . died? All the poem's tensions come to a head in this final question: 'what if' both dismisses and entertains doubt; 'Bewildered' exonerates from blame (it is no one's fault to be 'Bewildered') even as it implies confusion; if the rebels were guilty of 'excess', it was an 'excess of love'.

I. 76.   Connolly. James Connolly (1870–1916), trade-union leader. Commandant General of the Rising's forces.

I. 80.   born. The poem is concerned with a birth – the birth of tragic beauty.

25 September 1916.   This date, attached to the poem, makes us acutely aware of the poem's concern with time: time is involved in change on the one hand, as minute follows minute, but, on the other hand, the rebels have entered a realm of permanence: 'Now and in time to be', their actions have given rise to a 'terrible beauty'.

The Second Coming

Composed in 1919; first published in *The Dial* in 1920; published in *Michael Robartes and the Dancer* (1921). Like 'Easter 1916', the poem is concerned with a birth, this time the birth of a new era symbolized by the 'rough beast' (l. 21). The poem can be understood without knowledge of Yeats's 'system', but it serves to articulate with great power and some ambivalence the historical views set out in *A Vision*. A key term here is 'gyre', found in the first line, and used by Yeats to describe the spinning circular motion made by a cone, a spiralling vortex. The gyre is the 'principal symbol' of Yeats's system in *A Vision*.[1] More precisely, it is the image of two interpenetrating cones or gyres that constitute the essence of his understanding of personality, culture and history. 'The apex of each vortex' is, he writes, 'in the middle of the other's base', and this interlocking image is his 'fundamental symbol'[2], applicable to the opposition between 'subjective' and 'objective' people and eras, and suited perfectly to his view that poetry emerges from conflict. So, when the falcon turns 'in the widening gyre' (l. 1), Yeats describes the widening or ending of one gyre's movement, and implies the narrowing or beginning of the interlocking, opposed gyre. In historical terms, this means that as he imagines the end of one era, an ending accompanied by portents of catastrophe and chaos, he imagines, too, the ushering in of a new era. In a note in *Michael Robartes and the Dancer* (1921), Yeats wrote: 'All our scientific, democratic, fact-accumulating, heterogeneous civilization belongs to the outward gyre and prepares not the continuance of itself but the revelation as in

---

1   *A Vision* (1937), London: Macmillan, 1962, p. 67.
2   Ibid., p. 68.

a lightning flash . . . of the civilization that must slowly take its place'. This 'revelation' is the 'second coming', a phrase violently wrenched from its usual meaning of Christ's return to establish a heaven on earth, and made, rather, to describe the onset of a civilization or 'anti-civilisation'[3] founded on terrifying violence. Initially, as Jon Stallworthy's essay in Modern Criticism (**pp. 55–62**) reveals, Yeats anchored the poem in the aftermath of the First World War. Stallworthy argues that studies of the poem's manuscripts 'show how large a part the world situation of 1918–19 played in its conception and growth' (**p. 55**). In an early draft the poem began, 'The gyres grow wider and more wide / The hawk can no more hear the falconer / The germans to Russia to the place' (**p. 56**), alluding to the invasion of Russia by Germany in 1917–18. But Yeats's revisions untether the poem from the details of a specific time and place, and result in an imaginative vision of the breakdown of civilization. Central to the poem's effectiveness is its use of a jagged blank verse that moves from analysis in the first verse-paragraph to imagining in the second. In the first paragraph, the poet may record how 'Things fall apart; the centre cannot hold' (l. 3), but his voice is diagnostic and in control. In the second paragraph the poet no longer has an analyst's calm authority. Here, as he senses the onset of 'revelation' (l. 9), he is a medium for the 'vast image' that emerges out of '*Spiritus Mundi*' (l. 12) to haunt him, an image whose meaning he in part claims to 'know' (l. 18), yet whose full implications stir him to conclude – yet again – with a question. A disturbing aspect of the poem is that although Yeats conveys the menace of the 'rough beast', he, in effect, dismisses the Christian era as only 'twenty centuries of stony sleep' (l. 19). History condenses into a stark opposition between 'stony sleep' and imminent 'nightmare' (l. 20).

Notes to the Poem

l. 2.   *falcon . . . falconer*. Have been interpreted, respectively, as 'modern civilization' and 'Christ'; see A. Norman Jeffares (ed.), *Yeats's Poems* (1989), revised edn, London: Macmillan, 1991, p. 574.

l. 11.   *Hardly are those words out*. The poem's experience is literally catalysed by its own words, giving it grim immediacy. The youthful Yeats was a would-be mage. The mature poet summons up, in a seance-like poem, a frightening image.

l. 12.   *Spiritus Mundi*. Glossed by Yeats as 'a general storehouse of images which have ceased to be a property of any personality or spirit'.

l. 14.   *lion body . . . head of a man*. The sphynx-like shape is both unlike and like 'man'.

l. 17.   *indignant desert birds*. 'Indignant' at this new presence; the 'birds' contrast with the 'falcon' (they at least respond to the new threat, but share the falcon's inability to exert control over what is happening).

l. 22.   *Bethlehem*. That the beast usurps Christ's birthplace brings home shockingly the reversal of eras that is Yeats's theme.

---

3   John Unterecker, *A Reader's Guide to William Butler Yeats*, London: Thames & Hudson, 1959, p. 165.

A Prayer for my Daughter

Written in 1919; first published in *Poetry* in 1919 and in *The Irish Statesman* in 1919; published in *Michael Robartes and the Dancer* (1921). 'A Prayer for my Daughter' sets a vision of good against the 'storm' (l. 1) of war, modernity and 'intellectual hatred' (l. 57). Using eight-line stanzas rhyming *ababcddc*, mainly pentameters but with tetrameters in the fifth and seventh lines of each stanza, it reads like a reaction against the 'nightmare' evoked by 'The Second Coming', the poem that precedes it. Yeats prays for his daughter not to be so beautiful that she 'Lose natural kindness' (l. 22) and not to be consumed by fanaticism. The poem owes much of its force to the fact that it allows us to sense the dangers from which Yeats wishes to protect his daughter. These dangers have as their emblem the 'howling' 'storm' (l. 1) and they induce the 'gloom' (l. 8) that the poet mentions at the close of the first stanza. The reiterated use of 'scream' (ll. 10, 11) in the second stanza corresponds to a near-apocalyptic state of 'excited reverie' (l. 13) in the poet, who glimpses the horrors of 'future years' (l. 14), horrors bred out of 'the murderous innocence of the sea' (l. 16). This 'innocence' is the amoral innocence of a great natural power, and Yeats attributes a similar amoral innocence to historical forces. What human beings can do, the poem implies, is live according to a code that emphasizes the value of civilization, located by Yeats, on whose thinking Castiglione's *The Courtier* (1528) was a major influence, 'in custom and in ceremony' (l. 77), in the Anglo-Irish tradition of the Big House and Protestant aristocracy. Right choices can be made, the poem suggests, as it describes wrong choices suffered and made by Helen and Aphrodite (stanza 4). The poem raises the question of Yeats's attitude to gender issues. It is clear that Yeats is doing more than schooling his daughter in traditional, anti-feminist values. There is humour in his observations that Aphrodite suffered from 'Being fatherless' (l. 28) and that 'fine women eat / A crazy salad with their meat' (ll. 30–1). Moreover, beneath the humour, there is a continual reminder that the values he recommends are those that sustain others by sustaining the soul as it 'recovers radical innocence' (l. 66). This radical innocence is opposed to the earlier murderous innocence, and represents a major spiritual achievement, in which the ultimate guarantee of stability and happiness turns out to be not simply 'one dear perpetual place' (l. 48), but the soul itself. A trio of compound adjectives starting with 'self-' ('self-delighting, / Self-appeasing, self-affrighting', ll. 67–8) conveys this ideal. Throughout, Yeats's management of his stanza is attuned to his mingled feelings of dread and hope, and there is a tonal blend of lightness and firmness. So, at the poem's close the final assertions have an almost nonchalant ease; Yeats adopts an allegorical idiom that enacts the very traditionalism he is advocating. And yet the traditional is being advocated in a highly individual way. Yeats's values are being created as he writes.

Notes to the Poem

l. I *Once more the storm is howling.* The opening two words imply a typical Yeatsian scenario of recurrence; the next four words may echo William Blake's 'The Sick Rose', in which there is a 'howling storm'.
l. 4 *Gregory's wood.* Belonging to Lady Gregory.
l. 26 *fool.* Probably Paris, who abducted Helen from her husband, Menelaus.
l. 27 *that great Queen.* Aphrodite, goddess of love.
l. 29 *bandy-leggèd smith.* Hephaestos (Greek) or Vulcan (Roman), lame god of fire and maker of weapons; husband of Aphrodite.
ll. 54–6 *If there's no hatred . . . leaf.* The lines convey both the vulnerability of goodness (subjected to 'Assault and battery') and its inner strength (the storm cannot 'tear the linnet from the leaf', let alone the tree).
l. 59 *loveliest woman.* Maud Gonne.
l. 67 *self-delighting.* The soul in this state determines its own delights and concerns, and is not simply shaped by others, through, for example, feelings of hatred.

Sailing to Byzantium

Composed in 1926; first published in *October Blast* (1927); published as the opening poem of *The Tower* (1928). 'Sailing to Byzantium', written in four stanzas of *ottava rima* (eight iambic lines rhyming *abababcc*), is among the most distilled and concentrated examples of Yeats's lyric art. In a radio talk of 8 September 1921, Yeats said: 'Now I am trying to write about the state of my soul, for it is right for an old man to make his soul, and some of my thoughts upon that subject I have put into a poem called "Sailing to Byzantium".' Byzantium is the emblem of 'the search for the spiritual life' (a phrase from the radio talk) because it seemed to Yeats, as he put it in *A Vision*, as though 'in early Byzantium, maybe never before or since in recorded history, religious, aesthetic and practical life were one'.[1] Yet Yeats is divided about the desirability of focusing exclusively on 'the state of [his] soul' and, indeed, about the worth of Byzantium. The first stanza begins with a dramatic gesture of apparent rejection: 'That [Ireland] is no country for old men'. But the stanza is held by what it would reject, the world of sexuality, 'dying generations' (a phrase that compacts death and renewal), the transient but captivating stuff of physical living that composes a 'sensual music' persisting 'all summer long'. The last phrase implies that the appeal of the physical lessens with the onset of the winter of age; and when he describes 'all' as being 'Caught', Yeats suggests not only willing captivation, but

---

1 *A Vision* (1937), London: Macmillan, 1962, p. 279.

also a state of entrapment. Certainly, though, the neglected 'Monuments of unageing intellect' seems ponderous and remote by comparison with the sensual music that Yeats, against the grain of his manifest intention, hymns in this first stanza. In the second stanza Yeats turns with scorn on the condition of age, saying it can only be redeemed if 'Soul clap its hands and sing, and louder sing / For every tatter in its mortal dress'. Soul, minus definite article and receiving a strong stress, conveys its longing for spiritual life through the physical image of clapping and singing, and in this stanza 'unageing intellect' is a vital force, delighting in the study of 'its own magnificence', and prompting the poet's voyage to 'the holy city of Byzantium', where the name of the city rhymes triumphantly with the verb 'come'. After the polarities of 'sensual music' and 'Soul' have been set up, the poem moves, in the third stanza, to its emotional core; here, as Yeats longs for the sages to spiral their way out of their dimension and take him up into theirs, it is his suffering 'heart' that takes centre-stage, a heart that is 'sick with desire / And fastened to a dying animal' and, in an echo of Christ's words on the cross, 'knows not what it is'. The lines suggest the poet's torment: 'fastened' develops the hint of entrapment in the first stanza's 'Caught'; the tragic glamour of the first stanza's 'dying generations' shrinks to the drab terror implied by the poet's description of his body as a 'dying animal'. But in the act of praying to be gathered 'Into the artifice of eternity', Yeats glimpses the limitations of an imagined permanence. It is hard to agree with critics who dispute the presence of irony in 'artifice': Yeats implies that 'eternity' is both artistically shaped and something 'artificial', a pretence. In the final stanza, the poet offers an urbane diminuendo after this emotional climax; he imagines himself choosing his post-mortal shape from something made, not begotten, but the golden bird he strongly suggests he would like to be seems ornamental, a trivial plaything to amuse the Emperor. Moreover, his song would still be of time ('Of what is past, or passing, or to come'), for all his would-be escape from the temporal. As 'Byzantium' again rhymes with 'come', there is less a sense of triumph than of the inability of Yeats's holy city to free itself from the dimension of time. This impression is reinforced by the syntactical chime across the poem between 'Whatever is begotten, born, and dies' and the last line.

I

That is no country for old men. The young
In one another's arms, birds in the trees[2]
—Those dying generations—at their song,[3]
The salmon-falls, the mackerel-crowded seas,

2   These birds contrast with the 'form' 'set upon a golden bough' in the last stanza.
3   A central word in the poem: in the second stanza, 'Soul' must 'sing'; in the third, the poet prays that the sages will become 'the singing-masters' of his soul; in the fourth, he depicts himself as singing, after death, to the inhabitants of Byzantium.

Fish, flesh, or fowl, commend[4] all summer long   5
Whatever is begotten, born, and dies.
Caught in that sensual music all neglect
Monuments of unageing intellect.

II

An aged man is but a paltry thing,
A tattered coat upon a stick,[5] unless   10
Soul clap its hands and sing, and louder sing
For every tatter in its mortal dress,
Nor is there singing school but studying
Monuments of its own magnificence:
And therefore I have sailed the seas and come   15
To the holy city of Byzantium.

III

O sages standing in God's holy fire
As in the gold mosaic[6] of a wall,
Come from the holy fire, perne in a gyre,[7]
And be the singing-masters of my soul.   20
Consume my heart away; sick with desire
And fastened to a dying animal
It knows not what it is; and gather me
Into the artifice of eternity.

IV

Once out of nature I shall never take   25
My bodily form[8] from any natural thing,
But such a form as Grecian goldsmiths make
Of hammered gold and gold enamelling
To keep a drowsy Emperor awake;
Or set upon a golden bough to sing   30
To lords and ladies of Byzantium
Of what is past, or passing, or to come.
        1927

---

4 The mingling of Anglo-Saxon and Latinate words implies the poet's awareness of the claims of physicality and meditation, body and mind.
5 The image, used also by Yeats in 'Among School Children' (p. 166), is of the aged body as a scarecrow.
6 A simile, and yet the effect is to blur the distinction between real 'sages' and represented figures, as though Yeats were collapsing the distinction between 'God's holy fire' and 'art'.
7 Turn in a vortex.
8 Yeats imagines himself 'out of nature' (that is, dead), but needing a 'bodily form' (presumably implying reincarnation).

The Tower

Composed in 1925; first published in *The New Republic* and *The Criterion* in 1927; published in *The Tower* (1928). After the celebration, in however ambivalent a form, of 'the artifice of eternity', *The Tower* as a collection plunges more and more into the chaos of physical decay, emotional remorse and the horror of recent historical events (especially the Anglo-Irish War and the Irish Civil War). 'The Tower' is a poem of three sections, many moods and remarkable writing. It begins with the poet troubled, as in the third stanza of 'Sailing to Byzantium', by 'Decrepit age', imaged as something tied to him 'As to a dog's tail' and, at the end of the first section, as 'A sort of battered kettle at the heel'. The anguished opening question leads into a momentary affirmation of the power of the poet's 'Imagination', placed at the start of the line after three adjectives, and yet Yeats turns on this affirmation to say, 'It seems that I must bid the Muse go pack, / Choose Plato and Plotinus for a friend'. His unwillingness to settle for 'abstract things' and philosophical wisdom is evident, partly through the vigour with which his speaking voice, at once passionate and colloquial, sounds through the unobtrusive rhyming (the section consists, in effect, of four quatrains, each rhyming alternate lines).

Written in eight-line stanzas rhyming *aabbcddc*, and using pentameters interspersed with shorter lines, the second section depicts Yeats on 'the battlements' of his tower, bidding himself 'send imagination forth' (rather than telling the Muse to go pack), and questioning 'Images and memories' that are, as Yeats puts it in his note to the poem, 'associated by legend, story and tradition with the neighbourhood of Thoor Ballylee'. He calls up, in turn, 'Mrs. French', a redoubtable aristocrat who embodies the arrogance of Anglo-Ireland, and at whose behest a serving man 'Clipped an insolent farmer's ears'; Mary Hynes, 'A peasant girl commended by a song', a song so potent that it persuaded 'certain men' to attempt to see her, only to be led astray as they sallied forth by night and moonlight; and the 'blind' poet Anthony Raftery (c. 1784–1835) who composed the song about Mary Hynes. The recollection that Raftery was blind leads Yeats to recall that so, too, was Homer, and to long for the 'moon and sunlight', symbols, respectively, of communal and individual thought and feeling, to be bound together – even if the consequence will be to 'make men mad'. Here and throughout, images of light and dark, indeed of border states between the two, alert us to the poet's feelings about the efficacy of imagination.

An equivocal note about such efficacy and a readiness suddenly to change direction run though what follows, as Yeats recalls a creation of his own, 'Hanrahan', an imaginary poet, who features in a short story, 'Red Hanrahan' (1903), the plot of which is sketched in this part of the poem. A stranger ('ancient ruffian') transformed cards into hounds and a hare. Yeats claims to 'have forgotten' the upshot of his story (Hanrahan arrived at a house where a beautiful, weary woman sat; he was too tongue-tied to speak to her). Yeats incorporates this moment of amnesia to hint at a reluctance to pursue a plot with painful

personal implications, but recollection returns in the reference to 'the Great Memory', said to retain 'images' of 'men-at-arms' who formerly dwelt in the tower. The question Yeats would put to all those who 'trod upon these rocks or passed this door' is whether they raged 'As I do now against old age'. This sense of rage explains much of the controlled violence of the writing, at once obsessive and distracted, a tension caught in the rhyme scheme, whose initial couplets mimic obsessiveness, before the couplet form breaks. Yeats asserts that he needs his alter ego, Hanrahan, to help him deal with his preoccupation with love, and finishes the section with a remorseful sense of waste at failure in relationships with women. Yeats's verse rises to the artistic challenge of conveying a failure of ethical courage: 'admit you turned aside / From a great labyrinth', he writes in lines whose onward flow conducts us into a labyrinth.

The third section consists of a long passage of alternately rhymed trochaic tetrameters, sometimes trimeters, a metre suited to chant and incantation, but also, as the moving close reveals, to a falling away of intensity. Here Yeats leaves behind remorse, and composes his poetic 'will'. He reasserts his faith in his Anglo-Irish inheritance, rejects the spiritual wisdom of Plato and Plotinus, and affirms the human capacity to create meaning much as the 'mother bird' builds a nest for her young. Even 'Death and life' are human inventions, he declares, and yet in the midst of his assertions one can hear his need to face down doubt and opposition: the 'Mirror-resembling dream' may be 'superhuman', but it remains a 'dream', and in the closing lines Yeats effects one of his finest transitions as he readmits human weakness, 'the wreck of body, / Slow decay of blood', into the poetry. This time he thinks of eliminating awareness of such weakness not through superhuman feats of imagination but through recognition of mortality. Loss lessens in its capacity to inflict suffering; it now suggests merely 'a bird's sleepy cry / Among the deepening shades'.

I

What shall I do with this absurdity—
O heart, O troubled heart—this caricature,
Decrepit age that has been tied to me
As to a dog's tail?
           Never had I more
Excited, passionate, fantastical   5
Imagination, nor an ear and eye
That more expected the impossible—
No, not in boyhood when with rod and fly,
Or the humbler worm, I climbed Ben Bulben's[1] back,
And had the livelong summer day to spend.   10

---

1   A mountain in County Sligo.

It seems that I must bid the Muse go pack,
Choose Plato and Plotinus[2] for a friend
Until imagination, ear and eye,
Can be content with argument and deal
In abstract things; or be derided by   15
A sort of battered kettle at the heel.

II

I pace upon the battlements and stare
On the foundations of a house, or where
Tree, like a sooty finger, starts from the earth;
And send imagination forth
Under the day's declining beam, and call   5
Images and memories
From ruin or from ancient trees.
For I would ask a question of them all.
Beyond that ridge lived Mrs. French, and once
When every silver candlestick or sconce   10
Lit up the dark mahogany and the wine,
A serving-man, that could divine
That most respected lady's every wish,
Ran and with the garden shears
Clipped an insolent farmer's ears   15
And brought them in a little covered dish.

Some few remembered still when I was young
A peasant girl commended by a song,
Who'd lived somewhere upon that rocky place,
And praised the colour of her face,   20
And had the greater joy in praising her,
Remembering that, if walked she there,
Farmers jostled at the fair
So great a glory did the song confer.

And certain men, being maddened by those rhymes,   25
Or else by toasting her a score of times,
Rose from the table and declared it right
To test their fancy by their sight;
But they mistook the brightness of the moon
For the prosaic light of day—   30
Music had driven their wits astray—
And one was drowned in the great bog of Cloone.

---

2   Two ancient philosophers associated by Yeats with rejection of the physical.

Strange, but the man who made the song was blind;
Yet, now I have considered it, I find
That nothing strange; the tragedy began   35
With Homer that was a blind man,
And Helen has all living hearts betrayed.
O may the moon and sunlight seem
One inextricable beam,
For if I triumph I must make men mad.   40

And I myself created Hanrahan[3]
And drove him drunk or sober through the dawn
From somewhere in the neighbouring cottages.
Caught by an old man's juggleries
He stumbled, tumbled, fumbled to and fro   45
And had but broken knees for hire
And horrible splendour of desire;
I thought it all out twenty years ago:

Good fellows shuffled cards in an old bawn;[4]
And when that ancient ruffian's turn was on   50
He so bewitched the cards under his thumb
That all but the one card became
A pack of hounds and not a pack of cards,
And that he changed into a hare.
Hanrahan rose in frenzy there   55
And followed up those baying creatures towards—

O towards I have forgotten what—enough!
I must recall a man that neither love
Nor music nor an enemy's clipped ear
Could, he was so harried, cheer;   60
A figure that has grown so fabulous
There's not a neighbour left to say
When he finished his dog's day:
An ancient bankrupt master of this house.

Before that ruin came, for centuries,   65
Rough men-at-arms, cross-gartered to the knees
Or shod in iron, climbed the narrow stairs,
And certain men-at-arms there were
Whose images, in the Great Memory[5] stored,
Come with loud cry and panting breast   70

---

3 An imaginary poet and a main character in short stories included in *The Secret Rose* (1897).
4 Here, probably a barn; normally a fortified enclosure.
5 The Anima Mundi, a reservoir of universal images.

To break upon a sleeper's rest
While their great wooden dice beat on the board.

As I would question all, come all who can;
Come old, necessitous, half-mounted man;
And bring beauty's blind rambling celebrant;   75
The red man the juggler sent
Through God-forsaken meadows; Mrs. French,
Gifted with so fine an ear;
The man drowned in a bog's mire,
When mocking Muses chose the country wench.   80

Did all old men and women, rich and poor,
Who trod upon these rocks or passed this door,
Whether in public or in secret rage
As I do now against old age?
But I have found an answer in those eyes   85
That are impatient to be gone;
Go therefore; but leave Hanrahan,
For I need all his mighty memories.

Old lecher[6] with a love on every wind,
Bring up out of that deep considering mind   90
All that you have discovered in the grave,
For it is certain that you have
Reckoned up every unforeknown, unseeing
Plunge, lured by a softening eye,
Or by a touch or a sigh,   95
Into the labyrinth of another's being;

Does the imagination dwell the most
Upon a woman won or woman lost?[7]
If on the lost, admit you turned aside[8]
From a great labyrinth out of pride,   100
Cowardice, some silly over-subtle thought
Or anything called conscience once;
And that if memory recur, the sun's
Under eclipse and the day blotted out.[9]

---

6 Hanrahan. Yeats needs, he says, to draw on his experience of the complexities of love.
7 Presumably Maud Gonne is the 'woman lost'.
8 Yeats is ostensibly speaking to Hanrahan, his own creation, but the effect of the wording is self-
   address.
9 Yeats subtly avoids saying 'And if that memory recur'; he does not mean a specific memory, but a
   pain associated with the workings of memory itself.

It is time that I wrote my will;
I choose upstanding men[10]
That climb the streams until
The fountain leap, and at dawn
Drop their cast at the side   5
Of dripping stone; I declare
They shall inherit my pride,
The pride of people that were
Bound neither to Cause nor to State,
Neither to slaves that were spat on,   10
Nor to the tyrants that spat,
The people of Burke and of Grattan[11]
That gave, though free to refuse—
Pride, like that of the morn,
When the headlong light is loose,   15
Or that of the fabulous horn,[12]
Or that of the sudden shower
When all streams are dry,
Or that of the hour
When the swan must fix his eye   20
Upon a fading gleam,
Float out upon a long
Last reach of glittering stream
And there sing his last song.
And I declare my faith: 25
I mock Plotinus' thought
And cry in Plato's teeth,
Death and life were not
Till man made up the whole,
Made lock, stock and barrel   30
Out of his bitter soul,
Aye, sun and moon and star, all,
And further add to that
That, being dead, we rise,[13]
Dream and so create   35

---

10 These imagined heirs, engaged in fishing, recall the figure for whom Yeats proposes to write in 'The Fisherman'.
11 Edmund Burke (1729–97), Irish author and politician; Henry Grattan (1746–1820), politician who headed 'Grattan's Parliament' before the Act of Union (1800), which he opposed. Both men supported Catholic Emancipation; both are examples for Yeats of a great eighteenth-century tradition of Anglo-Irishness.
12 A never-ending horn of plenty, 'fabulous' because extraordinary and the stuff of fable.
13 Deliberately recalls a central tenet of Christianity, that Jesus rose from the dead, but adapted to Yeats's own vision of everything as created out of the 'bitter soul' of mankind. Embittered, spurred on by dreams, human beings create reality.

Translunar Paradise.[14]
I have prepared my peace
With learned Italian things
And the proud stones of Greece,
Poet's imaginings   40
And memories of love,
Memories of the words of women,
All those things whereof
Man makes a superhuman
Mirror-resembling dream.   45

As at the loophole there
The daws chatter and scream,
And drop twigs layer upon layer.
When they have mounted up,
The mother bird will rest   50
On their hollow top,
And so warm her wild nest.

I leave both faith and pride
To young upstanding men
Climbing the mountain side,   55
That under bursting dawn
They may drop a fly;
Being of that metal made
Till it was broken by
This sedentary trade.[15]   60

Now shall I make my soul,
Compelling it to study
In a learned school
Till the wreck of body,
Slow decay of blood,   65
Testy delirium
Or dull decrepitude,
Or what worse evil come—
The death of friends, or death
Of every brilliant eye   70
That made a catch in the breath—
Seem but the clouds of the sky
When the horizon fades;

14 A paradise beyond the control of the moon; the *OED* also gives 'visionary' and 'insubstantial' as
   meanings of 'translunar'.
15 Writing poetry.

Or a bird's sleepy cry[16]
Among the deepening shades.

   1926

Meditations in Time of Civil War

First section composed in 1921; the others in 1922–3; first published in *The Dial* in 1923 and in the *London Mercury* in 1923; published in *The Tower* (1928). In this sequence Yeats moves into recent Irish history. The 'Civil War' of the title is the Irish Civil War of 1922–3, fought between those who accepted the treaty signed with England in 1922, creating the Irish Free State but leaving Northern Ireland as part of Great Britain, and those who opposed the treaty on the grounds that they refused to accept a partition of the island of Ireland; the military wing of the latter faction was the Irish Republican Army. Yeats is immersed in public events and solitary thought in the sequence, which takes as its central theme the conflict between a poet's dreams of order and the chaos of history. The first section, five stanzas written in *ottava rima,* reflects on cultural achievement. Associated by Yeats with 'Ancestral Houses', such achievement is represented, first of all, as an overflowing fountain, an expression of 'life's own self-delight'. Yet such an image, however true of a poet such as Homer, seems less appropriate than that of a 'sea-shell flung' out of the past, at once 'marvellous' and 'empty'. In the remaining stanzas of this section Yeats is troubled by the fear that aristocratic culture is built on some original violence, on the longing experienced by 'Bitter and violent men' for the 'sweetness' that is their antithesis. As a result there may be some intertwining of 'greatness' and 'violence', so that once the 'violence' has been left behind the 'greatness' may vanish. Such thoughts are voiced as disturbed questions. In the second section, three ten-line stanzas rhyming *abcabcdeed* and mingling longer and shorter lines, Yeats describes his house and the world beyond his window. The description makes us aware of a poet living among his images: the 'rose' that might 'break' out of 'stony ground' is 'symbolic'; the house itself with winding stair and candle recalls Milton's Platonist in *Il Penseroso*, a forerunner of the occult Yeats; and the poet depicts himself as seaching for 'Befitting emblems of adversity'. In the third section, made up of couplets, Yeats focuses on one such emblem, 'Sato's' 'sword', given to him as a present and emerging, so Yeats speculates, from a culture that valued lack of change. Yet asserting that 'only an aching heart/ Conceives a changeless work of art', Yeats brings back into play ideas of conflict, opposition, things generating their opposites, and the section closes with an intuition of revolutionary change ascribed to one with 'waking wits'. The heart aches because it fears loss and desires permanence. A culture may exalt an

---

16 The last of three bird images in section III: the dying 'swan', associated with a 'fading gleam' and the 'mother bird' building her nest are its predecessors. All bear on the predicament of the poet.

ideal of permanence. But the 'aching human heart' is also a constant presence: constantly driven to find some new expression of its desire for changelessness.

The fourth section, three stanzas of *ottava rima*, takes up the theme of inheritance in relation to the poet himself. Yeats fears for the future should his descendants be unworthy of him; should that happen, he wishes that his house might be visited by 'desolation', and yet, convinced that everything moves in cycles, he is able to conclude the section by asserting the worth of friendship and love, and the lasting value of the tower (symbol, among other things, of his poetic labours). In the fifth section Yeats turns to the outside world and in three five-line stanzas of iambic tetrameters, rhyming *abaab*, he sets himself as solitary poet against two men of action: an 'affable Irregular' fighting for the anti-treaty side and 'A brown Lieutenant' fighting for the Irish Free State. When he complains to the latter of 'the foul weather', his complaint is directed at the recent historical climate as well as literal storms. Counting 'feathered balls of soot', rather as he numbered the swans in 'The Wild Swans at Coole', the poet turns back to his solitary 'chamber, caught / In the cold snows of a dream'. These 'cold snows' constitute his own inner weather, and show him possessed by his commitment to poetry, here represented as something frozen and imprisoning.

The sixth section builds on previous hints of imminent ruin to confess, with personal urgency, 'My wall is loosening', analyses the condition of imprisonment, uncertainty and brutality engendered by 'fantasies' (a rebuke to the poet's own preoccupation with 'dream') and articulates a longing for nurturing and sweetness, as, in the refrain, Yeats pleads that the 'honey-bees' 'Come build in the empty house of the stare'. These four stanzas, each of five lines rhyming *abaab*, convey a different relationship between sweetness and violence than was imagined in the first section. Now Yeats sees natural sweetness as an antidote to the horror of civil war. He accepts that there may be some connection between his isolation and the barricades thrown up by civil war, and between his fantasies and the country's enmities. In the seventh section, he ends the poem dwelling on what he calls, in the first of five eight-line stanzas rhyming *ababcdcd*, 'Monstrous familiar images'. These 'images' are 'familiar' from previous sections (we meet, for example, a mist like blown snow and a moon like an unchangeable sword), yet they are caught up in the mood of reverie sweeping through the poem. The second stanza shows the poet in the act of being taken over in imagination by mob violence. In contrast, the third stanza reveals a further longing for 'sweetness', though this time the sweetness, indebted to a memory of a painting by Gustave Moreau, is bejewelled and narcissistic. The fourth stanza replaces the 'rage' of the second and the 'self-delighting reverie' of the third with a vision of 'brazen hawks', by which Yeats implies a culture founded on logical rationalism and dominated by the 'indifferent multitude': indifferent, among other things, to art. In the fifth stanza he turns back to the ongoing, never fully satisfied or satisfying, quest of the poet trying to make sense; the lines offer, at best, two cheers for the poetic vocation.

I

Ancestral Houses

Surely among a rich man's flowering lawns,
Amid the rustle of his planted hills,
Life overflows without ambitious pains;
And rains down life until the basin spills,
And mounts more dizzy high the more it rains   5
As though to choose whatever shape it wills
And never stoop to a mechanical
Or servile shape,[1] at others' beck and call.

Mere dreams, mere dreams! Yet Homer had not sung
Had he not found it certain beyond dreams   10
That out of life's own self-delight had sprung
The abounding glittering jet; though now it seems
As if some marvellous empty sea-shell flung
Out of the obscure dark of the rich streams,
And not a fountain, were the symbol which   15
Shadows the inherited glory of the rich.

Some violent bitter man, some powerful man
Called architect and artist in, that they,
Bitter and violent men, might rear in stone
The sweetness that all longed for night and day,   20
The gentleness none there had ever known;
But when the master's buried mice can play,
And maybe the great-grandson of that house,
For all its bronze and marble, 's but a mouse.[2]

O what if gardens where the peacock strays   25
With delicate feet upon old terraces,
Or else all Juno from an urn displays
Before the indifferent garden deities;
O what if levelled lawns and gravelled ways
Where slippered Contemplation finds his ease   30
And Childhood a delight for every sense,
But take our greatness with our violence?

What if the glory of escutcheoned[3] doors,
And buildings that a haughtier age designed,

---

1 Yeats feared that the present age exalted the mechanical and servile. This first stanza uses the
   movement of the *ottava rima* to mimic the generous overflowing that is its theme.
2 The colloquial phrasing conveys a sense of contempt.
3 Marked by shields with armorial bearings.

The pacing to and fro on polished floors   35
Amid great chambers and long galleries, lined
With famous portraits of our ancestors;
What if those things the greatest of mankind
Consider most to magnify, or to bless,
But take our greatness with our bitterness?   40

II

My House

An ancient bridge,[4] and a more ancient tower,
A farmhouse that is sheltered by its wall,
An acre of stony ground,
Where the symbolic rose can break in flower,
Old ragged elms, old thorns innumerable,   5
The sound of the rain or sound
Of every wind that blows;
The stilted water-hen
Crossing stream again
Scared by the splashing of a dozen cows;   10
A winding stair, a chamber arched with stone,
A grey stone fireplace with an open hearth,
A candle and written page.
Il Penseroso's Platonist toiled on
In some like chamber, shadowing forth   15
How the daemonic rage[5]
Imagined everything.
Benighted travellers
From markets and from fairs
Have seen his midnight candle glimmering.   20

Two men have founded here. A man-at-arms[6]
Gathered a score of horse and spent his days
In this tumultuous spot,
Where through long wars and sudden night alarms
His dwindling score and he seemed castaways   25
Forgetting and forgot;
And I, that after me
My bodily heirs may find,
To exalt a lonely mind,
Befitting emblems of adversity.   30

---

4   The next thirteen lines lack a main verb as Yeats produces an inventory of the symbols among
    which he lives.
5   A supernatural creative force; 'rage' occurs later in the poem (see section VII).
6   The first known owner of the tower, a member of the de Burgo family.

My Table

Two heavy trestles, and a board
Where Sato's gift,[7] a changeless sword,
By pen and paper lies,
That it may moralise
My days out of their aimlessness.   5
A bit of an embroidered dress
Covers its wooden sheath.
Chancer had not drawn breath
When it was forged. In Sato's house,
Curved like new moon,[8] moon-luminous,   10
It lay five hundred years.
Yet if no change appears
No moon; only an aching heart
Conceives a changeless work of art.
Our learned men have urged   15
That when and where 'twas forged
A marvellous accomplishment,
In painting or in pottery, went
From father unto son
And through the centuries ran   20
And seemed unchanging like the sword.
Soul's beauty being most adored,
Men and their business took
The soul's unchanging look;
For the most rich inheritor,   25
Knowing that none could pass Heaven's door
That loved inferior art,
Had such an aching heart
That he, although a country's talk
For silken clothes and stately walk,   30
Had waking wits; it seemed
Juno's peacock screamed.[9]

---

7 A gift made to Yeats in Portland, Oregon, by a Japanese admirer.
8 The sword, apparently changeless, is also a symbol of the changing moon.
9 An image used by Yeats as a portent of the collapse of a civilization: 'A civilisation is a struggle to
   keep self-control . . . The loss of control over thought comes towards the end; first a sinking in upon
   the moral being, then the last surrender, the irrational cry, revelation – the scream of Juno's
   peacock', A Vision (1937), London: Macmillan, 1962, p. 268.

IV

My Descendants

Having inherited a vigorous mind
From my old fathers, I must nourish dreams
And leave a woman and a man[10] behind
As vigorous of mind, and yet it seems
Life scarce can cast a fragrance on the wind,   5
Scarce spread a glory to the morning beams,
But the torn petals strew the garden plot;
And there's but common greenness after that.

And what if my descendants lose the flower[11]
Through natural declension of the soul,   10
Through too much business with the passing hour,
Through too much play, or marriage with a fool?
May this laborious stair and this stark tower
Become a roofless ruin that the owl
May build in the cracked masonry and cry   15
Her desolation to the desolate sky.

The Primum Mobile[12] that fashioned us
Has made the very owls in circles move;
And I, that count myself most prosperous,
Seeing that love and friendship are enough,   20
For an old neighbour's friendship[13] chose the house
And decked and altered it for a girl's love,[14]
And know whatever flourish and decline
These stones remain their monument and mine.

V

The Road at My Door

An affable Irregular,[15]
A heavily-built Falstaffian[16] man,

---

10 Yeats's daughter, Anne Butler Yeats, and his son, Michael Butler Yeats.
11 Thus reversing the breaking 'in flower' of the 'symbolic rose' of section II.
12 Prime source of action or motion; from the name given to the outermost sphere, added in the Middle Ages to the Ptolemaic system, supposed to revolve round earth in 24 hours carrying with it the contained spheres (*OED*).
13 Lady Gregory who lived close by at Coole Park.
14 Yeats's wife, Georgie Yeats.
15 A member of the Irish Republican Army.
16 Like Sir John Falstaff, comic figure in Shakespeare's two *Henry IV* plays and *The Merry Wives of Windsor*.

Comes cracking jokes of civil war
As though to die by gunshot were
The finest play under the sun.   5

A brown Lieutenant[17] and his men,
Half dressed in national uniform,
Stand at my door, and I complain
Of the foul weather, hail and rain,
A pear-tree broken by the storm.   10

I count those feathered balls of soot
The moor-hen guides upon the stream,
To silence the envy in my thought;
And turn towards my chamber, caught
In the cold snows of a dream.   15

VI

The Stare's Nest by My Window

The bees build in the crevices
Of loosening masonry, and there
The mother birds bring grubs and flies.
My wall is loosening; honey-bees,
Come build in the empty house of the stare.[18]   5

We are closed in, and the key is turned
On our uncertainty; somewhere
A man is killed, or a house burned,
Yet no clear fact to be discerned:
Come build in the empty house of the stare.   10

A barricade of stone or of wood;
Some fourteen days of civil war;
Last night they trundled down the road
That dead young soldier in his blood:
Come build in the empty house of the stare.   15

We had fed the heart on fantasies,
The heart's grown brutal from the fare;
More substance in our enmities
Than in our love; O honey-bees,
Come build in the empty house of the stare.   20

---

17 In the Irish National army.
18 Yeats's note says that the word is 'our West of Ireland name for a starling'.

VII

*I see Phantoms of Hatred and of the Heart's Fullness and of the Coming
Emptiness*

I climb to the tower-top and lean upon broken stone,
A mist that is like blown snow is sweeping over all,
Valley, river, and elms, under the light of a moon
That seems unlike itself, that seems unchangeable,
A glittering sword out of the east. A puff of wind   5
And those white glimmering fragments of the mist sweep by.
Frenzies bewilder, reveries perturb the mind;
Monstrous familiar images swim to the mind's eye.

'Vengeance upon the murderers,' the cry goes up,
'Vengeance for Jacques Molay.'[19] In cloud-pale rags, or in lace,   10
The rage-driven, rage-tormented, and rage-hungry troop,
Trooper belabouring trooper, biting at arm or at face,
Plunges towards nothing, arms and fingers spreading wide
For the embrace of nothing; and I, my wits astray
Because of all that senseless tumult, all but cried   15
For vengeance on the murderers of Jacques Molay.

Their legs long, delicate and slender, aquamarine their eyes,
Magical unicorns[20] bear ladies on their backs.
The ladies close their musing eyes. No prophecies,
Remembered out of Babylonian almanacs,   20
Have closed the ladies' eyes, their minds are but a pool
Where even longing drowns under its own excess;
Nothing but stillness can remain when hearts are full
Of their own sweetness, bodies of their loveliness.
The cloud-pale unicorns, the eyes of aquamarine,   25
The quivering half-closed eyelids, the rags of cloud or of lace,
Or eyes that rage has brightened, arms it has made lean,
Give place to an indifferent multitude, give place
To brazen hawks.[21] Nor self-delighting reverie,
Nor hate of what's to come, nor pity for what's gone,   30

19 Jacques Molay was burned at the stake in 1314; he was Grand Master of the Templars. Yeats's note
    says: 'A cry for vengeance because of the murder of the Grand Master of the Templars seems to me
    fit symbol for those who labour from hatred.'
20 Yeats describes a painting by Gustave Moreau, *Ladies and Unicorns*, of which there was a print in
    a room at Thoor Ballylee.
21 In a note Yeats writes: 'I suppose that I must have put hawks into the fourth stanza because I have a
    ring with a hawk and a butterfly upon it, to symbolize the straight road of logic, and so of
    mechanism, and the crooked road of intuition: "For wisdom is a butterfly and not a gloomy bird of
    prey." '

Nothing but grip of claw, and the eye's complacency,
The innumerable clanging wings that have put out the moon.

I turn away and shut the door, and on the stair
Wonder how many times I could have proved my worth
In something that all others understand or share;   35
But O! ambitious heart, had such a proof drawn forth
A company of friends, a conscience set at ease,
It had but made us pine the more. The abstract joy,
The half-read wisdom of daemonic images,
Suffice the ageing man as once the growing boy.[22]   40
    1923

Nineteen Hundred and Nineteen

First published in *The Dial* and the *London Mercury* in 1921 (entitled in the latter journal 'Thoughts upon the Present State of the World'); published in *The Tower* (1928), where it was first called by its present title. In keeping with the voyaging backwards through time of *The Tower*, 'Nineteen Hundred and Nineteen' travels beyond the Civil War to the violent struggle for independence preceding it. The poem conducts *The Tower* further into chaos. The sequence takes its title from the first year of the violent Anglo-Irish War (1919–21) fought between the Irish Republican Army and the Black and Tans (so called because they wore a mixture of military and constabulary uniforms), made up chiefly of British soldiers demobilized from the First World War. Yeats wrote of the sequence that the poems 'are not philosophical but simple and passionate, a lamentation over lost peace and lost hope'.[1] The sequence at once resists and bears out the system laid out in *A Vision*: resists, because it suggests that the effort of human beings to piece their 'thoughts into philosophy' is doomed to fail; bears out, because it sees the recent violence as symptomatic of the cyclical nature of history. So, the line, 'Herodias' daughters have returned *again*' (emphasis added) uses 'again' to imply that the 'daughters' have 'returned' before. In some ways, the sequence reads as a speeded-up, more bitterly cynical reprise of 'Meditations'. In the first section, six stanzas in *ottava rima*, Yeats laments the loss of beautiful artefacts ('ingenious lovely things') from ancient Athens as a prelude to lamenting the loss of what, bitterly, he calls 'many pretty toys' recently possessed by his own culture. These include a just legal system, liberal optimism about the future and an army more for show than action. There is a strong suggestion that 'we' were

22 Yeats echoes Wordsworth's 'Ode: Intimations of Immortality', ll. 68–9: 'Shades of the prison-house begin to close/Upon the growing boy'.

1 Allan Wade (ed.), *The Letters of W. B. Yeats*, London: Hart-Davis, 1954, p. 668.

complacent to suppose 'All teeth were drawn', and in the terse, powerfully shocking fourth stanza the poet turns to the present state of things in which 'days are dragon-ridden', 'the nightmare/Rides upon sleep' and 'a drunken soldiery' can leave 'the mother' (the definite article giving her iconic status) 'murdered at her door,/To crawl in her own blood'. Liberal hopes have gone up in smoke, since what history teaches is that we 'are but weasels fighting in a hole', a line and off-rhyme that mock the effort 'to bring the world under a rule'. The last two stanzas seek some appropriate stance in the face of loss, but such a search is undercut by the all-subverting question: 'Man is in love and loves what vanishes,/What more is there to say?'

In the second section, ten lines rhyming *abcabcdeed*, a rhyming that enacts the winding motions of the dance, Yeats offers a different image of a 'dragon', this time a 'dragon of air' created by Loie Fuller's troupe of dancers as they danced with silk looped round sticks. Though the image is of artistic triumph, Yeats concludes with an image of 'men' as 'dancers' that is far from reassuring since 'their tread/Goes to the barbarous clangour of a gong'. The third section, using the same rhyming scheme as the second section, dwells more openly on the poet and the nature of the 'solitary soul' (picking up the emphasis on 'ghostly solitude' towards the close of the first section). Yeats develops a comparison between such a soul and a swan, bringing out the swan's 'pride' and courage, and the threat of 'approaching night'. He concedes that any person caught up in 'secret meditation' 'Is lost amid the labyrinth that he has made', and repeats a Platonic argument that it would be best for human beings to move into the next cycle of incarnation without their 'works'; vanishing here is seen as 'lucky' by contrast with the lament for 'what vanishes' in section 1, a typical instance of the doubling back on a position, idea or mood often to be found in a Yeatsian poem. The section ends with the swan imagined as having 'leaped into the desolate heaven', as though it had got beyond the 'night', only to find that 'heaven' is 'desolate'. Yeats comments on the 'image' he has just produced; it brings 'a rage/To end all things', an emblem of finality and possible futility that makes a mockery of the poet's 'laborious life', his devotion to 'The half-imagined, the half-written page'. The moment sparks off a return to the scorn expressed in section 1 for dreams of mending 'Whatever mischief seemed/To afflict mankind', where 'seemed' implies that the diagnosis itself may have been at fault. In the fourth section, a short quatrain, this tone of self-contempt crystallizes; the pursuit of 'honour and truth' was, the poet implies, hypocritical since human beings are essentially no better than weasels.

In the fifth section Yeats chants a song of mockery, as though riding the wave of the scorn and contempt expressed earlier, and invites himself and us to 'mock' 'the great', 'the wise' and 'the good'. In a typical turn, however, the section finishes with a command to 'Mock mockers after that'; 'mockery' may be a temporary relief, but it is not a stance the poet can embrace without dissatisfaction. The sixth and last section returns to Yeats in a mode and mood that might be described as apocalyptic but reined-in or pent-up. The section,

among Yeats's most compelling passages, consists of eighteen lines, breaking into three six-line units, each rhymed *abcabc*. Yeats condenses in the section references to or contrasts with much of what has gone before: for 'The guardsmen's drowsy chargers' of section I, he substitutes the menacing 'violence of horses'; earlier, 'All men' were 'dancers', but here the stage is taken up by 'Herodias' daughters'; the poet's 'image' of the swan gives way to a 'tumult of images'; the man lost in his own 'labyrinth' is replaced by 'Their purpose in the labyrinth of the wind'; the wind that blows through the section suggests that the poet cannot 'bar that foul storm out', to use a phrase from section V; the 'nightmare' that 'Rides upon sleep' in section I is echoed by what 'lurches past' the eye of the poet's horrified imagination at the close. The cycle of history does not usher in a new redemptive era, but an era whose symbol is a fiend (Robert Artisson) and his mortal worshipper (Lady Kyteler). Yeats's occult images allow him, as at the end of 'The Second Coming', to gaze into the abyss. The sole positive to emerge is the unflinching nature of that gaze. See M. L. Rosenthal's account of the final section in the extract included in Modern Criticism (**pp. 80–3**).

I

Many ingenious lovely things are gone
That seemed sheer miracle to the multitude,
Protected from the circle of the moon
That pitches common things about. There stood
Amid the ornamental bronze and stone   5
An ancient image[2] made of olive wood—
And gone are Phidias'[3] famous ivories
And all the golden grasshoppers and bees.

We too had many pretty toys when young:
A law indifferent to blame or praise,   10
To bribe or threat; habits that made old wrong
Melt down, as it were wax in the sun's rays;
Public opinion ripening for so long
We thought it would outlive all future days.
O what fine thought we had because we thought   15
That the worst rogues and rascals had died out.

All teeth were drawn, all ancient tricks unlearned,
And a great army but a showy thing;

---

2   Of Athene in the Erechtheum on the Acropolis at Athens.
3   A great Athenian sculptor (*c.* 490–423 BC).

What matter that no cannon had been turned
Into a ploughshare?[4] Parliament and king   20
Thought that unless a little powder burned
The trumpeters might burst with trumpeting
And yet it lack all glory; and perchance
The guardsmen's drowsy chargers would not prance.

Now days are dragon-ridden, the nightmare   25
Rides upon sleep: a drunken soldiery
Can leave the mother, murdered at her door,[5]
To crawl in her own blood, and go scot-free;
The night can sweat with terror as before
We pieced our thoughts into philosophy,   30
And planned to bring the world under a rule,
Who are but weasels fighting in a hole.

He who can read the signs nor sink unmanned
Into the half-deceit of some intoxicant
From shallow wits; who knows no work can stand,   35
Whether health, wealth or peace of mind were spent
On master-work of intellect or hand,
No honour leave its mighty monument,
Has but one comfort left: all triumph would
But break upon his ghostly solitude.[6]   40

But is there any comfort to be found?
Man is in love and loves what vanishes,
What more is there to say? That country round
None dared admit, if such a thought were his,
Incendiary or bigot could be found   45
To burn that stump on the Acropolis,
Or break in bits the famous ivories
Or traffic in the grasshoppers or bees.

II

When Loie Fuller's[7] Chinese dancers enwound
A shining web, a floating ribbon of cloth,

---

4   Echoes Isaiah 2:4: 'and they shall beat their swords into plowshares . . .. nation shall not lift up
     sword against nation, neither shall they learn war any more.'
5   Alludes to Eileen Quinn, shot by Black and Tan soldiers 'from a passing lorry', as Lady Gregory
     recorded in her journal on 5 November 1920.
6   Such 'solitude' seems the only possible refuge; 'ghostly' may be intended literally as well as meta-
     phorically to allude to the soul's experience after death.
7   American dancer (1862–1928), danced at the Folies Bergères in Paris, using lengths of silk wound
     round sticks.

It seemed that a dragon of air
Had fallen among dancers, had whirled them round
Or hurried them off on its own furious path;
So the Platonic Year[8]
Whirls out new right and wrong,
Whirls in the old instead;[9]
All men are dancers and their tread
Goes to the barbarous clangour of a gong.

5

10

III

Some moralist or mythological poet[10]
Compares the solitary soul to a swan;
I am satisfied with that,
Satisfied if a troubled mirror[11] show it,
Before that brief gleam of its life be gone,
An image of its state;
The wings half spread for flight,
The breast thrust out in pride
Whether to play, or to ride
Those winds that clamour of approaching night.

5

10

A man in his own secret meditation
Is lost amid the labyrinth that he has made
In art or politics;
Some Platonist[12] affirms that in the station
Where we should cast off body and trade
The ancient habit sticks,
And that if our works could
But vanish with our breath
That were a lucky death,
For triumph can but mar our solitude.

15

20

The swan has leaped into the desolate heaven:
That image can bring wildness, bring a rage
To end all things, to end
What my laborious life imagined, even
The half-imagined, the half-written page;
O but we dreamed to mend

25

---

8 A cycle lasting 36,000 years; see *A Vision* (1937), London: Macmillan, 1962, p. 248.
9 The 'whirling' in and out is chaotic; the 'new' is whirled out, the 'old' in.
10 Possibly Shelley in *Prometheus Unbound*, II, v, 72–3: 'My soul is an enchanted boat/Which, like a sleeping swan, doth float'.
11 The phrase captures Yeats's sense of the relationship in this poem between language and experience.
12 Possibly Thomas Taylor (1758–1835).

Whatever mischief seemed
To afflict mankind, but now
That winds of winter blow
Learn that we were crack-pated when we dreamed.   30

IV

We, who seven years ago
Talked of honour and of truth,
Shriek with pleasure if we show
The weasel's twist, the weasel's tooth.

V

Come let us mock at the great
That had such burdens on the mind
And toiled so hard and late
To leave some monument behind,
Nor thought of the levelling wind.   5

Come let us mock at the wise;
With all those calendars whereon
They fixed old aching eyes,
They never saw how seasons run,
And now but gape at the sun.   10

Come let us mock at the good
That fancied goodness might be gay,
And sick of solitude
Might proclaim a holiday:
Wind shrieked—and where are they?   15

Mock mockers after that
That would not lift a hand maybe
To help good, wise or great
To bar that foul storm out, for we
Traffic in mockery.   20

VI

Violence upon the roads: violence of horses;[13]
Some few have handsome riders, are garlanded
On delicate sensitive ear or tossing mane,

---

13 These horses are seen as portents of disaster, giving way at the close to an even more frightening portent.

But wearied running round and round in their courses
All break and vanish, and evil gathers head: 5
Herodias' daughters[14] have returned again,
A sudden blast of dusty wind and after
Thunder of feet, tumult of images,
Their purpose in the labyrinth of the wind;
And should some crazy hand dare touch a daughter   10
All turn with amorous cries, or angry cries,
According to the wind, for all are blind.
But now wind drops, dust settles; thereupon
There lurches past, his great eyes without thought
Under the shadow of stupid straw-pale locks,   15
That insolent fiend Robert Artisson[15]
To whom the love-lorn Lady Kyteler[16] brought
Bronzed peacock feathers, red combs of her cocks.
    1919

Leda and the Swan

Composed in 1923 (date appended); first published in *The Dial* in 1924; published in *The Tower* (1928). The poem, a sonnet of great compression and power, alludes to the myth of the rape by Leda, wife of Tyndareus, King of Sparta, by Zeus in the form of a swan. As a result of their coupling, Leda laid three eggs.[1] One egg contained Castor and Clytemnestra, one Helen and Pollux. The third remained unhatched, and, in so far as it asks to be given contemporary historical resonance, the poem may be wondering 'what would break the third shell'.[2] Yeats interprets the rape of Leda as an 'annunciation that founded Greece' and the historical era running from 2000 BC to AD 1.[3] The birth of Helen led to the Trojan War, fought over Helen's abduction by Paris from her husband, Menelaus, brother of Agamemnon. Agamemnon, commander of the Greek army, was murdered by his wife, Clytemnestra, on his return from Troy. Preoccupied by act and consequence, the poem is engrossed in a myth treated by various Renaissance painters, notably Michelangelo, whose painting of *Leda and the Swan*

14 Conflates Herodias' daughters (the most famous of whom was Salome, who demanded John the
   Baptist's death after dancing for Herod) with the Sidhe, Irish pagan goddesses who dwell in the
   wind.
15 Yeats calls him 'an evil spirit much run after in Kilkenny at the start of the fourteenth century'.
16 Dame Alice Kytler, a witch of the fourteenth century, alleged to have killed three husbands by
   poisoning them and to have summoned evil spirits. Yeats read accounts of her trial for witchcraft.

1 According to the version of the myth described in *A Vision* (1937), London: Macmillan, 1962,
   p. 51.
2 Ibid.
3 Ibid., p. 268.

was admired by Yeats. According to Yeats, the poem had its origins in a request made by George Russell ('AE') for a poem for the *Irish Statesman*. Yeats, reflecting on the nature of historical change in the last two centuries, 'thought "Nothing is now possible but some movement, or birth from above, preceded by some violent annunciation." My fancy began to play with the Leda and the Swan for metaphor and I began this poem; but as I wrote, bird and lady took such possession of the scene that all politics went out of it, and my friend tells me that "his conservative readers would misunderstand the poem." ' Interestingly Yeats writes of the process of composition – 'bird and lady took such possession of the scene' – in a way that suggests his imagination had an analogous experience to that of Leda. Yeats himself is taken possession of by 'metaphor'; the artist's mind, on this reading, is invaded by vast images out of Spiritus Mundi, images of sexuality and war. Whether 'all politics went out' of the poem is disputable. The gender politics, for one thing, of the frightening rape have provoked discussion; if there is an emphasis on masculine aggression and violence ('A sudden blow', 'the staggering girl', 'nape caught in his bill'), there appears to be a counter-suggestion in phrases such as 'terrified vague fingers' and 'her loosening thighs' that Leda partly consented to the assault. The poem presents the relationship between swan and Leda as more than one of dominance by the former of the latter. Even as Leda is said to be 'mastered by the brute blood of the air', the poem asks whether she 'put on his knowledge with his power', a question that invites us to imagine that the mortal woman assumed the 'knowledge' of a god. The last line evokes a spent, post-coital indifference, but in 'could let her drop', Yeats implies that the god was, previously, not wholly master of the situation. Politics re-enters via the imagery of 'broken wall' and 'burning roof and tower', an imagery that cannot but recall 'Meditations in Time of Civil War' and 'Nineteen Hundred and Nineteen', with (for example) the former poem's 'My wall is loosening' and the latter poem's horror at the ravage wrought by 'Incendiary and bigot'. Noting the post-Treaty date appended to the poem (1923), Declan Kiberd reads it as an allegory of Yeats's complicated feelings about England's relation to Ireland (see Modern Criticism, **pp. 83–4**). Intriguingly, for all its power, the poem is puzzled by the full implications of its images and ends in a not wholly graspable, let alone answerable, question.

A sudden blow:[4] the great wings beating still
Above the staggering girl, her thighs caressed[5]
By the dark webs, her nape caught in his bill,
He holds her helpless breast upon his breast.

How can those terrified vague fingers push   5
The feathered glory from her loosening thighs?

---

4   The phrase's blow-like abruptness was not achieved without effort: in the first printing the opening read: 'A rush, a sudden wheel, and hovering still/The bird descends'.
5   Among the suggestions of something not merely brutal in the rape.

And how can body, laid in that white rush,[6]
But feel the strange heart beating where it lies?

A shudder in the loins engenders there[7]
The broken wall, the burning roof and tower   10
And Agamemnon dead.[8]
Being so caught up,
So mastered by the brute blood of the air,
Did she put on his knowledge with his power
Before the indifferent beak could let her drop?
        1923

Among School Children

Composed in 1926; first published in *The Dial* and in the *London Mercury* in 1927; published in *The Tower* (1928). Yeats's prose draft for the poem reads as follows: 'Topic for poem – School children and the thought that live [life] will waste them perhaps that no possible life can fulfil our dreams or even their teacher's hope. Bring in the old thought that life prepares for what never happens.' Written in the *ottava rima* stanza that Yeats favoured for poems of meditation, 'Among School Children' enacts a twisting, turning journey of thought and feeling – significantly, a frequent mark of punctuation is the dash, used in five of the eight stanzas. The poem is full of fluctuations of mood, incorporating the sardonic, the tragic, the ironic and the affirmative. It begins with Yeats, a 'sixty-year-old smiling public man', visiting a school in County Wexford (St Otteran's School). As if in reaction to such a version of himself, Yeats takes us, at the start of the second stanza, into his inner life of 'dream'. He recalls a 'Ledaean body' (Maud Gonne, 'Ledaean' because often compared by Yeats to Helen of Troy, daughter of Leda) and a tale by Maud 'That changed some childish day to tragedy'. In an anticipation of the final vision of unity, the effect of the tale was to generate such sympathy that he and Maud seemed like halves of a single self. In the third stanza Yeats carries further the unfolding of a process of thought ('And thinking of that fit of grief or rage'), and wonders whether Maud as a girl resembled any of the children on whom he looks. The poetry's pulse quickens when speculation becomes imaginative event, signalled by 'thereupon'. Maud 'stands before [him] as a living child'. This making present of a past self leads the

---

6 The absence of 'his' or 'her' before 'body' creates momentary uncertainty about whose body is being referred to; but the subsequent phrase makes clear that it must be Leda's.

7 The 'shudder' means the act of insemination that begets a series of catastrophic consequences, but it could also imply an orgasm experienced by Leda or mutually; 'there' presumably means in 'the loins' (Leda's).

8 The break after this phrase marks a shift in the poem from the enactment of 'power' to a questioning about 'knowledge'.

poet to think of what he calls 'Her present image'. Yeats ponders that hollow-cheeked image and thinks, too, of the effect of age on himself, now 'a comfortable kind of old scarecrow'. The next stanza asks whether any mother would think the pain of childbirth worth enduring, were she able, at her child's birth, to see the child 'With sixty or more winters on its head'. The poem's underlying preoccupation with mutability surfaces in stanza VI, when Yeats mentions with cavalier absence of respect three philosophers who wrestled with the problem: Plato, Aristotle and Pythagoras. Despite their eminence, they were all subject to the indignities of old age and are dismissed in the stanza's last line as 'Old clothes upon old sticks to scare a bird'. The penultimate stanza turns to 'images', both those worshipped by nuns and those by mothers. The images worshipped by nuns differ from those worshipped by mothers since they claim a greater permanence. 'And yet', Yeats says, 'they too break hearts'. All images, the broken-off sentence asserts, are would-be 'Presences' that hold our fear of absence at bay and 'symbolise' 'all heavenly glory'. Yeats invokes these Presences as 'self-born mockers of man's enterprise'. The phrasing is highly condensed here; the Presences are 'self-born' because they seem at once autonomous, generated by themselves, and projected, to be generated by the selves that worship them. They 'mock' 'man's enterprise' because their change-lessness derides the human fear of change. Yet, drawing on an older sense of 'mock', they also mock man's enterprise by virtue of imitating it; expressing the human need for permanence, they concede a fear of change. In the final stanza Yeats attempts to salvage something from the poem's overall pessimism. He returns to the theme of 'Labour', brought to the poet's mind, in part, by the consideration of childbirth. Yeats says that labour can be identified with 'blossoming or dancing' when it cancels our sense of being creatures who are self-divided, caught between the demands of body and soul. The feeling of unity occurs 'where' self-division is absent. If the reader asks 'where might that "where" be located?', one answer, reinforced by the position of 'where' at the end of the line, is 'in this poem'. The poem concludes with two questions that suggest the impossibility of reducing images to their constituent parts: the chestnut-tree illustrates a 'blossoming' that is organic and interconnected; the dancer cannot be separated from the dance. The questions result in an implicit affirmation. Yet the fact that this affirmation is expressed through images in a poem that has just expressed ambivalent feelings about 'images' cannot be overlooked. For a reading of the poem alert to its exaltation of images of women at odds with those favoured by De Valera's Catholic Ireland, see the excerpt from Elizabeth Cullingford in Modern Criticism (**pp. 76–80**).

I

I walk through the long schoolroom questioning;
A kind old nun[1] in a white hood replies;
The children learn to cipher and to sing,
To study reading-books and histories,
To cut and sew, be neat in everything   5
In the best modern way—the children's eyes
In momentary wonder stare upon
A sixty-year-old smiling public man.[2]

II

I dream of a Ledaean body, bent
Above a sinking fire, a tale that she   10
Told of a harsh reproof, or trivial event
That changed some childish day to tragedy—
Told, and it seemed that our two natures blent
Into a sphere from youthful sympathy,
Or else, to alter Plato's parable,[3]   15
Into the yolk and white of the one shell.

III

And thinking of that fit of grief or rage
I look upon one child or t'other there
And wonder if she stood so at that age—
For even daughters of the swan can share   20
Something of every paddler's heritage—
And had that colour upon cheek or hair,
And thereupon my heart is driven wild:
She stands before me as a living child.

IV

Her present image floats into the mind—   25
Did Quattrocento finger[4] fashion it
Hollow of cheek as though it drank the wind
And took a mess of shadows for its meat?

---

1 Reverend Mother Philomena.
2 Yeats was now a Senator of the Irish Free State and had been awarded the Nobel Prize.
3 The parable is the story told by Aristophanes in Plato's *Symposium* to explain sexual difference and attraction. Originally, Aristophanes says, men and women were part of a whole being until Zeus divided each being into two; hence, Love came into being as people sought a reintegrarted wholeness.
4 A fifteenth-century painter. In one of its first printings, in the *London Mercury*, August 1927, the poem read 'Da Vinci finger'.

And I though never of Ledaean kind
Had pretty plumage once—enough of that,   30
Better to smile on all that smile, and show
There is a comfortable kind of old scarecrow.

V

What youthful mother, a shape upon her lap
Honey of generation[5] had betrayed,
And that must sleep, shriek, struggle to escape   35
As recollection or the drug decide,
Would think her son, did she but see that shape
With sixty or more winters on its head,
A compensation for the pang of his birth,
Or the uncertainty of his setting forth?   40

VI

Plato thought nature but a spume that plays
Upon a ghostly paradigm of things;[6]
Solider Aristotle[7] played the taws
Upon the bottom of a king of kings;
World-famous golden-thighed Pythagoras[8]   45
Fingered upon a fiddle-stick or strings
What a star sang and careless Muses heard:
Old clothes upon old sticks to scare a bird.

VII

Both nuns and mothers worship images,
But those the candles light are not as those   50
That animate a mother's reveries,
But keep a marble or a bronze repose.
And yet they too break hearts—O Presences
That passion, piety or affection knows,
And that all heavenly glory symbolise—   55
O self-born mockers of man's enterprise;

---

5   Sexual pleasure. Yeats's note reads: 'I have taken the "honey of generation" from Porphyry's essay
    on "The Cave of the Nymphs," but find no warrant in Porphyry for considering it the "drug" that
    destroys the "recollection" of pre-natal freedom. He blamed a cup of oblivion given in the zodiacal
    sign of Cancer.'
6   Alludes to Plato's theory that reality existed in an ideal world of forms ('ghostly paradigm') of
    which this world ('nature') was an imitation.
7   Aristotle (384–322 BC) was 'solider' than Plato because less contemptuous of physical reality; he
    believed that reality consisted of form inhering in matter. Aristotle was also the tutor of Alexander
    ('a king of kings', l. 44); hence the 'taws', a form of birch.
8   The adjective 'golden-thighed' was used of Pythagoras (c. 582–507 BC) in classical times. Pythag-
    oras was credited with finding ways of describing musical pitch in mathematical terms.

Labour is blossoming or dancing where
The body is not bruised to pleasure soul,
Nor beauty born out of its own despair,
Nor blear-eyed wisdom out of midnight oil.   60
O chestnut-tree, great-rooted blossomer,
Are you the leaf, the blossom or the bole?
O body swayed to music, O brightening glance,
How can we know the dancer from the dance?[9]

A Dialogue of Self and Soul

Composed in 1927; first published in *The Winding Stair* (1929 edition). The poem, written in eight-line stanzas that rhyme *abbacddc* and employ shorter lines among their pentameters, is a debate between 'Self', whose allegiance is to this world, and 'Soul', who wishes to focus on a world beyond conflict, body and thought. It recalls metaphysical poems such as Andrew Marvell's 'A Dialogue between the Soul and the Body', but Yeats departs from the dialogue form by removing one of his speakers half way through. Soul opens by recommending meditation on escape from the physical; it seeks the 'breathless starlit air' (I. I. 4). Self, by contrast, is caught up with symbols of things of this world: the sword wound round with material from a Japanese lady's dress, things 'Emblematical of love and war' (I. I. 19). Soul advocates deliverance from what it calls 'the crime of death and birth' (I. I. 24); Self asserts its right 'to commit the crime once more' (I. I. 32). Soul, then, concludes the first part by dwelling on that 'quarter' of the moon where identity is lost and the self and heaven are one, but the cost of such absorption is also admitted in the part's final line: 'But when I think of that my tongue's a stone' (I. I. 40). Soul has reached a point where it has run out of words, and all of the second part is spoken by Self. This is partly because Soul has said all it wishes to say, partly because Self's own words articulate a self-quarrelling. Self speaks out for acceptance of living, but this acceptance is movingly fraught and tension-ridden; the life that Self accepts is, the writing makes only too clear, full of suffering, pain, error, humiliation, blindness and emotional violence. Self urges the casting out of remorse, and claims it (or 'he', since Self's voice is indistinguishable from Yeats's by the end) can 'forgive myself the lot' (II. I. 27), a remark that counters Soul's view that 'Only the dead can be forgiven' (I. I. 39). The poem finishes with an assertion of the omnipresence of blessing wherever the likes of Yeats's 'Self' are to be found. It illustrates the refusal of Yeats to write poems that merely advocate the virtues of his system; as Harold

---

9   The question can be read as Yeats's rejection of knowing as an analytical, dividing activity.

Bloom writes, 'The poem's largest irony is that the Soul is an esoteric Yeatsian, and the Self a natural man'.[1]

Notes to the Poem

l.l.1   *the winding ancient stair*. Of Thoor Ballylee, Yeats's tower.
l.l.7   *That quarter . . . done*. 'That quarter', according to Yeats's system, is the last phase of the lunar months, when (in Phrase 27, for example), 'If [a man] possess intellect he will use it but to serve perception and renunciation. His joy is to be nothing, to do nothing, to think nothing', *A Vision* (1937), London: Macmillan, 1962, p. 180. The repetition of 'thought' in successive lines implies Soul's view of its ultimate futility.
l.l.10   *Sato's ancient blade*. See 'My Table' in 'Meditations in Time of Civil War'.
l.l.25   *Montashigi*. A fifteenth-century Japanese sword-maker.
l. 28–9   *I set / For emblems*. Yeats draws explicit attention to the process of fashioning emblems or symbols here and elsewhere in his later poetry.
l.l.35   *blind*. Will be picked up and redefined by Self, for whom it is a condition of ordinary living to be 'blind', not of some quasi-mystical intuition.
l. 37   *Is . . . Known*. Technical terms in Yeats's system, but their meaning is clear: being and ideal, and subjective knower and objective knowledge are one, in the condition described by Soul.
ll.l.30   *We must laugh*. Yeats switches from 'I' to 'We' at the close, as though establishing a community with all who can bring to life an acceptance that is creatively exultant.

Byzantium

Composed in 1930; first published in *Words for Music Perhaps and Other Poems* (1932); published in *The Winding Stair* (1933 edition). Yeats's prose draft (written in 1930) reads: 'Describe Byzantium as it is in the system [laid out in *A Vision*] towards the end of the first Christian millennium. A walking mummy. Flames at the street corners where the soul is purified, birds of hammered gold singing in the golden trees, in the harbour [dolphins] offering their backs to the wailing dead that they may carry them to Paradise.' The poem is a sequel to 'Sailing to Byzantium' that wants to travel further 'out of nature' than its predecessor. Yeats may have been prompted to write the poem by the criticism made by T. Sturge Moore of the earlier poem: 'Your *Sailing to Byzantium*, magnificent as the first three stanzas are, lets me down in the fourth, as such a

goldsmith's body is as much nature as a man's body, especially if it only sings like Homer and Shakespeare of what is past or passing or to come to Lords and Ladies'.[1] 'Byzantium' takes up Moore's implicit challenge to evoke in greater detail the nature of life after death. It shares with 'Sailing to Byzantium' a wish to leave behind the 'unpurged' (l. 1) physical world and, like many of Yeats's poems, it conducts us into a symbolic plot that is tense with conflict. The poem's form is suited to the expression of conflict; it employs an eight-line stanza rhyming *aabbcddc*, a rhyme scheme that lends itself to a movement from initial assertion to quickened complication, an effect reinforced by the way Yeats uses the shorter fourth, sixth and seventh lines in each stanza. A five stanza poem, it is a symbolic drama in five acts. In the first stanza the poet sets himself to purify the 'unpurged images of day' (l. 1); these images 'recede' (l. 1), along with the 'reson-ance' (l. 3) of sound produced by the 'great cathedral gong' (l. 4) and the 'song' of 'night-walkers' (prostitutes) (l. 3); the 'drunken soldiery are abed' (l. 2). The poem imagines the disappearing of the sensuous and the sensual. The mention of Byzantium's 'great cathedral' (St Sophia) leads Yeats to assert in symbolic terms the contempt for 'man' felt by art, 'A starlit or a moonlit dome disdains / All that man is' (ll. 5–6). What 'man is' is further defined as the sentence unwinds as 'mere complexities' (l. 7) and 'The fury and the mire of human veins' (l. 8). But already something rebels in the poem against 'disdain' for 'All that man is'; that short line, ostensibly sending packing human pretensions, covertly invites us to feel that 'All that man is' cannot be easily disdained. In the second stanza Yeats enters a world beyond the physical and sees, floating before him, a ghostlike form that defies definition, 'an image, man or shade' (l. 9). Ultimately he sees it as 'more image than a shade' (l. 10), which suggests that it is, first and foremost, a poet's imagining. This mummy-like corpse is imagined as unwinding 'the winding path' (l. 12), the tortuous passage between life into death, and the whole stanza dwells on a convergence of opposites: though lacking in 'breath', the 'mouth' (l. 13) of someone 'out of nature' may 'summon' (l. 14) or be summoned by (the syntax is artfully open) 'Breathless mouths' (l. 14). Yeats hails 'the superhuman' (l. 15) in this meeting with what lies beyond life; but his self-conscious allusions to Coleridge and Tennyson (see notes) will not allow his greeting to be straightforwardly affirmative. The third stanza develops the image of the golden bird in the last stanza of 'Sailing to Byzantium'. Again definition proves elusive – 'Miracle, bird or golden handiwork' (l. 17), Yeats writes – but his concern is with an artefact that boasts the superiority of its 'changeless metal' (l. 22) over 'Common bird or petal' (l. 23) (and over 'all complexities', l. 24) because it is 'by the moon embittered' (l. 21): that is, it is provoked to disdain by the fact that human or natural things are subject to change. In the fourth stanza Yeats imagines a 'midnight' (l. 25) moment when a supernatural transcending of human limitation takes place in the city (on 'the

1   Ursula Bridge (ed.), *W. B. Yeats and T. Sturge Moore: Their Correspondence 1901–1937*, New York: Oxford University Press, 1953, p. 162.

Emperor's pavement', l. 25) as 'spirits' (l. 28) are purged of 'all complexities of fury' (l. 29) associated with their 'blood-begotten' (l. 28) state; images of flames dominate the stanza, but these flames are purifying and cannot destroy anything. The fifth stanza turns to the moment when these spirits arrive at Byzantium, at once city of art and of the dead, borne by dolphins who are linked, via 'mire and blood' (l. 33), with sensuality. The spirits are hammered into post-mortal shape by the 'smithies' (l. 34) (poets, artists) who serve the Emperor. These smithies turn the flux ('flood', l. 34) of the real sea into images and representations, 'Marbles of the dancing floor' (l. 36). These 'marbles' 'Break' (tame) 'bitter furies of complexity' (l. 37). But 'complexity' is now the possession of 'bitter furies', not simply of 'fury', and will not easily be broken and disciplined. Indeed, as the syntax works itself out, the marble floors have to deal with an endless, incoming torrent of 'Fresh images' (l. 39), images that culminate in the final line's reference to 'That dolphin-torn, that gong-tormented sea' (l. 40): what one might call the 'real sea' of experience, torn by sensual conflicts and spiritual aspirations. In 'Byzantium' Yeats produces a meditation that is beautifully structured round a series of relentlessly reworked words (and their cognates) — words such as *complexity, fury, images* and *beget* — only to point up the final inadequacy of structures, systems and artefacts.

Notes to the Poem

l. 7   *complexities*. 'Complexity' is the state of being composed of more than one, or of many, parts. The word suggests an intricacy that the speaker at this stage is attempting to regard with scorn.

l. 11   *Hades' bobbin*. Possibly based on the 'spindle' mentioned in Plato's myth of Er, alluded to by Yeats in 'His Bargain': 'Who talks of Plato's spindle; / What set it whirling round? / Eternity may dwindle, / Time is unwound'. Yeats's image is of a bobbin round which the cloth of a mummy is wound; were this cloth to be unwound, the lines suggest, the 'winding path' leading from death to life or life to death could be traced.

l. 16   *death-in-life and life-in-death*. See Coleridge's lines in 'The Ancient Mariner': 'The Nightmare LIFE-IN-DEATH was she, / Who thicks man's blood with cold', and Tennyson's line in 'Tears, Idle Tears': 'O Death in Life, the days that are no more'. Both antecedents represent their condition as something undesirable.

l. 19   *golden bough*. May allude to the golden bough by which Aeneas was able to move through the underworld in *Aeneid*, VI.

l. 20   *cocks of Hades*. Associates the artefact with the birds crowing in the underworld.

l. 33   *Astraddle*. A word that emphasizes the physicality of the 'Spirit after spirit' (l. 34).

l. 37   *bitter furies*. 'Bitter' recalls the bird 'by the moon embittered' (l. 21); this time, though, bitterness is experienced on behalf of change rather than because of it.

The Gyres

Composed 1936–7; first published in *New Poems* (1938). In this and ensuing poems, we move into Yeats's late poems. These poems are often concerned with the fate of civilizations and the best way of confronting their inevitable destruction. This concern can take one into troubling regions of Yeats's later thought, as in *On the Boiler*, a work whose emphasis on eugenics (the 'science' of 'race improvement') is dangerously close in spirit to the fascist ideologies popular in Europe in the 1930s. (For a balanced assessment of Yeats and fascism, see Elizabeth Cullingford's essay in Modern Criticism, **pp. 74–6**.) In many of these poems, there is at moments a creative embrace of the worst life can inflict; in 'The Gyres' Yeats refers to such an embrace as 'tragic joy', a phrase that indicates an intense experience of life as tragic drama. In 'A General Introduction for My Work', Yeats writes of 'the sudden enlargement of their vision' experienced by Shakespeare's tragic protagonists at climactic moments of their plays, and goes on to remark, 'I have heard Lady Gregory say, rejecting some play in the modern manner sent to the Abbey Theatre, "Tragedy must be a joy to the man who dies" ' (see **p. 32**). As always in Yeats, though, a countercurrent makes itself felt in his late works, and at certain moments the poems make us aware that 'tragic joy' may be inadequate as a response to human suffering. Some critics, notably Harold Bloom, have expressed scepticism about the vision that pervades the late works; writing of 'Lapis Lazuli', for example, Bloom says sardonically: 'Inhumane nonsense is not always the best foundation for aesthetic judgement, and perhaps we might be a little wary of "the message of affirmation" Yeats is bringing us'.[1] At their finest, though, these poems present 'affirmation' as a position adopted with desperate optimism in the face of war, suffering and death.

'The Gyres', written in three stanzas of *ottava rima* (eight iambic lines rhyming *abababcc*), alludes in its title to Yeats's image of the interlocking spinning cones that govern historical change. For Yeats, each era of history is imagined as a vortex that turns as it progresses; the resulting movement is a gyre. The poem proceeds with a wild gusto, as of someone hysterically laughing off fears. He asks an alter ego or an anti-self called 'Rocky Face' to 'look forth' (l. 1) since a time of change is approaching, the implication being that what will be required is a 'rocky' yet exultant acceptance of change. The change does not seem to be for the best; 'ancient lineaments are blotted out' (l. 4), for example. Yet, unlike 'The Second Coming', 'The Gyres' does not posit a change that is historically specific. A series of present-tense assertions blends the contemporary with the past, as though all were taking place in some current now: so, present crisis coexists with Empedocles' theory of the inextricability of 'Concord' and 'Discord' (see notes) and with the death of Hector and the destruction of Troy. 'We that look

1   Harold Bloom, *Yeats*, New York: Oxford University Press, 1970, p. 438.

on', Yeats writes, 'but laugh with tragic joy' (l. 8). The use of 'but' there may hint that others will find insufficient this response of detached 'joy', albeit 'tragic joy', and the second stanza begins by facing down possible objections to the attitude to suffering proposed by the poem. 'What matter?' (ll. 9, 11, 15) is a repeated question that appears to wish to be answered 'It is no great matter at all', yet the reference to 'numb nightmare' (l. 9) and the stained 'sensitive body' (l. 10) provokes the counter-response, 'It matters a great deal'. In the third stanza, 'What matter?' (l. 18) is heard for a final time in response to the assertion that conduct, work and the soul are all growing coarse. The poem contains within itself an undercurrent of doubt about the positions being asserted, an under-current that does much to prevent it from being mere rant. Concluding with a long, carefully judged sentence, Yeats expresses his trust in the ability of 'Those that Rocky Face holds dear' (l. 18) to restore (or 'disinter', l. 22) a culture based on 'workman, noble and saint' (l. 23), as the 'gyre' (l. 24) to which they belong returns. The poem's close attempts to fuse faith in human agency and determinist acceptance. The anticipated gyre is 'unfashionable' (l. 24) not only because out of sympathy with the current age but also because it cannot be shaped or 'fashioned' by human beings

Notes to the Poem

l. 1   *Old Rocky Face*. 'Delphic Oracle' is Mrs Yeats's annotated gloss; Shelley's *Ahasuerus* in *Hellas* who has witnessed 'Cycles of generation and of ruin' (l. 154) has also been suggested.

l. 2   *Things . . . thought*. The line implies that there is in any dominant body of 'Thoughts' a built-in self-destructive mechanism.

l. 6   *Empedocles*. A Greek philosopher (*c.* 493–*c.* 433 BC); quoted at the outset of Yeats's discussion of the gyres in *A Vision* on the antithetical, mutually generating nature of Concord and Discord (see *A Vision* (1937), London: Macmillan, 1962, pp. 67–8). What is striking is the almost knockabout way Yeats describes his thought; the tone, flippant yet desperate, is in keeping with a poem that begins with an exclamatory shriek at the bringing forward of a homespun symbol.

l. 7   *Hector*. Son of Priam (the king of Troy) and chief soldier among the Trojans; his death in single combat at the hands of Achilles was one of the factors contributing to the sack of Troy ('a light' refers to the fires burning the city).

ll. 13–14   *For painted forms . . . but not again*. Yeats denies that he will feel longing for the past 'again'; this may be because he thinks it is inevitable that it will reappear.

ll. 21–2   *dark . . . nothing*. Further Yeatsian images for that key moment in his thought, the moment of pure potentiality when an age is about to turn into its opposite.

l. 24   *again*. Off-rhymed with 'run', preventing recurrence from seeming too straightforward; in the previous stanza, 'again' off-rhymes with 'gone' and rhymes with 'stain'.

Lapis Lazuli

Composed in 1936; first published in the *London Mercury* in 1938; published in *New Poems* (1938). The poem was inspired by the gift of a carving in lapis lazuli (a precious stone) given to Yeats as a present for his seventieth birthday by the young poet Harry Clifton, to whom the poem is dedicated. Yeats wrote: 'someone has sent me a present of a great piece carved by some Chinese sculptor into the semblance of a mountain with temple, trees, paths and an ascetic and pupil about to climb the mountain'.[1] The poem was written in 1936, the year of the outbreak of the Spanish Civil War and of Hitler's occupation of the Rhineland, and a time of great political tension. It meditates on the role of art in the face of catastrophe. Its five rhymed verse-paragraphs approach this subject in connecting yet surprising ways, their transitions refusing to explain themselves and relying on the reader to supply the linking sense. The poem's rhythms and moods are equally full of expressive changes. In the first paragraph Yeats mimics the reported view of 'hysterical women' (l. 1) who condemn artists for fiddling while the world burns, or slides towards war. The verse suggests, though, that war will always be with us through its references both to 'Aeroplane and Zeppelin' (l. 6), associated with the First World War, and to 'King Billy' (l. 7), associated with the Battle of the Boyne in 1690 between William of Orange and James II. The tone is mockingly aloof from the women's fears. In the alliterative beat of 'Pitch like King Billy bomb-balls in' (l. 7), there is a mirthless flippancy that prepares us for the clear-sighted acceptance of war's devastation in the paragraph's last line. Yeats's manner implies his sympathy with 'poets that are always gay' (l. 3), the first use of an adjective (meaning spiritedly upbeat and joyous despite the fact of catastrophe) that will become central in the poem. The next paragraph brings forward what Yeats thinks of as an appropriate response to disaster: a response he has already in 'The Gyres' called 'tragic joy' and is demonstrated at its artistic best in Shakespearean tragedy. Like the heroes and heroines of Shakespeare's plays, people should 'perform their tragic play' (l. 9) and 'not break up their lines to weep' (l. 15); they should aim, Yeats implies, at 'Gaiety transfiguring all that dread' (l. 17), both withstanding and bearing triumphant witness to 'Tragedy wrought to its uttermost' (l. 20). Life is a serious play that may (indeed, should) end in 'Black out' (l. 19), a triple allusion to extinction, the obliterating of lights during an air-raid and the sudden darkening of a theatre stage. The next section switches abruptly from the theatre to an evocation of the fate of civilizations, built up with labour and toil, before being summarily 'put to the sword' (l. 27). Yeats dwells on the loss of the sculptures of Callimachus, an Athenian sculptor of the fifth century BC, describing his achievements with great power. The paragraph's conclusion is one of tragic acceptance and of the pleasure of recreating what has been destroyed, as, in a

---

1   Dorothy Wellesley (ed.), *Letters on Poetry from W. B. Yeats to Dorothy Wellesley*, London: Oxford University Press, 1964, p. 8.

sense, the poet himself has just done in his description of the sculptor's 'handi-work' (l. 29), where the syntax does much to make us see what we are told no longer exists. The fourth paragraph moves to the lapis lazuli sculpture. Yeats first gives an unadorned account of the sculpture, as though he were writing a catalogue description. But in the word 'doubtless' (l. 47) in the fifth paragraph he makes us aware of the poet's scrutiny of the artwork, of his mind and imagination at work. In this final paragraph the presence of the poet's imagin-ation comes to the fore, as he permits himself to interpret accidental cracks as features of the landscape and wonders where the 'Chinamen' are climbing. 'I / Delight to imagine them' (ll. 49–50), Yeats writes, clarifying his subjective involvement in an imagined scene, the word 'I' taking a strong stress at the line's end. For all Yeats's own gloss in a letter that emphasizes the gap between the East and the West ('the east has its solutions always and therefore knows nothing of tragedy. It is we, not the east, that must raise the heroic cry'),[2] the Chinamen exemplify the stance recommended by the poet. Looking out on 'all the tragic scene' (l. 52), they supply 'mournful melodies' (l. 53) with 'Accomplished fingers' (l. 54), and retain that quality of gaiety that Yeats prizes. The serenity of the East and the intensity of the West (as exemplified by Shakespeare) approach from opposite ends of the spectrum the state of tragic joy. See the reading of the poem by J. R. Mulryne in Modern Criticism (**pp. 66–9**).

Notes to the Poem

l. 1   *I have heard.* Yeats's use of this formula distances himself from anything too 'hysterical' in his account of what the 'hysterical women' are alleged to have said.

l. 4   *For . . . know.* Yeats sardonically mimics the hackneyed phrases of those who feel artists are insufficiently responsible.

l. 6   *Zeppelin.* A large airship, capable of being guided, used by the Germans to bomb London in the First World War.

l. 7   *Pitch like King Billy bomb-balls in.* Yeats borrows and adapts from the ballad 'The Battle of the Boyne', lines of which read: 'King James he pitched his tent between / The lines for to retire / But King William threw his bomb-balls in / And set them all on fire'.

ll. 10–11   *There struts Hamlet . . . Cordelia.* The lines suggest that people live out roles in a Shakespearean tragedy.

l. 15   *Do not . . . weep.* See 'A General Introduction for My Work': 'no actress has ever sobbed when she played Cleopatra, even the shallow brain of a pro-ducer has never thought of such a thing' (**p. 32**).

l. 24   *It.* 'Tragedy', which has already been 'wrought to its uttermost' (l. 20).

II. 29–32   *No handiwork . . . stands.* By delaying the verb 'stands', Yeats allows us to dwell for several lines on Callimachus' vanished creations.

II. 45–6   *water-course or an avalanche / Or lofty slope.* The use of 'or' indicates that the poet is imagining different possibilities, 'reading' the sculpture by releasing his imagination, rather as he invites us to read his poem.

I. 55   *their eyes.* The word 'eyes' is repeated three times to bring out the unflinching steadiness of the musicians' stare.

Beautiful Lofty Things

First published in *New Poems* (1938). The poem celebrates people Yeats admired. It depends less on rhyme than on the repetition of the same word in the rhyme position. It consists of irregular alexandrines stretched in length in accordance with feeling, and offers a different version of tragic acceptance from that found in 'The Gyres' and 'Lapis Lazuli'. The theory of cyclic recurrence advanced in those poems vanishes in favour of elegiac celebration of the unique beauty and nobleness of individuals: one reason for the high proportion of named people, including Maud Gonne, the only time she is named in Yeats's poetry. All the people named are caught in an attitude of heroic singleness, as when the poet's father first mollifies, then teases, 'a raging crowd' (l. 2) at the Abbey Theatre, and Augusta Gregory (here given her 'august' first name rather than her title) tells a would-be assassin where she can be found. As in 'Easter 1916', individuals are turning into mythic figures in the poem, a process clinched by the comparison of Maud to Pallas Athene (rather than Helen), and by the summarizing phrase, 'All the Olympians' (l. 12). But the Olympians are kept in touch with ordinary life; Maud is 'waiting a train' (l. 10), and in the final phrase, 'a thing never known again' (l. 12), Yeats ends on a muted note, as if too moved by emotion to aim at anything fancier than a relatively commonplace form of words. Here, for once in Yeats, 'again' is used to dismiss the possibility of return.

Notes to the Poem

I. 1   *O'Leary's noble head.* For John O'Leary, see note 3 to 'September 1913' (**p. 116**).

I. 2   *My father.* John Butler Yeats (1839–1922) was present at the debate in 1907 at the Abbey Theatre following the riots about Synge's *The Playboy of the Western World*.

I. 4   *plaster Saints.* The phrase undermines the Irish Catholic view of the country as a 'land of scholars and saints' by suggesting the saints are bogus.

I. 5   *Standish O'Grady.* Standish James O'Grady (1866–1928), historian and novelist, a central figure in the Irish literary revival. There may be a joke on the name 'Standish', given that the character is evidently standing with some difficulty, 'supporting himself between the tables'.

l. 6   *high nonsensical.* Yeats conveys delighted admiration at O'Grady's torrent of drunken nonsense by allowing the two adjectives to play against one another; 'high' picks up the suggestion of something 'elevated' in 'lofty' (title and first line).

l. 7   *great ormolu table.* 'Ormolu' is a gilded bronze used in decorating furniture; Yeats uses the word to evoke the aristocratic finery of Lady Gregory's house.

l. 10   *Pallas Athene.* Greek goddess of wisdom.

Under Ben Bulben

Composed in September 1938; first published in the *Irish Times* (1939); published in *Last Poems and Two Plays* (1939). In this poem, written a few months before his death in a rhythm close to chant, Yeats reasserts his major convictions and composes his epitaph in the final lines. The poem has the feel of a buoyant last will and testament; free from the questions that haunt 'Man and the Echo', it has an affirmative, at times strident, tone (drafts were entitled 'Creed' and 'His Convictions'). In the opening section Yeats begins with an imperative to himself and his reader to 'Swear' (I. l. 1) by visionary, occult forces and invokes the 'sages' (I. l. 1) associated with Shelley's Witch of Atlas and 'superhuman' (I. l. 6) 'horsemen' and 'women' (I. l. 5), figures who appear to come from Irish myth. Yeats sees these riders as having achieved 'Completeness' (I. l. 9) and imagines them haunting 'the wintry dawn' (I. l. 10). A single line, set apart, promises us 'the gist of what they mean' (I. l. 12), and in the second section that 'gist' is explained; it hinges on a belief in reincarnation, and on the view that human beings shuttle between commitment to a larger community, 'race', and to individual development, 'soul' (II. l. 3). In the third section Yeats comes dangerously close to praise of 'violence' (III. l. 10) as he returns to the theme of completeness: the bitter words of John Mitchel (1815–75), an Irish nationalist, who desired 'war' (III. l. 2) with England are quoted to suggest that 'some sort of violence' (III. l. 10) is needed if human beings are to 'accomplish fate' (III. l. 11). Yeats's nationalist feelings show themselves here; but his words restate his long-held belief that achievement is possible through 'conflict'. Section IV instructs artists to 'do the work' (IV. l. 1), that is, provide artistic forms that 'Bring the soul of man to God' (IV. l. 4). As he does in another late poem, 'The Statues', Yeats praises 'Measurement' (IV. l. 6) as the basis of Western art. Found in works produced by Egyptian and Greek artists, 'Measurement', with its implications of ordered vision, finds its supreme embodiment in Michelangelo's paintings in the Sistine Chapel and in 'Quattrocento' (fifteenth-century) paintings, and is apparent, too, in the work of later artists such as William Blake and Samuel Palmer. The section finishes, though, with a sense that 'Confusion' (IV. l. 31) has since taken over, and in section V Yeats urges 'Irish poets' to 'learn your trade' (V. l. 1) and value

'whatever is well made' (V. l. 2). In particular, he wishes them to celebrate the alliance between the 'peasantry' (V. l. 7) and 'Hard-riding country gentlemen' (V. l. 8) that he sees as central to Irish culture and as the driving force behind what he calls 'the indomitable Irishry' (V. l. 16). The final section meditates on the poet's epitaph; it writes about the setting and wording of this epitaph in a present tense that has about it a quality of stilled permanence. The words cut on limestone are 'By his command' (VI. l. 8); they use 'no conventional phrase' (VI. l. 6). Yeats, at the end, asserts his poetic 'command' and scorn of the 'conventional'. The epitaph itself is chiselled, cold, superior to 'life' and 'death' (VI. l. 10); it bids the 'superhuman' 'Horseman, pass by!' (VI. l. 11) The last command implies both that the grave of Yeats is a fitting place for such a figure to pass and that the poet is indifferent even to the attentions of such a figure. Few poems imagine a posthumous existence with such force, and the sense that the poet and his work will 'air in immortality' (l. l. 8) is strong.

Notes to the Poem

l. l. 2   *Mareotic Lake*. Shelley's visionary character, the Witch of Atlas, passes on her journey down the Nile 'By Moeris and the Mareotid Lakes'.
l. II. 5–7   *horsemen . . . pale, long-visaged company*. Recalls the Sidhe, the gods of Irish myth, who dwell among the wind.
III. l. 1   *Mitchel's prayer*. In his *Jail Journal*. The 'prayer' mocks the words 'Send peace in our time'.
IV. l. 5   *cradles*. Associated with the phases of the moon.
IV. l. 8   *Phidias*. See the first section of 'Nineteen Hundred and Nineteen'.
IV. l. 17   *Quattrocento*. See 'Among School Children', stanza IV.
IV. l. 28   *Calvert*. Edward Calvert (1799–1883), painter; *Wilson*. Richard Wilson (1714–82), painter; *Claude*. Claude Lorraine (1600–82), French painter.
IV. l. 30   *Palmer's phrase*. Samuel Palmer (1805–81), painter.
V. l. 6   *Base-born . . . base beds*. Later Yeats was prone to the expression of such eugenicist views.
VI. l. 3   *An ancestor*. Reverend John Yeats (1774–1846), Yeats's great-grandfather.
VI. II. 9–11   *Cast . . . by!* Yeats cancelled the first line of this epitaphic quatrain, which was 'Draw rein, draw breath'; as a result the only end-word in the poem without a rhyme is 'death'.

Long-legged Fly

First published in the *London Mercury* in 1939; published in *Last Poems and Two Plays* (1939). With its use of a refrain and repetitive structure, 'Long-legged Fly'

deploys techniques associated with the ballad, a form much practised by Yeats in his late work. The poem presents three vignettes – Caesar in his tent, 'eyes fixed upon nothing' (l. 7), Helen of Troy practising 'a tinker shuffle / Picked up on a street' (ll. 17–18), and Michelangelo working in the Sistine chapel – to suggest the far-reaching consequences of some hushed moment of concentration. It has in common with poems such as 'The Gyres' and 'Lapis Lazuli' a preoccupation with the fate of 'civilisation', but its angle of approach is quite different. The poem begins each of its three stanzas with an emphatic 'That' (meaning 'In order that'), yet the reader is struck by the distance between an apparent moment of idleness, play or slow work and the ultimate outcome. Silence is the condition of creativity, a silence that outstrips and makes possible human creativity. In the first stanza the vantage-point is of some Roman soldier aware of Caesar ignoring the spread-out 'maps' (l. 6), contemplating 'nothing' (l. 7), in order to win the 'great battle' (l. 2) of maintaining 'civilisation' (l. 1). In the second stanza the command is to 'Move most gently if move you must' (l. 13) in order that Helen can 'Practise a tinker shuffle' (l. 17), forming her identity in so doing, an identity that will lead to the destruction of Troy and her legendary reputation for beauty. In the third stanza, silence is sought for Michelangelo, so that he can produce paintings that will provoke and give form to erotic longing. The refrain suggests that each figure has learnt how to let the mind move 'upon silence' (ll. 10, 20, 30). The mind moves upon silence in two senses: it broods on, and allows itself to be borne along by, something vaster than itself.

Notes to the Poem

l. 5   *Caesar.* Julius Caesar (*c.* 102–44 BC).
l. 10   *moves upon silence.* The phrase recalls Genesis 1:2, 'And the Spirit of God moved upon the face of the waters'; here, though, what moves upon the water is not the 'Spirit of God' but 'a long-legged fly'. At the same time, the 'mind' of all three figures is able to create by virtue of moving upon silence; to that extent the allusion to Genesis involves comparison as well as contrast.
l. 11   *topless towers.* Alludes to Faustus' address to Helen of Troy (or a spirit impersonating Helen) in Christopher Marlowe's *Doctor Faustus* (1604), 5. 1. 94–5: 'Was this the face that launched a thousand ships / And burnt the topless towers of Ilium?'
l. 22   *The first Adam.* The first promptings of sexual feeling (playing on the phrase 'old Adam' meaning sinful nature innate in people); also alludes to Michelangelo's painting in the Sistine Chapel of God giving life to Adam.

Man and the Echo

First published in the *Atlantic Monthly* and the *London Mercury* in 1939, with, in the latter case, the above title; published in *Last Poems and Two Plays* (1939), with the title 'The Man and the Echo'. The poem recalls 'A Dialogue of the Self and Soul' in its concern with 'night' and the soul, and uses a traditional form (that of the 'Echo' poem) to convey powerful and highly dramatic self-searching. Among Yeats's most self-examining poems, its trochaic tetrameters and couplet-rhymes lull the ear before three questions nagging at a sleepless old man close to death are sprung: did his nationalist play, *Cathleen ni Houlihan* (1902), contribute to the Easter Rising and subsequent executions of the rebel leaders? Did he in some way contribute to the breakdown of an unnamed woman (probably Margot Ruddock, a young dancer and actress (1907–51) whom Yeats met in 1934 and with whom he had a close relationship that ended painfully)? Should he have spoken out to secure the preservation of a wrecked 'house' (probably but not solely Coole Park)? These questions are offered as instances of how 'all seems evil' (l. 17), making the 'Man' long for death, a longing repeated by the 'Echo'. The Man reacts against this longing, however, and rejects it as cowardly and fruitless. He describes, in a long sentence, the 'spiritual intellect's great work' (l. 20) of seeking to ensure 'That all's arranged in one clear view' (l. 31). The passage has an exultant doggedness as it describes the search for self-understanding, the discovery of significance, purgation of error, and acceptance of oblivion. When the Echo repeats the Man's 'Into the night' (ll. 36, 37), the first impression is of tragically serene acceptance. But in the Man's final speech, questions begin again: asking whether we shall 'rejoice' 'in that great night' (l. 38), Yeats concedes uncertainty about our identity after death. The assurance of *A Vision*, with its detailed account of the soul's state after death as it re-enters the wheel of incarnation, falls away here, and vanishes after the next question, as bare and unanswerable a question as Yeats asks himself and us throughout his work: 'What do we know but that we face / One another in this place?' (ll. 39–40) After that moment of total agnosticism, Yeats breaks away from the developing plot of his poem to say he has 'lost the theme' (l. 41); possibilities of 'joy or night seem but a dream' (l. 42), and he returns to the physical world of suffering and mortality, embodied in the cry of 'A stricken rabbit' (l. 45), a cry that distracts the poet's thought. The last line deserves attention: 'distracts' (l. 46) is a verb emerging from the off-rhyming sounds of 'hawk' (l. 43), 'struck' (l. 43), 'rock' (l. 44) and 'stricken' (l. 45), and it conveys an inability to concentrate on the 'spiritual intellect's great work'. Yeats's 'thought' (l. 46), by which he means not only a process of thinking but a body of systematized ideas, is finally 'distracted' in this poem.

4

Further Reading

Further Reading

This section is highly selective, in accordance with the format of the series. All the books and articles mentioned elsewhere in this volume are worthy of attention.

Editions of Yeats's Poetry

Undergraduates reading Yeats for the first time are recommended to consult one or more of the following:

Albright, Daniel (ed.), *W. B. Yeats: The Poems* (1990), London: Dent, 1994. Probably the best single 'Collected Poems' for students because of its wealth of stimulating commentary.
Jeffares, A. Norman (ed.), *Yeats's Poems* (1989), revised edn, London: Macmillan, 1991. Invaluable notes and appendices, including a guide to pronouncing Irish words in Yeats.
Larrissy, Edward (ed.), *W. B. Yeats*, Oxford Authors, Oxford: Oxford University Press, 1997; reissued in *The Major Works* series. Excellent selection of poetry and prose, with very good notes. Has line-numbered texts – as do all the editions recommended, except for that edited by Jeffares.
Webb, Timothy (ed.), *W. B. Yeats: Selected Poems*, Harmondsworth: Penguin, 1991. Excellent introduction, with particularly useful and intelligent notes.

Editions of Yeats's Prose

Two very helpful collections are:

Jeffares, A. Norman (ed.), *Selected Criticism and Prose*, London: Macmillan, 1980. An immensely valuable selection that ranges expertly across essays and letters.
Welch, Robert (ed.), *Writings on Irish Folklore, Legend and Myth*, Harmondsworth: Penguin, 1993.

Biographies

Yeats's life and art are so intertwined it is highly recommended that at an early stage students read one or more of the following:

Brown, Terence, *The Life of W. B. Yeats: A Critical Biography* (1999), Oxford: Blackwell, 2001. This eloquent 'critical' biography is concerned with both the life and the work, and is packed, among other things, with readings that register the disquieting power of Yeats's imagination.

Ellmann, Richard, *Yeats: The Man and the Masks* (1948), Oxford: Oxford University Press, 1979. Synthesizes interpretation and biography. A classic work on the poet.

Jeffares, A. Norman, *W. B. Yeats: A New Biography*, London: Continuum, 2001. A mine of information and balanced judgements, this study focuses on 'the multiplicity of the man, who began to write as a dreaming idealist, became a satiric sceptic, and finally a conserver' (p. xix).

Selected Criticism

Bloom, Harold, *Yeats*, New York: Oxford University Press, 1970. Idiosyncratic but at its best a valuable reading of the poetry as a whole.

Cullingford, Elizabeth, *Yeats, Ireland and Fascism*, London: Macmillan, 1981. Vital for grasping some of the complexities of an issue that remains central to thinking about later Yeats. The same critic has also produced groundbreaking work on 'gender and history' (see the extract in Modern Criticism, **pp. 76–80**) and edited a fine Casebook, *Yeats: Poems, 1919–1935*, Basingstoke: Macmillan, 1984, which includes seminal pieces by Allen Tate, George Orwell (concerned about Yeats's fascism), R. P. Blackmur and Yvor Winters (at his most judiciously imperious, taking exception to Yeats's 'Silly ideas'), among many others.

Larrissy, Edward, *W. B. Yeats*, Plymouth: Northcote House, 1998. Independent and thoughtful contribution to the 'Writers and Their Work' series; emphasizes the presence in Yeats of 'the characteristic Anglo-Irish sense of division' (p. 7).

Longenbach, James, *Stone Cottage: Pound, Yeats and Modernism*, New York: Oxford University Press, 1988. A fine study of the personal and literary relations between Pound and Yeats, and perhaps the best assessment of their affinities and differences in relation to modernism.

MacNeice, Louis, *The Poetry of W. B. Yeats* (1941), London: Faber and Faber, 1967. Still among the best introductions to Yeats's poetry, Irishness and thought.

Pierce, David (ed.), *W. B. Yeats: Critical Assessments*, 4 vols, Mountfield, near Robertsbridge: Helm Information, 2000. Wide-ranging selection: vol. 1 concentrates on 'Contemporary Reviews'; vol. 2 on 'Assessments: 1889–1959'; vol. 3 on 'Assessments: 1960–1979'; vol. 4 on 'Assessments 1980–2000'. An essential tool for studying Yeats's critical reception.

Rosenthal, M. L., *Running to Paradise: Yeats's Poetic Art*, New York: Oxford University Press, 1994. A beautifully succinct and perceptive book that reminds us that, when all is said, fascination with Yeats is generated by his art. Required reading.

Stallworthy, Jon (ed.), *Yeats: Last Poems*, London: Macmillan, 1968. Still the best first place to go (after annotated editions) for critical work on the late poems.

Index

Note: numbers in **bold** indicate main or substantial entries.